In a Classroom of Their Own

DISSIDENT FEMINISMS

Elora Halim Chowdhury, Editor

A list of books in the series appears at the end of this book.

In a Classroom
of Their Own

The Intersection of Race and Feminist Politics in All-Black Male Schools

KEISHA LINDSAY

**UNIVERSITY OF
ILLINOIS PRESS**
Urbana, Chicago, and Springfield

Support for this research was provided by the University
of Wisconsin–Madison's Office of the Vice Chancellor
for Research and Graduate Education.

Cataloging-in-Publication Data is available from the
Library of Congress
ISBN 978-0-252-04173-0 (cloth: alk.)
ISBN 978-0-252-08335-8 (paper: alk.)
ISBN 978-0-252-05040-4 (ebook)

Contents

Acknowledgments

I am writing these acknowledgements in the parking lot of my daughter's school. This somewhat unorthodox state of affairs is a reflection of my often-harried life as an academic parent. It is also evidence of what I have learned while completing this book—that it is possible to engage in scholarly writing anywhere. By anywhere, I mean not only in school parking lots but also in public libraries, mall food courts, public parks, airports, hotel lobbies, karate studios, hospital waiting rooms, fast-food restaurants, and sometimes even in one's own driveway.

While I wrote this book in all manner of places, I did not do so without support. *In a Classroom of Their Own* owes much of its existence to assistance from the University of Wisconsin–Madison in the form of a pre-tenure sabbatical sponsored by the Institute for Research in the Humanities, research and project assistance from the Vilas Life Cycle Professorship program, and a book manuscript workshop sponsored by the Department of Political Science. Subvention support for this research was also provided by the University of Wisconsin–Madison's Office of the Vice Chancellor for Research and Graduate Education with funding from the Wisconsin Alumni Research Foundation.

I am equally grateful for the support that I have received from past and present colleagues in the Department of Gender and Women's Studies, the Department of Political Science, the African Diaspora and the Atlantic World Research Circle, and other academic units at the University of Wisconsin–Madison. Thank you to Myra Marx Ferree, Judith Houck, Janet Hyde, Christina Ewig, Aili Tripp, Ellen Samuels, Susan Friedman, Jennie Higgins, Julie D'Acci, Annie Menzel ,Helen Kinsella, Dan Kapust, Michelle Schwarze, John

Zumbrunnen, Jimmy Klausen, Tejumola Olaniyan, Jim Sweet, and Steve Stern for offering productive, critical commentary on my formal and informal presentations of various portions of this book. I owe an extra special thank you to Jane Collins for reading and commenting on multiple drafts with amazing speed and insight, for offering wonderful guidance about the publication process, and for exemplifying a kindness and concern that is hard to come by in the academy or elsewhere.

I also want to acknowledge Eunjung Kim, Pernille Ipsen, Steve Kantrowitz, Linn Posey-Maddox, Christy Clark-Pujara, and Aida Levy-Hussen, who have personally supported me during the book-writing process and who have served as great models for how to craft research that has significance within and beyond the college classroom. Jane Gordon, Tiffany-Willoughby Herard, Mary Hawkesworth, Cathy Cohen, Lawrie Balfour, Robert Gooding-Williams, Neil Roberts, Lance McCready, Gladys Mitchell, Mara Marin, and other mentors and colleagues from further afield have also been instrumental in helping me to craft several of the arguments that appear in this book.

Thanks, too, to my anonymous reviewers for their critical and constructive readings and to Dawn Durante, my acquisitions editor at the University of Illinois Press. Dawn never wavered in her support of this book despite various delays. Alice Falk and Julie Gay also provided invaluable developmental editing and copyediting, respectively, during the book-writing process.

To my best friend Sandra Knight Reese, I am grateful that you never doubted my ability to complete the manuscript even when the way forward looked grim. I am also indebted to Nyaneba Nkrumah, Jennie Mollica, Lisa Berry, Karen Botsoe, Eugene Botsoe, Enith Martin Williams, Maziki Thame, Aretha Brown, Taitu Heron, and other friends for the support they offered during the many challenging life events that seemed to accompany every stage of writing this book. To all of my Hylmann, Lindsay, Amoah, and Akyea extended family members—especially Doreth Hylmann and Desmond Lindsay—thanks for keeping my spirits up and my mind sharp with laughter, various family intrigues, and the latest political news from Jamaica and Ghana.

My life partner, Gideon, has been my rock of stability over the past few years. When he was very sick I took care of him. When he got better he took care of me by taking over the day-to-day running of our household, reminding me that it was okay to "disappear" to write, suggesting that I take breaks to pamper myself, and by remaining convinced that I could and would complete this book. Our daughter, Sena, was equally supportive—albeit in her unique "diva"-like way. She repeatedly encouraged me to take a break from writing by playing with her doll-baby "sister" Ama, wearing more pink clothing, watching more television, learning to love all things "princessy," playing Lego Friends, and by embracing her own high-energy zest for life.

Finally, I am eternally grateful to my parents—both of whom died while I was writing this book. My father, Louis Lindsay, was my first and best academic mentor and teacher. During my childhood he introduced me to Bob Marley's political thought and music. During my teenage years he exposed me to Walter Rodney, George Beckford, Frantz Fanon, and other giants of radical Caribbean political thought. As an adult, I learned from him the importance of putting black pride and anti-racism into practice in America (or in what he described as "the belly of the beast") as a student, worker, immigrant, and parent. My mother, Audrey Lindsay, was the ultimate renaissance woman—divorced mother of one, lab technician, small-business owner, middle- and high-school teacher, cofounder of a local black women's investment club, volunteer GED instructor, proud "grandmom," and the recipient of a doctorate in education at age fifty-five. From her I learned the importance of resilience, positive thinking, and dignity as the best means of surviving and thriving in the face of the seemingly overwhelming odds that often come from living life as black woman.

In a Classroom of Their Own

Introduction

A Separate Class of Boys

On December 6, 2010, Kaleem Caire, president of the Urban League in Madison, Wisconsin, formally petitioned the city's board of education to establish Madison Preparatory Academy, or "Madison Prep." Caire's petition was part of a months-long campaign to convince city leaders and residents that Madison needed a new kind of educational institution—a publicly funded, all-male school specifically designed to improve the academic achievement of boys of color. Caire made the case for Madison Prep by arguing that the city's schools should address the needs of all students and by emphasizing that he and his supporters were intent not only on "developing another school" but also on "changing the whole way" that schools are "set up" in Madison and farther afield (qtd. in Schubert 2011).

Caire's push for Madison Prep occurred against the backdrop of Wisconsin's status as one of the worst places in the nation to educate a black child (Wisconsin Council on Children and Families 2013; Becker 2015). Madison, the state capital, exemplifies this troubling reality. Ninety percent of the city's white students graduate within six years, compared to only 59 percent of black students (Madison Metropolitan School District 2016). Equally disturbing is the more than 50 percent gap between black children's and white children's reading proficiency levels in grades three, four, and five and the fact that only 12 percent of black middle school students are proficient in math, compared with 69 percent of their white peers (Madison Metropolitan School District 2016).

Making the Case for and against All-Black Male Schools

Although Kaleem Caire's petition ultimately failed, his effort to establish Madison Prep was warmly received among its target population—young black males. Tyler Beck, the youngest board member of the proposed school, encouraged city leaders to "hop on board" with Madison Prep because it was "offering a solution" for black males, like himself, who generally fail in traditional public schools (qtd. in Comp 2011). Fifth-grader Ryan Felix-Moth welcomed the chance to attend Madison Prep because doing so meant that he would no longer "feel kind of embarrassed" about being the only black boy in his class ("District Leaders Learn More" 2010).

Local conservatives lauded Caire not only for proposing an educational model designed to meet black boys' needs but also for doing so in a manner that strove to reduce state control over local schools, embraced mandatory school uniforms and other supposed means of fostering black boys' sense of self-responsibility, and recognized the financial and educational benefits of hiring non-union teachers who could work longer hours than their unionized counterparts (Blaska 2011; Severson 2011). Such right-of-center praise for Madison Prep was remarkable, given that conservatives in Madison and throughout Wisconsin have generally been hostile to feminist-led efforts to address gender-related inequalities in the state's schools and have long resisted antiracist activists' calls for greater government attention to and spending on underachieving black students.

Numerous left-of-center Madisonians also supported establishing Madison Prep. Some of these supporters saw the school as key to ensuring that Madison's black students and white students have the same chance to thrive in the city's classrooms. Other liberal supporters, particularly from Madison's black community, lauded Caire's desire to recruit teachers and administrators of color as an important means of diversifying the city's overwhelmingly white and frequently racist teaching and administrative cadre. That a significant number of Madison's liberal residents publicly embraced Madison Prep was far from expected, given their well-established support for teachers' unions, frequent praise for racially integrated and coeducational schooling, and general hostility toward Republican-supported efforts at educational reform.

The unusual political bedfellows in favor of Madison Prep did not go unnoticed. Local commentators alternatively described the bipartisan coalition supporting the school's establishment as "crucial" and "odd" (Ruff 2012; Blaska 2011). While Kaleem Caire's attempt to establish Madison Prep and the politically diverse support his attempt attracted were unprecedented in Madison, this was hardly the case in the rest of the country. In 1991 Clifford

Watson, a Detroit-based black male educator, spearheaded the opening of the first all-black male school (ABMS) in the nation. Author and motivational speaker Jawanza Kunjufu has spoken and written extensively about why black boys fail in school and about the need for educational alternatives, including ABMSs, to remedy their failure. Fellow black male educators Tim King and David Banks are ardent proponents of ABMSs and presently head two networks of separate schools for black boys—Chicago's Urban Preparatory Academies as well as the Eagle Academies in New York and New Jersey.

As was the case in Madison, the black-male led effort to establish ABMSs nation wide has been well received across the political spectrum. President George H. W. Bush, the Nation of Islam's Louis Farrakhan, Facebook founder Mark Zuckerberg, and former Democratic presidential candidate Hillary Clinton have all championed ABMSs. This across-the-aisle support is financial as well as rhetorical. The left-leaning Open Society Foundation backs abortion rights and antiracist criminal-justice reform. It is also a major donor to the Eagle Academies and to the Coalition of Schools Educating Boys of Color (COSEBOC), an educational advocacy organization in favor of ABMSs. The right-of-center Walton Family Foundation sponsors efforts to outlaw abortion and affirmative action and has also sponsored ABMSs, including Albany's Brighter Choice schools and Chicago's Urban Preparatory Academies.

The push for ABMSs is not without critics. Political scientist Willie Legette (1999) and several other black male commentators argue that ABMSs are detrimental to black children's psychological, academic, and socioeconomic well-being. Kenneth Clark, whose research influenced the Supreme Court's decision to end school segregation, declares of such schools: "This is contrary to everything that we were fighting against and everything that the research says about the benefits of learning Black and White, male and female together" (qtd. in Whitaker 1991, 18). Devon Carbado (1999), a law professor, concludes that the discourse in favor of ABMSs "ignores the degree to which Black girls are burdened by racism, discards the particular educational difficulties with which Black girls are confronted, and . . . creates the false impression that the educational status of Black female adolescents is such that they are not in need of these kinds of academies" (7).

The American Civil Liberties Union (ACLU) rejects ABMSs on the basis that they unconstitutionally deny children equal access to publicly funded education. The organization asserts, more particularly, that Title IX legislation allows gender-segregated schooling only when girls' and boys' schools are separate administrative and educational entities, are equally resourced, and are premised on a legally sound rationale for each class subject and grade in which single-gendered teaching is offered—none of which is applicable

to most proposed or existing AMBSs (ACLU 2011). As part of its broader
public education campaign to convey the dangers of single-gender schools,
the ACLU (2012) has crafted numerous policy briefs and has issued cease-
and-desist letters to multiple ABMSs.

Many feminists, including members of the Feminist Majority Foundation
and the National Organization of Women Legal Defense Fund (NOWLDF),
are equally vociferous critics of single-gender schooling for black boys. Members of both organizations emphasize that ABMSs perpetuate the scientifically
unfounded assumption that girls and boys have "naturally" different learning
needs and styles and also that such schools obscure data that suggest that
black boys' academic performance does not improve when they are schooled
separately from girls (Halpern et al. 2011; Feminist Majority Foundation 2014;
Pahlke, Hyde, and Allison 2014; National Organization of Women 2006;
National Organization of Women Legal Defense Fund 1991). Several black
feminist critics emphasize that both black girls and black boys are underachieving in school relative to their white peers and that the achievement gap
between black girls and white girls is often higher than that between black
boys and white boys (hooks 1996; Pratt-Clarke 2010; Williams 2004).

Despite, or perhaps because of, these criticisms, the black-male led effort
to establish ABMSs and the politically diverse supporters who have embraced
this effort raise two important questions for those of us concerned about race
and gender-based inequality in the classroom and beyond. Does the push for
ABMSs signal a new, more expansive recognition of structural racism in the
classroom? Or is the effort to establish such schools evidence that conservative whites are trying to divide traditional left-of-center educational alliances
and that the nation remains wedded to rigid, gender-biased presumptions
about what good schooling looks like?

This book broadens the scope of inquiry regarding ABMSs' diverse and
seemingly incongruous political supporters in Madison and across the nation.
It argues that the consensus in favor of ABMSs among ideologically diverse
groups who are frequently at loggerheads over a range of other issues is neither surprising nor contradictory. Instead, these groups' embrace of ABMSs
makes sense, given that many black male proponents of such schools frequently make antifeminist as well as antiracist claims about black schoolboys'
experience of oppression—claims that appeal to liberals and conservatives
alike. In other words, my examination of the campaign to establish ABMSs
addresses the complex politics that scholars, policymakers, educators, and
parents face and are sometimes not so willing to face as they try to determine
what equitable schooling looks like in the nation's classrooms. As such, *In a
Classroom of Their Own* is more than an interrogation of the pros and cons

of single-gender schooling for black boys. It is also a work in political theory with a heavy insistence on practice—one that gives heave to the complexities of experience and power that multiple participants in the discourse on ABMSs make clear.

Other book-length discussions of black males and schooling either focus on black boys in coeducational schools or pay short shrift to the simultaneously antifeminist and antiracist politics at work in the push for ABMSs. Examples of the former include Pedro Noguera's (2008) *The Trouble with Black Boys*, Ann Ferguson's (2001) *Bad Boys*, and Tyrone Howard's (2013) *Black Male(d)*—all of which use teacher-student interactions as well as black boys' own viewpoints to illuminate the structural forces that harm black males and/or Latinos in coeducational public schools and to posit reforms for counteracting these forces. Examples of the latter include Juliette Williams's (2016) *The Separation Solution*, which critiques the antifeminist politics that undergirds the push for single-sex schools for boys of all races, as well as Ronnie Hopkins's (2007) *Educating Black Males*, which constructs ABMSs as a key means of challenging racism. Finally, Edward Fergus, Pedro Noguera, and Margary Martin's (2014) *Schooling for Resilience* insightfully acknowledges both the antiracist politics and the "traditional ideas of manhood and masculinity" that undergird the push for ABMSs, but does not detail why and how these "ideas" harm black girls in and outside of the classroom (157).

The Discursive and Material Reality of ABMSs

An important, antiracist impetus informs the effort to establish separate schools for black boys. Consider, for example, the following declaration from Jawanza Kunjufu (2013)—a prominent black male proponent of ABMSs:

> For a White male to be suspended, one of three things has to be present: a gun, a knife, and bloodshed. For a Black male to be suspended, there doesn't have to be a gun, a knife, or bloodshed. He can be suspended because the teacher does not like the way he looks at her . . . the way he walks . . . his tone . . . what he says . . . his eye contact . . . the fact that he walks away from her . . . his swagger. Can you imagine, a Black male is suspended because of his swagger! (77)

Conceptualizing the Antiracist Politics of ABMSs

Kunjufu's comments are part of a broader, antiracist commentary at the heart of the discourse in support of ABMSs—one that routinely queries how and why teachers engage in systemically racist behavior, including but not limited to expelling and suspending black boys at disproportionately high rates relative to other students. The answer, many of these proponents emphasize, is that the nation's overwhelmingly white teaching force embraces racist stereotypes of black people as inferior beings whose primitive physicality predisposes them to violence against whites and, more broadly, to engaging in socially deviant acts such as "playing the dozens, using slang . . . [and] wearing pants with loosened belts" (Chiles 2014; Ransaw, Majors, and Moss 2016; Majors and Billson 1993, 14). According to this reasoning, black boys are "ignored, discouraged, and disinvited to learn" by racist educators who are motivated by anything but "equality, freedom, and rationality" (Midgette and Glenn 1993, 72; see also Diop 2009). The result of such racial bias, psychiatrist and ABMS supporter Alvin Poussaint (1996) concludes, is not only "the lack of real representation of blacks as teachers and principals in the school system." It is also that black boys are frequently taught by "white teachers who do not have anything in their educational background to prepare them to deal with children from a different ethnic group."

There is copious evidence that black boys do, in fact, experience systematic racial disadvantage in the classroom. Whites make up 82 percent of all teachers but only 52 percent of the nation's students; blacks are 16 percent of all students but a mere 7 percent of teachers (Boser 2014). Of equal concern is the fact that the nation's predominantly white teaching force places inexplicably high numbers of black boys in so-called special-education classes. Black boys are three times more likely than white boys to be classified as "educable mentally retarded," one and a half times more likely to be classified as having "learning disabilities," and twice as likely to be deemed "emotionally disturbed" (Ford 1996; Jordan 2005).

To make matters worse, black boys have long been suspended from school at higher rates than white boys. In 1999 nearly 41 percent of black high-school boys were suspended, compared with only 25 percent of their white male peers. The comparable figures in 2014 for boys of all ages were 20 percent versus 6 percent (Henderson 2014; U.S. Department of Education 2011). Black males are also more likely to drop out of high school than white males. In 1997, 13.3 percent of black boys dropped out of high school, compared with only 8.5 percent of white boys. In 2015 the figures were 7.1 percent and 5.7 percent, respectively (U.S. Department of Education 2016).

It is this all-too-real racial achievement gap that motivates many black males to regard ABMSs as the best means of ameliorating black boys' racial oppression in the classroom. Consider the following declaration from Tim King (2011), founder of the Urban Prep Academies for black boys:

The grim statistics are well known, but bear repeating: here in Chicago, close to 60% of Black boys do not graduate from high school, and only one in forty receive a bachelor's degree by age 25. In the fall of 2006, we opened Urban Prep Charter Academy for Young Men–Englewood Campus, the nation's first all-male charter public high school, knowing that we had to do something differently to succeed. (191)

"Mr. C.," an Urban Prep teacher, is more explicit in casting ABMSs as a key antiracist tool. He argues that while the "media makes the Black man look so bad," schools like Urban Prep are "[b]reaking stereotypes that Black men are not smart" and are doing so by graduating students from "the hood" whose academic performance parallels that "of any kid who [comes] out of Evanston Township High School [a high achieving, predominantly white school in suburban Chicago]" (qtd. in B. Williams 2013, 102).

Marlon James, an education professor, similarly depicts the establishment of ABMSs as an important means of challenging racism. He argues, more specifically, that such schools can and do counter under-resourced classrooms, inattentive teachers, and other common manifestations of structural racism in the educational system. James cites as evidence ABMSs students' own insights regarding what distinguishes their schools from other, more conventional ones. These insights include everything from "I know how to multiply now" and "I could not read when I came here, but now I can" to "They care about us" and "My [old] teacher just did not care" (qtd. in James 2010, 177–78).

David Banks, head of the Eagle Academies, posits an even more expansive link between establishing ABMSs and challenging systemic racism. He emphasizes, first, that black boys in conventional public schools are "far more likely" than whites not just to "receive a principal's suspension" but also to display their concomitant "frustration" via criminal violence that lands them in the "juvenile corrections system" and, ultimately, in adult prisons (2014, 13). Banks concludes, second and most significantly, that ABMSs, including his own, can counter this troubling reality:

We chose to concentrate our attention on the most underperforming group of young men—inner-city boys of color—so we decided to found [the first] Eagle Academy as a single-sex school in a "prison-pipeline" neighborhood. We refused to cherry-pick the best available students, and we pledged to open our doors to all comers. . . . [G]iven the supports they need, young men can achieve excellence in both scholarship and character. (2015, 15, 16)

On Banks' account, ABMSs are not only key to eradicating institutional racism in the classroom; such schools also produce academically successful black males who are, as such, well positioned to navigate the structural racism that informs the so-called "school to prison" pipeline. Sociologists Anthony Mitchell and James Stewart (2013) similarly conclude that ABMSs stem the tide of black boys' systemically based "educational failure" and, in so doing, reduce the likelihood that said boys will experience a "lifetime of under-employment and institutionalization" (387).

Reading ABMSs as Antifeminist Politics

While an obvious antiracist sentiment pervades the discourse in favor of ABMSs, it is also true that many black male supporters of such schools espouse an antifeminist politics that obscures the extent of black girls' own oppression in the classroom. Absent, for instance, in much of the discussion in favor of ABMSs is any recognition that while black boys are far more likely to be suspended than white boys, it is also true that black girls are more likely to be assigned to special-education classes and to be suspended from school than white girls (U.S. Department of Education 2014; Crenshaw, Ocen, and Nanda 2015). Black girls, moreover, have the lowest SAT scores of all female students and are less likely than other girls to obtain College Readiness Benchmark Scores on the ACT (Smith-Evans et al. 2014). In sum, black girls and black women are not academic superstars who routinely outperform all other social groups. Instead, *both* black females and black males are underachieving relative to their white counterparts (Crenshaw, Ocen, and Nanda 2015; Pratt-Clarke 2010).[1] Helen Neuborne (1991), former executive director of the NOWLDF, sums up this reality when she concludes, "The statistics of school failure, drug addiction and violence call for a national effort to save the next generation of young men from a cycle of poverty and despair. But urban girls are drowning too."

This "drowning" continues once black girls leave school. While all blacks enjoy fewer returns to education than white males, black females are most disadvantaged in this regard. The median income of black female and black male high-school dropouts is $19,300 and $25,200, respectively. Just as disconcerting is the reality that black women high school graduates earn only $100 more per year than black males who leave school early (O'Sullivan, Mugglestone, and Allison 2014). Black female dropouts are also less likely to complete their GED and more likely to be unemployed than their male peers (U.S. Department of Education 2014).

In contending that most black male supporters of ABMSs ignore this and other evidence of young black women's academic underachievement, I am by no means impugning the good intentions of many of the proponents of these schools. On the contrary, as Pedro Noguera (2012) correctly asserts, the push for ABMSs is generally "being carried out by individuals who are sincere and well-meaning about their desire to 'save' young men of color" (11). What prevails, nevertheless, in much of the discourse in favor of ABMSs is the flawed, antifeminist assumption that professional women, including women teachers, inevitably exercise their status as *women* in ways that harm the males in their charge (English 2003). Consider how English professor Ronnie Hopkins draws on the classroom-based insights of fellow ABMSs supporter, Spencer Holland, to argue that women teachers' "feminine" ways are "inhibiting" black male students' academic success:

> You sit in a classroom of kindergarten–first grade boys, they won't do the dancing they won't do the singing. . . . The teacher demonstrates a skill or concept and says, "Come on children, show me, come on." And the little boy says, "I ain't doing that." Her gestures, her demonstrations are always feminine. Sometimes she has on all these long fingernails, and rings on every finger, earrings going. . . . [W]e have got to start looking at what is going on in that classroom that is inhibiting Black boys from succeeding, and one of the most salient things that [has] jumped out at me [is that] they won't copy women. (Holland, qtd. in Hopkins 1997, 69–70)

Another antifeminist assumption is at work in the discourse that promotes ABMSs—namely, that black boys underachieve because women teachers refuse to acknowledge that all boys have unique, biologically based learning needs and styles. Ilandus Hampton, an assistant school superintendent, captures this perspective when he laments the fact that the nation is beset by "feminized public school rooms" which are "geared towards the learning styles of girls and are largely taught by females." The unsurprising result, according to Hampton and fellow ABMSs advocate R. Perez Gaitling (2014), is that educators and administrators mistakenly assume that boys can sit quietly and work independently despite their "naturally" masculine visual and kinesthetic way of learning (Hampton 2015, 9). The difficulty with this perspective, as feminist critics make clear, is that there is no scientific evidence that boys and girls have inherently different, biologically derived learning styles (Halpern et al. 2011; Klein et al. 2014). Nor is it true that black boys' academic performance improves when they are schooled separately from girls (Pahlke, Hyde, and Allison 2014).

Kaleem Caire of Madison Prep posits yet another antifeminist argument—that black boys underachieve, in part, because they are forced to learn alongside black girls, who the boys themselves readily admit are "the number-one distraction" in school (cited in Schubert 2011).[2] Marcus, a black male student, articulates exactly this view when he argues that the best way forward is to establish schools where heterosexual black boys "can't flirt with anybody":

> So going to a [school with girls] . . . we were used to just sitting in the back of the bus and just watching everything. Quickly we saw we have to figure out what we're going to do to be able to keep our grades up because there's no women in here [at this ABMS]. None of them are going to help us with our homework; we can't flirt with anybody to do our homework. It's just my homeboy who wasn't paying attention because I wasn't paying attention. So, we quickly had to find a way to be able to help each other out. (qtd. in Fletcher 2013, 107)

Marcus and Caire's suggestion, that black girls are sexual provocateurs who lure black boys from the worthy path of academic discipline and success, draws on a longtime, antifeminist argument against co-education—that members of the opposite sex are dangerous distractions.[3] As was the case in the early 1900s, this argument erroneously assumes that all schoolboys are heterosexual and will consequently achieve only when they are not forced to divide their energies between their schoolwork and their (hetero)sexually attractive female classmates, who almost always lure them from the path of academic success (Pahlke, Hyde, and Allison 2014; Fergus, Noguera, and Martin 2014).

"Endangered" Urban Black Males, the "Boy Crisis," and Neoliberal Educational Reform

Black male supporters of ABMSs do more than presume that boys have social and learning needs that cannot be addressed in racist, female-led classrooms. As I detail later, many of these supporters also take it for granted that these needs are best met when black boys are free to partake in a neoliberal-inspired educational marketplace made possible by vouchers, open enrollment, and the privatized management of public schools. Other supporters regard ABMSs as an important tool in the broader fight against the "boy crisis" in education—one in which boys of all races are more likely to be characterized as having learning disabilities, to be assigned to special-education classes, to underperform on standardized tests, and to otherwise underachieve relative to their female peers. Still other proponents regard ABMSs as key to dismantling the achievement gap between predominantly white suburban schools and largely black urban schools. A final group of proponents characterize their support for such schools as part of their broader quest to illuminate as well as remedy what numerous academic and popular commentators make clear—that black males are an "endangered" species in the classroom and elsewhere.

In a Classroom of Their Own uses these supporters' understandings of neoliberal educational reform, concerns about a boy crisis in education, worries about racial inequalities in urban schools, and belief that black males are endangered to detail *how* and *why* the push for ABMSs rests on antiracist and antifeminist politics alike. On the one hand, as I make clear in chapter 1, neoliberal-inspired educational reform and the notion of a transracial crisis in boys' education provide black male advocates of these schools with a normative and institutional framework within which to advance their antifeminist politics. A case in point is these supporters' claim that ABMSs represent "equal opportunity" or are a means of leveling the educational "playing field" for all students and, in so doing, ensuring that black boys, like boys of all races, are finally taught in ways that are attentive to their supposedly gender-specific, biologically based educational needs. That black males are most burdened by racism's harmful effects—a key assumption in the narrative on endangered black males—also undergirds many ABMS advocates' empirically unfounded, antifeminist claim that black schoolboys are necessarily more disadvantaged than their female peers. Many of these advocates also cite black boys' underachievement in urban schools not just as evidence that such schools are underfunded relative to their suburban counterparts but also to validate the antifeminist argument that black single mothers, are, by definition, unwilling and unable to properly rear their sons.

On the other hand, black male advocates of ABMSs use the narrative on endangered masculinity, established understandings about racism in urban schools, and efforts at neoliberal educational reform to advance a politics that challenges racism. Many of these advocates note, for instance, that black schoolboys are endangered or at risk of being rendered socially and economically obsolete because of their racist white teachers' biased disciplinary practices. Numerous black male advocates of ABMSs argue, too, that the neoliberal-inspired privileging of "choice"—be it in relation to school, healthcare, and otherwise—is actually a racist code word that masks reduced government spending on social services that blacks especially need. Other advocates not only critique the unequal political economy of urban schools. They emphasize that this inequality is racialized precisely because it stems from the state's failure to distribute adequate material goods and resources to *black* students in the nation's central cities.

Learning from Intersectional Experience

Many black male supporters of ABMSs who articulate a simultaneously antifeminist and antiracist politics do so by way of intersectionality—the analytical framework pioneered by black feminists to illuminate how racial, gendered, and other kinds of disadvantage reinforce each other (Combahee River Collective 1983; Crenshaw 1991). On most accounts, to embrace intersectionality is to reject a dichotomous or binary approach in which race, gender, and other hierarchies of power are taken as "distinct and isolated realms of experience" operating along "independent axes" (Brah and Phoenix 2004, 80). Intersectional theorizing also rejects derivative analyses that posit a single, key oppression, like class, as the one from all others follow. Intersectionality differs, too, from additive models of oppression, which presume, for instance, that black women are subject to the double burden of racial plus gendered oppression or to the tri-fold oppression of race, class, and gender (Collins 2008).

My reading of how ABMSs' black male supporters embrace intersectionality illuminates, contrary to what many feminists suggest, that intersectional analysis is not a necessarily feminist construct but is, instead, a politically fluid framework that can be used to advance a range of political agendas, including those that advance gender-biased understandings of how children learn. For example, many black male supporters of ABMSs embrace the logic of intersectionality when they presume that black boys underachieve not because they are black or because they are males but because they are *black males* who are subject to a particularly debilitating kind of masculinized racism. According to these advocates, such masculinized racism involves, among other things, racist, white women teachers' repeated failure to either acknowledge or attempt to accommodate their black male students' testosterone-driven or "naturally" aggressive learning style.

My analysis of ABMSs also raises controversial questions about intersectionality's utility. Does unmooring intersectionality from its black feminist orientation limit black women's and black girls' ability to identify and articulate their own oppression at the crossroads of race and gender, be it in the classroom or elsewhere? What, moreover, does reconceptualizing intersectionality as something other than a necessarily feminist analytical framework suggest about its capacity to challenge oppressive politics? The answer, which I detail in chapter 2, is that intersectional analysis is not a zero-sum phenomenon in which focusing on one group's oppression at the junction of race and gender means ignoring the disadvantage of another group or groups. Instead, intersectional analysis makes it possible to do something starkly different—to explore how the intersectional subjectivity of social groups, including black women, informs and is informed by the intersectional status of other groups.

Dialectics and the Politics of Experience

Of course, it is quite possible for social groups to articulate a simultaneously liberatory and oppressive politics without embracing the logic of intersectionality. This exact phenomenon is evident among women who rightly challenge their patriarchal oppression as "women" *and* do so on the flawed, oppressive assumption that "real" women are white. There are many blacks, moreover, who rightly resist their racial subordination as "blacks" and do so on the erroneous assumption that "real" black people are heterosexual. What, then, is the way forward? How else are we to understand why members of disadvantaged social groups, including but not limited to black male advocates of ABMSs, make experiential claims that challenge as well as reinscribe gendered and other hierarchies of power?

A key explanation, which I outline in chapter 3, is that there is a dialectic between "experience" and "politics" that frames how disadvantaged social groups, including ABMSs' black male advocates, articulate their oppression. On one hand, experiencing racism's harmful effects motivates these advocates to embrace an antiracist politics that justifiably critiques white privilege in schools. On the other hand, these advocates' understanding of *why* they experience racism is shaped by a less-than-ideal patriarchal politics that presumes that young black males underachieve because they are forced to learn in "overly" feminized classrooms.

Other feminist theorists advance the notion of a dialectic reality between making experiential claims and embracing a specific kind of politics. Nancy Hartsock (1990) asserts that women who think and speak critically about their experience of oppression can attain a feminist "standpoint" or politics that exposes the inequitable world that "men have constructed" *and* that this standpoint is sometimes antifeminist because how women acquire it is "conditioned by" their oppressive social "locations" (32).[4] Joan Scott (1999) concludes that although appeals to experience "essentialize identity and reify the subject," it is *also* true that the very act of historicizing and critically analyzing, rather than blindly accepting, why certain people occupy categories such as "woman" encourages the conditions necessary for a new kind of political resistance that undermines traditional, patriarchal understandings of gender (37–38).

Absent from Hartsock's, Scott's, and other feminist theorists' recognition that women and other social groups make experiential claims that both foster and stymie a politics of resistance, is a detailed accounting of what the political "messiness" of making such claims looks like within the context of tangible public policy, especially policy with mutually constructing racial and gendered effects. I take up this task by doing two things. First, I detail E. Frances White's (1990) conception of "discursive dialectics" or the notion that black people and other oppressed groups' appeals to experience resist and reproduce inequalities of power because these groups utilize "counter discourses" that both challenge and "operate on the same ground" as "dominant ideolog[ies]" (79). Second, I provide concrete evidence of how this "discursive dialectics" is manifest within the narrative in support of ABMSs. I pay particular attention to how black male supporters of such schools articulate black boys' experience of oppression in ways that foster antiracist politics *and* reinscribe the flawed, patriarchal assumption that women and girls are necessarily complicit in black males' oppression. My aim, again, is to highlight—within the parameters of a concrete policy initiative—"discursive dialectics" or the reality that social groups' experiential claims challenge and reinscribe hierarchies of power.

My argument, that social groups' experience-based claims are, by definition, politically fluid, is inspired by but goes beyond the work of Gayatri Spivak (1988a, 1988b, 1990, 1993a, 1993b) and Iris Young (1994), who recognize and attempt to transcend the often polarizing terms of the debate regarding the emancipatory potential, or the lack thereof, of experience-based politics. Like these feminist theorists, I acknowledge the liberatory possibilities and limitations of making experiential claims. Unlike them, I do not attempt to construct a new, less problematic kind of experiential claim (such as Spivak's "strategic essentialism") as the way forward. I emphasize, instead, that no such terrain exists, given that assertions about experience are often already enmeshed in liberatory as well as oppressive politics.

From Non-Ideal Experience to Coalitional Power

In a Classroom of Their Own makes a final, major argument—that while no ideal experiential claim exists, it *is* possible for disadvantaged groups to recognize this reality and to build antiracist as well as feminist political coalitions around it. Black male proponents of ABMSs are no exception. Many of these proponents embrace elements of a normative-critical understanding of power that make them both willing and able to critically analyze the assumptions and demands associated not merely with their own but also with their feminist critics' experiential claims. To embrace a normative-critical understanding of power is to be suspicious of the material, political, and social harm caused by domination; to recognize the reality of plural, interconnected forms of domination; and to understand that we cannot challenge domination until we identify how our own history leads us to hold views that legitimate harm (hooks 2004, Crenshaw 2000, Pettit 1999, Young 1990).

In arguing that many black male advocates of ABMSs subscribe to a normative-critical understanding of power, I assume, as do a wide array of feminist and other social and political theorists, that power is exercised in ways (via decision making, agenda setting, and/or determining the parameters of what is true) that result in the domination of one or more social groups over others (Dahl 1961, Lukes 1974, Collins 2008). Catherine MacKinnon (1989) captures this reality when she argues that the differences between men and women are "defined by power." The difficulty, MacKinnon goes on to explain, is not that society places little value on these differences. It is, rather, that they are recognized in ways that render men's relationship with women little more than "the velvet glove on the iron fist of domination" (219).

At the same time, I regard a normative-critical theory of power as not only providing a critique of domination but also serving as a generative resource from which oppressed groups can envision new pathways for their emancipation. According to the latter reading, power is that which allows us to decide what is in our interests, to recognize that we have the ability to shape our life circumstances, and to do so in ways that advance what is in our self-interest (Yeatman 1997; Hartsock 1983a, 1983b). The result of this process is often empowerment or a "grassroots" or "bottom-up" social, political, and/or economic "reaction against the authority of large-scale, hierarchical, and bureaucratic institutions, and a turn toward emancipatory projects based upon some vision of self-actualization and/or self-determination" (Freire 1970; hooks 1984; Biewener and Bacqué 2015, 59).

This two-pronged approach is valuable on several fronts. To begin with, it overcomes a key difficulty associated with describing power as either empowerment or domination—namely, that the former minimizes the degree to which social groups can become empowered by dominating others while the latter obscures the extent to which even dominated groups can exercise power over others (Allen 1998). Put another way, conceptualizing power as both empowerment and domination makes it possible to understand how and with what consequences social groups, including black male proponents and feminist critics of ABMSs, are privileged as well as oppressed.

Second, defining power in this way captures the reality of "structuration" or the degree to which patriarchal labor markets, racist classrooms, and other oppressive social structures limit our ability to make decisions solely of our own choosing and that these structures exist because we have the agency or are empowered to (re)produce them (Giddens 1984). Finally, a normative-critical theory of power, with its parallel emphases on domination and empowerment, leaves room for a third reading of power as that which is manifest in collective acts carried out by individuals and groups who are united not by a shared or fixed set of identities or identifications but by their commitment to cooperate to resist subordination (Allen 1999).

Most significant is how and with what effect black male advocates of ABMSs subscribe to a normative-critical understanding of power. I answer this question, in chapter four, by drawing on a specific case—a roundtable on ABMSs co-sponsored by the National Urban League and the Carnegie Corporation—that is composed of both black male supporters and black feminist critics of these schools. The black men who participate in this round-table critique structural racism, regard the harms inflicted upon children as a gross violation of human rights, detail how black men's experience of racism is gendered, and recognize their own complicity in perpetuating harmful stereotypes of black boys' capacity for academic achievement.

Put more succinctly, these men articulate important tenets of the norma-tive-critical understanding of power that I describe above. Equally signifi-cant is that doing so makes these black male supporters of ABMSs willing to and capable of critically interrogating the political assumptions and de-mands associated with their own and with their feminist challengers' ap-peals to experience. What these supporters discover in the process is that their own appeals to experience are both antiracist and antifeminist and that their feminist critics similarly make experiential claims that resist as well as perpetuate existing inequalities of power. For instance, on the roundtable I analyze, several black male supporters of ABMSs recognize that their own assumption—that black males are necessarily oppressed in white, "overly" feminized classrooms—not only challenges structural racism but also per-petuates gender-based oppression by denying black males' own capacity to subordinate black women and black girls. Many of these same supporters also understand that when feminist critics demand a moratorium on ABMSs, they are often motivated not just by a valid liberatory desire to challenge many of these schools' gender-biased, Afrocentric curricula but also by the flawed notion that such curricula are necessarily and always antifeminist.

Finally, interrogating the political assumptions and demands that come with their own and with their feminist challengers' appeals to experience, positions many of ABMSs' black male proponents to recognize that they and their opponents are not necessarily united by a shared experience of oppres-sion. They are instead united by a shared conundrum—how to navigate the reality that their respective experiential claims help as well as harm black children of *all* genders. Far from mere speculation on my part, there is tangible evidence that black male supporters of ABMSs recognize this reality. Some of these supporters express concern that while depicting black boys as oppressed in white, female-dominated classrooms highlights an important dimension of young black males' racial victimization, this approach also minimizes the gender-specific manner in which all black children, including black girls, are racially oppressed. Other supporters note that while feminists are right to point out that the gender-biased, Afrocentric curricula of some ABMSs harms black girls, the reality is that such criticism, when paired with a demand to close ABMSs, runs the risk of limiting both black girls' and black boys' opportunity to learn and be self-empowered in antiracist classrooms.

Practicing the Politics of Experience

Simply deducing that ABMSs' black male proponents can form antiracist and feminist coalitions when they acknowledge and attempt to remedy the flaws in their own and in their feminist critics' experiential claims is not enough. For doing so provides little concrete insight about either the kind of spaces that allow groups to collectively navigate the contradictory politics of their own and others' appeals to experience or how such coalition building helps to determine the kind of criteria that must be in place to create classrooms in which black boys and black girls alike can thrive.

My aim here is not to push for a specific or "thick" model of coalition building. Nor is it to specify particular pedagogical, curricular, disciplinary, or other policies in the nation's schools. It is, rather, to make the case, as I do in the concluding chapter of this book, that black male supporters of ABMSs and the feminists who criticize them are best positioned to navigate the contradictory politics associated with their appeals to experience when they use accessible, community-based spaces—from barbershops to public libraries—to do so. Furthermore, critics and proponents of ABMSs who engage in this kind of coalition building foster black children's academic and social well-being in the classroom if and when they engage in a particular process of educational advocacy—one that emphasizes the importance of public schools while criticizing the quality of such schools available to black children.

Educational advocacy, so defined, recognizes that taxpayer-funded schools are an important means of addressing oppression *and* that oppressed groups are most often burdened with having to live with inferior public goods, including subpar public schools. Such advocacy is successful when it is beholden to two norms. The first norm is that public schools should foster black people's capacity for self-determination in the face of intersectional oppression. In highlighting this norm, I recognize that much of ABMSs' appeal stems from the fact that teachers and administrators in these schools recognize black people's yearning for and ability to define educational goals and pursue educational desires of their own choosing. At the same time, without a focus on intersectionality, such educational self-determination is possible not for the majority of black people but, rather, for the limited number—like heterosexual, middle-class black men—who are subject to a single form of oppression.

The second norm is that such schools succeed when they enable black students to perpetually (re)define what life in a democratic polity looks like. My two-pronged assumption here is that public schools foster democracy and that the kind of democracy that they make available to black students is limited, at best. In the final analysis, educational advocacy, as I define it, does not resolve the normative tension inherent in the politics of experience or the fact that disadvantaged social groups' appeals to experience both further and undermine a politics of resistance. What my understanding of such advocacy does provide is a set of norms according to which black men, women, and other social groups can navigate this tension in productive and potentially emancipatory ways.

A Short History of ABMSs

The late nineteenth and early twentieth centuries marked a period in which coeducation for all children was viewed with suspicion. It is hardly surprising, then, that many of the educational opportunities available to blacks, from the time of slavery and well into the twentieth century, were segregated by gender. Spelman College, founded in 1881 by white missionaries, taught young black women the liberal arts as well as concrete vocational skills (Williams 2004). The Daytona Literary and Industrial School for Negro Girls and the National Training School for Negro Girls, founded in 1909 and 1904, respectively, pro-vided young black women with technical and vocational training in domestic science, teaching, and nursing with the hope that they might achieve a modi-cum of "economic self-sufficiency" as domestic workers (McCluskey 1993).

The late nineteenth and early twentieth centuries also saw the emergence of missionary-founded and -financed secondary and tertiary institutions for young black men, including Morehouse College which was established 150 years ago in Atlanta, Georgia. Other, now-defunct all-black secondary and/or tertiary institutions originally established solely for males include Biddle University and St. Emma's Industrial and Agricultural School, founded in the late 1800s, as well as Boggs Academy, Harbison Agricultural College, and St. Augustine's Seminary, which were opened in the early 1900s (United Presbyterian Church in the U.S. General Assembly 1920; Morton 1975; Weldon 2010).

These ABMSs were part of a broader effort by nineteenth- and early-twentieth-century European and North American missionaries, industrialists, and moral reformers to establish single-gender educational institutions throughout the colonized world. Other examples of such institutions included secondary schools for the sons of West African chiefs (Berman 1977; Oliver 1952). Far more prevalent were single-gender industrial and vocational schools—from Jamaica's Hope Industrial School for Boys, which prepared its students for agricultural labor, to colonial Belgian domestic-training institutes or "foyers sociaux" that taught African women European-oriented cooking, sewing, and nursing skills (Roper 2013; Hunt 1990).

These all-female schools, as well as single-gender institutions for black boys, were meant to produce "Taylorized" workers for the rapidly expanding factory-based economy of the United States, to provide laborers and skilled tradesmen for colonial, agriculture-based economies, or to supply a cadre of local elites that Europeans could rely on to help run their respective colonies (Walker 2013; Roper 2013). Most of the black women and girls who attended the single-gender schools I describe above were being prepared to serve as housewives or to provide domestic labor for white and/or colonial households, the kind of labor that made it possible not only for middle-class white men to work outside the home and away from their land but also for their wives and children to experience labor-free domesticity (Brooks 2008; Gaitskell 1983).

It is not enough, however, to simply conclude that single-gender schools for blacks were designed to sustain whites' social and economic supremacy; doing so obscures the extent to which these institutions, particularly those in the United States, also fostered a gender-specific sense of racial pride, respectability, and "uplift." For example, many schools for black women and black girls challenged the racist assumption that blacks, including black women, are too immoral to earn a living based on something other than degeneracy (Williams 2004, McCluskey 1993). Numerous teachers and students in all-male institutions similarly regarded their very existence as an important, antiracist act. In 1896 black North Carolina congressman George White captured this sentiment when he proudly declared that all-male Biddle University represented both black men's and the entire race's progression "slowly but surely" away from the "foul valley" of enslavement "to the top" of the nation's socioeconomic and moral hierarchy (qtd. in Greenwood 2001, 149). Seventy-one years later Edward Jones (1967), a Morehouse alumnus, similarly described the school's mission, to cultivate and enable black males' "self-respect and dignity," as a key means of challenging white supremacy:

> Morehouse College, since its humble, inauspicious beginnings . . . has been dedicated to the task of building men: first by enlightening their minds, then by freeing them from the shackles of a psychological conditioning brought about by nearly two hundred and fifty years of slavery. The task of [its] first educators was not simply one of inculcating knowledge, which of itself tends to make men free, but also one of rehabilitation—of repairing the psychological damage done to the souls of enslaved men who needed to be taught self-respect and dignity even in a degrading environment where the social and political *status quo*, by laws and mores, was diametrically opposed to such teachings. (10–11)

At the same time, unlike separate schools for black women and black girls, which sought to challenge stereotypes of black women as sexually promiscuous, there was often little in the underlying ethos of the ABMSs of the late nineteenth and early twentieth centuries that lent itself to feminist politics. Instead, the opposite was frequently the case. Many students, educators, and donors associated with these schools presumed that their central mission was to restore black men to their "natural" status as leaders of black women and, by extension, of the race. Morehouse College is, again, an important departure point for illuminating this fact. Consider the following 1899 declaration from John Hope (1899), a year after his appointment as a Classics professor at Atlanta Baptist College (now Morehouse College) and seven years before he was selected as the first black president of the same institution: "As much as us Negroes are in need of men, it [is] a great calamity for our women to act as substitutes . . . and the surest way for our men to become more manly is for our women to become more womanly."

Financial constraints brought on by the Depression, combined with gradual loosening of de facto segregation in public schools, led many of the nation's earliest all-black male secondary and tertiary institutions either to accept women and girls or to close their doors during the 1960s and early 1970s (Durham 2003; Lohmann 2013). This hiatus, however, was relatively short lived. In March 1990 the "Ad Hoc Group of Concerned Educators," a Detroit-based group troubled by the poor academic performance of black students, particularly black male students, convened a conference—"Improving Self-Concept for At-Risk Black Students, with Emphasis on Saving the Black Male." Conference attendees, who showed up in larger-than-expected numbers, approved a resolution demanding that local politicians and the Detroit Board of Education host hearings on "the crisis of the African American Male" (Watson and Smitherman 1996, 37). The board, in response, formed a "Male Academy Task force which, in November 1990, recommended the establishment of a "Male Academy" (later called the Malcolm X Academy) to "change the odds for 'at-risk male students'" and to "save a generation" of the city's children (Detroit Public Schools, qtd. in Watson and Smitherman 1996, 40).

Both the board's decision and many blacks' enthusiastic reaction to it are best understood against the backdrop of Detroit's socioeconomic status, or lack thereof, in the early 1990s. In 1990, 22.2 percent of Detroit's predominantly black residents were unemployed, compared with 11.4 percent of blacks and 4.8 percent of whites nationwide (Levine and Callaghan 1998; U.S. Department of Labor 2011). Just as disturbing was the 34.8 percent of Detroit's black residents who lived in poverty in 1990 (Levine and Callaghan 1998). The comparable national rate was 31.9 percent for blacks and 10.7 percent for whites (U.S. Census Bureau 1991).

While the high unemployment and poverty rate of Detroit's black residents was disturbing, it was hardly surprising. By 1990 the city had experienced a significant decline in automobile manufacturing, which had been responsible for much of the black population's rapid growth and relative prosperity after World War II (Sugrue 2014; Farley, Danzinger, and Holzer 2000). Deindustrialization was not the only source of the city's economic woes, however. Detroit's white population decreased by 1.4 million between 1950 and 1990 (Hartigan 2013). These rapidly retreating whites, many of whom fled to the suburbs, took their purchasing power with them and left everything from decreased property values to retail "deserts" in their wake (Sugrue 2014).

With white flight and deindustrialization came the erosion of the city's tax base and corresponding inability to fully pay for roads, police officers, and other municipal services. The city's schools were not exempt. In 1990, the same year Detroit's school board granted permission to open a "Male Academy," per capita spending on students was $5,093 compared with $7,889 in 1970 (Deskins 1996). Moreover, the city's high school dropout rate was 18.8 percent—sharply higher than the national rate of 12.1 percent for all students and 13.2 percent and 9 percent for blacks and whites, respectively (Deskins 1996; U.S. Department of Education 2012). This racial achievement gap and its effects were gendered. While Detroit's black students were generally more likely to drop out of school than their white counterparts, the dropout rate for black males (54 percent) was higher than for black females (45 percent) (Pratt-Clarke 2010). In addition, while blacks as a whole earned less than their white peers, the mean hourly wage for young black women with a high school diploma was almost 50 percent less than that for comparably educated young black men (Farley, Danzinger, and Holzer 2000).

It was the masculinized dimension of Detroit students' racial oppression that ultimately captured the attention of the city's school board and other black advocates of the Male Academy (Pratt-Clarke 2010). The possibility of an all-black male school in Detroit was not, however, met with unanimous support. Several white and black commentators from the city and across the country criticized the proposed Male Academy (Williams 2016; Pratt-Clarke 2010). These critics included Shawn Garrett, a Detroit parent, who filed suit (*Garrett v. Board of Education*) in conjunction with the NOWLDF and the ACLU to thwart the academy's opening. The suit inspired accusations that Garrett and other black critics of the academy were "race traitors" who were colluding with white feminists intent on denying black Detroiters autonomy over their own schools and communities (Pratt-Clarke 2010; Watson and Smitherman 1996).

Garrett v. Board of Education ultimately resulted in an August 1991 court order mandating that girls be allowed to enroll in the Male Academy. The academy, officially named the Malcolm X Academy, opened in September 1991 with a student body that was only 7 percent female. This stark gender imbalance stemmed from the fact that local community organizations pressured black parents not to enroll their daughters. In addition, the court order that mandated girls' admission to the Malcolm X Academy stipulated that only 25 percent of enrolled students had to be girls, gave permission for boys to start school one week earlier than girls, and required girls but not boys to submit to a one-week application period. The result was arguably "a male-centered administration, a male-focused classroom environment . . . and a predominantly male student body" (Pratt-Clarke 2010, 123). In other words, the academy *was* the nation's first ABMS except in the narrow, legalistic eyes of the court.

The 2002 No Child Left Behind Act and 1996 reforms to Federal Title IX legislation eventually gave public schools more freedom to segregate students, including black students, by gender. It is far from surprising, then, that more than forty ABMSs have been proposed or established—mainly in the South, the Midwest, and the Northeast since the Malcolm X Academy opened its doors in 1991 (see Appendix). There are few signs of abatement on the horizon. Charleston, South Carolina's Prestige Academy and Washington, D.C.'s first all-male public high school, Ron Brown Preparatory High School, opened their doors in 2016. Not only that, multiple surveys reveal that more than 60 percent of all blacks and 70 percent of black educators are in favor of single-gender schools, including separate schools for black boys (Mitchell and Stewart 2010; Dawson 2001). This support exists across the ideological spectrum of black politics. Afrocentric scholars and activists argue that such schools offer an effective means of exposing black boys to African histories and cultures (Causey 2015). Black conservatives regard ABMSs as a form of "self-help" that enables black boys to benefit from growing socioeconomic opportunities in light of racism's supposed decline (Keyes 1996; Williams, qtd. in Meyers 1992). Black liberal supporters contend that these schools provide black boys with an "equal opportunity" to achieve academically (Laing 2010; King, qtd. in M. Davis 2006).

A Word about Terminology, Methodology, and Case Selection

Several important terms recur throughout this book. When I use "ABMSs" in this introductory chapter and in subsequent chapters, I am describing "whole schools." Such schools are publicly funded primary, middle, or secondary institutions, composed solely or primarily of black male students. Whole schools are also populated by faculty, staff, and students who make a formal commitment to improving the academic and social well-being of black boys (Hopkins 1997). I focus on "whole school" ABMSs because they have generated the greatest popular and scholarly attention and, thus, constitute the most productive point from which to consider the advantages and disadvantages of the experience-based politics of social groups, particularly that of black males. Other models of single-gender schooling for black boys include "evolving" male schools that are in the process of establishing gender-specific pedagogical, curricular, and other interventions, as well as coeducational schools that allow black boys to meet in single-gender classes at one or more times throughout the day in order to achieve specific academic and behavioral goals. Finally, school-associated programs provide black boys with all-black male academic tutoring, male mentorship, and other gender- and race-specific learning opportunities (Hopkins 1997).

In a Classroom of Their Own employs discourse analysis to illuminate how and with what consequences black male supporters of ABMSs construct black boys as victims of racist, "overly" feminized classrooms. I understand "discourse" to be the sum total of the "manifestoes, records of debates or meetings, actions of political demonstrators, newspaper articles, slogans, speeches, posters, satirical prints, statutes of associations, pamphlets, and so on" associated with a particular group, location, or moment in time (Sewell 1980, 8–9). To engage in discourse analysis is to identify and interrogate how these and other kinds of texts are socially constructed. Two assumptions inform my approach to discourse analysis. First, discourse is never articulated or acted upon in isolation but is instead resisted, rejected, or otherwise challenged by one or more social groups. Second, the meaning of any given discourse is a function not only of specific words or sentences but also of "broader speech episodes" or "contextual factors" which are "multifaceted, ever evolving, dialectical, and conflict-rived" (Johnston 2002, 67).

I make particular use of policy discourse analysis, which "focuses on the discursive construction of policy problems and on the effects, including the lived effects, of the policies which accompany particular constructions" (Bacchi 1999, 48). Engaging in such analysis means recognizing that social and public policies are themselves discursive phenomena that both regulate and create material and other inequalities of power. This approach illuminates how scholars, policymakers, and the general public construct a given social problem (black boys' academic underachievement) and position a specific policy (the establishment of ABMSs) as the best means of solving the problem.

The multiple "paradigms of inquiry" present in policy discourse analysis also make use of the strengths while mitigating the limitations of interpretive, critical, and poststructural perspectives of the social world (Allan 2012). I utilize an interpretive approach to identify the cognitive constructs or the key norms, rationales, assumptions, and silences that proponents of ABMSs utilize to find, recognize, and label such schools as the best means of improving black boys' academic outcomes. My simultaneous use of a critical approach to inquiry ensures that I not only identify but also challenge the inequalities that are so often central to policy-oriented process of meaning making, including the push for ABMSs. I do so, in part, by illuminating the institutional norms and structures that shape the nation's classrooms and by paying attention to the traditionally silenced voices or "counter-stories" of those, including black boys and black girls, who are disadvantaged by many of these norms and structures (Ladson-Billings 2000).

Policy discourse analysis's poststructural paradigm also allows me to address what many critically oriented policy scholars do not—that research subjects are rarely as coherent as first glance suggests. This kind of policy analysis approach challenges or renders problematic both the "givenness" of a policy intervention as well as who is widely regarded as being advantaged and/or disadvantaged by said intervention (Allan 2012, 49). To engage in such analysis is to recognize, in sum, that "[w]e cannot simply assume the 'pre-discursive existence' of . . . 'unified' subjects of policymaking" (Gottweis 2003, 254). This approach reveals, for instance, that the academically underachieving black male subject at the center of the discourse in favor of ABMSs is neither inevitable nor self-evident but, rather, the contingent result of well-established rules that posit "blackness" as a masculine phenomenon.

Finally, I focus my analysis on a specific case or happening, the effort to establish ABMSs, because the discourse regarding these schools is both expansive and detailed. Participants in the discourse include conservatives, liberals, scholars, activists, lawmakers, parents, teachers, and students. This breadth reflects the extent to which the discourse is at the center of rather than on the periphery of the nation's political consciousness. This centrality, in turn, means that the push to open ABMSs is a productive point of departure for exploring which specific material, ideological, and discursive circumstances in contemporary American society are most associated with the simultaneously emancipatory and oppressive experiential claims of ABMSs' black male proponents. The preponderance, diversity, availability, and sheer detail of the written documents about ABMSs—legal briefs, charter school proposals, school brochures, school newsletters, newspaper and magazine articles, academic books, scholarly journals, conference papers, transcripts of public meetings, blog postings, and Web sites—also makes such schools a desirable reference point for thinking about how and why social groups make politically fluid claims about their experience of oppression.

1 Choice, Crisis, and Urban Endangerment

Officials associated with Urban Preparatory Academies recently found themselves in the unusual position of having to fend off negative press. In June 2015 Urban Prep's board of directors terminated seventeen, or one in six, teachers from its three Chicago-based ABMSs. The fired teachers used local and national media outlets to accuse "Urban Prep" of "union-busting" or, more specifically, of firing them a few weeks after they had voted to join the Chicago Alliance of Charter Teachers and Staff (Sanchez 2015; Woo 2015). An array of parents, students, and other observers asserted that the fired teachers provided invaluable intellectual and social guidance for Urban Prep's students who are, like other black boys across the country, "at-risk" (Stone 2015) and, more pointedly, that the firings were racist because most of the affected teachers were black (Becerril and Zionts 2015). Other pundits emphasized that Urban Prep's chief executive officer, Tim King, was right to challenge teachers' unions, including the Chicago Alliance of Charter Teachers and Staff, precisely because their members are "over 90 percent White and overwhelmingly female" and are, consequently, inclined to embrace "a suburban White female platform at the expense of Black, Latino, and poor children of all colors" (Muhammad 2016).

In a letter to parents, Tim King emphasized that he and other school officials were concerned that unionization might harm the schools' "ability to remain steadfast . . . in making Urban Prep students the first priority." King further lamented the fact that so many Illinois-based unions are against so-called school choice, as evidenced by their "opposition to a bill designed to provide equal funding to charter schools" and by their general criticism of the "achievements" of schools like Urban Prep (King 2015). In spite of, or perhaps because of, King's rhetoric, Urban Prep ultimately offered to rehire the terminated teachers and agreed to hand them $250,000 in severance and back pay under a settlement authorized by the National Labor Relations Board.

In an effort to bring closure to the matter, Evan Lewis, chief operations officer of Urban Prep Academies, emphasized in a January 2016 press release that pursuing this path was ultimately in the "best interest" of the academies and of its students (Lewis 2016). The reality, however, is that the story regarding Urban Prep teachers' effort to unionize is far from complete. The teachers are still negotiating with management to determine the exact terms of their initial contract. Not only that, the fact that critics and supporters alike have responded to Urban Prep teachers' unionization efforts in ways that both challenge antiblack racism and denigrate white women teachers' status, as women, is further evidence of the need to ask an important question. Why does the discourse in favor of ABMSs so often disturb the boundary between liberatory and oppressive politics? Successfully answering this question rests, in part, on recognizing that the push for these schools emerges and is resonant within a specific socioeconomic context.

The rest of this chapter details the material and discursive environment in which black male proponents of ABMSs embrace both antiracist and antifeminist politics. I begin by situating these proponents' antifeminist politics within ongoing conversations about a universal "boy crisis"—one in which young males of all races are purportedly forced to learn in female-dominated and, thus, harmful classrooms. I then discuss how many black male supporters of ABMSs not only subscribe to the widespread notion that black males are nearly "endangered" but also do so in ways that both challenge systemic racism in the classroom and legitimate the gender-biased notion that high-achieving, sexually distracting black girls are complicit in young black males' underachievement.

ABMS supporters' simultaneously antifeminist and antiracist politics also comes to the fore within well-entrenched concerns about the nation's urban schools. Put more specifically, many advocates of these schools rightfully posit black boys' underachievement as a gender-specific manifestation of racism in urban schools and do so on the flawed antifeminist assumption that said boys underachieve because they, rather than black girls, are most burdened by racism in inner-city classrooms. The final section of the chapter reveals that many of these same supporters make the antiracist argument that neoliberal educational reforms disproportionately harm black students and advance the antifeminist notion that such reforms, if properly implemented, can address black boys' supposedly inherent or biologically informed learning needs.

All Boys against All Girls

In 2006, some fifteen years after the Malcolm X Academy opened its doors in Detroit, Pulitzer Prize–winning journalist Peg Tyre (2006) expressed concern that boys of all races and social backgrounds are increasingly underachieving relative to girls:

> [B]oys across the nation and in every demographic group are falling behind. In elementary school, boys are two times more likely than girls to be diagnosed with learning disabilities and twice as likely to be placed in special-education classes. High-school boys are losing ground to girls on standardized writing tests. The number of boys who said they didn't like school rose 71 percent between 1980 and 2001. (30)

Journalist and author Richard Whitmire (2011) similarly declared five years later that "something has gone awry with all boys." He cited, as evidence, the many "white middle class boys" whose "woes are masked by the plethora of second and third-tier colleges more than willing to admit slacker male freshmen whose parents can pay full tuition."

From Pro-ABMS Discourse to a Transracial Boy Crisis

Whitmire's and Tyre's sentiments are part of the scholarly, popular, and policy-oriented boy-crisis narrative[1] that emerged in the late 1990s. Key themes in much of this narrative echo and are arguably appropriated from the antifeminist ethos present in the discourse in favor of ABMSs (Williams 2013). First, like purveyors of the narrative in support of separate schools for black boys, psychologist Judith Kleinfeld (2006), family therapist Michael Gurian (2007), and other boy crisis commentators (Sommers 2013; Pollack 1999) assume that boys underachieve because schools have been "feminized" by women teachers who cater to girls' social and intellectual strengths by creating classrooms in which passive compliance and verbal communication or "sitting and reading" are the main measures of student success (Gurian 2007, 35). Others who trumpet the boy crisis, including popular writer and physician Leonard Sax (2016), agree with many black male proponents of ABMSs that girls' very presence in the classroom makes eager-to-impress boys "misbehave" in ways that impede their education, long-term ability to find jobs, psychological ability to avoid self-destructive violence and, by extension, their future capacity to function as socially and morally upstanding patriarchs (Sax cited in "No Boys Allowed" 2002; see also Wright 2103, Leonhardt 2014).

Finally, as is the case with black male advocates of ABMSs, many who warn of a boy crisis in education also make the case for gender-segregated schools on the gender-biased, scientifically unfounded assumption that boys and girls have distinct, biologically based learning needs (Williams 2016). Leonard Sax is chair of the governing board of the National Association for Single-Sex Public Education, whose members argue that "the brains of girls and boys differ in important ways . . . [that] are genetically programmed and are present at birth" (National Association for Single-Sex Public Education 2017). Fellow boy-crisis purveyor and conservative scholar Christina Hoff Sommers argues that ABMSs and other single-sex schools meet boys' seemingly inherent gender-specific "interests, propensities and needs" (2013a, 87) and, in the process, help close the "growing boy gap in education" (2013b). Michael Gurian (2007, 2014) strives to alleviate this gap by way of the Gurian Institute—an organization that provides teacher training on and promotes research about the efficacy of single-gender schools by emphasizing, among other things, how such schools can "remov[e] the distraction of girls when puberty sends the hormones into overdrive" (Gurian Institute 2017).

Gurian's and other similar efforts have paid off. While there is no definitive count of all-boys schools in operation across the nation, several sources put the number at eighty, compared with only three in 1990 (Williams 2016). The public, moreover, has been receptive to these schools. A 2008 nationwide survey revealed that more than one-third of Americans believe that parents should have the choice to enroll their child in a single-gender school; only one-quarter of Americans disagree (Howell, West, and Peterson 2008). While state-level data is harder to ascertain, a 2010 survey in South Carolina revealed that 79 percent of students enrolled in single-gender classrooms felt that their general attitude toward school had improved, 94 percent of these children's parents believed that their offspring were more likely to complete high school, and 85 percent of their teachers reported increased student effort (Reuters 2010).

These findings are particularly striking given the data, which suggests there is no transracial crisis in boys' education (DiPrete and Buchmann 2013; Anderson 2014). It is true that high-school girls earn better grades than their male peers and that women outnumber men at the tertiary level. At the same time, boys continue to outperform girls on the math sections of the SAT and ACT college entrance exams, boys' grades have remained the same or improved since the 1990s, and the percentage of males graduating from high school and obtaining bachelor's degrees is at an all-time high (American Association of University Women 2008; DiPrete and Buchmann 2013). Furthermore, boy crisis commentators (Wright 2013; Leonhardt 2014) who argue that academically underachieving boys ultimately lose out to women in the labor market, ignore the reality that while men's median wages have declined and their unemployment has increased since the late 1970s, they continue to earn more and to have higher levels of employment (in the case of white men) than women (American Association of University Women 2016).

From Boy Crisis to ABMSs

It is not merely the case that commentators who trumpet a boy crisis appropriate several of the key antifeminist tenets present in the discourse in support of ABMSs. The opposite is also true—most black male advocates of these schools embrace the notion of a transracial boy crisis.[2] Doing so has a twofold, antifeminist utility for these advocates. To begin with, embracing the idea of a universal crisis in boys' education allows these advocates to further legitimize the erroneous idea that black girls are always more successful in school relative to their male peers. One such supporter is educator Norman Johnson, who embraces Michael Gurian's "brain science," or the notion that feminized classrooms put boys at a "neurological" disadvantage, to emphasize a specific point—that black girls are inevitably on an "academic fast track" relative to their black male peers (qtd. in Blacknews.com 2008; see also Goff and Johnson 2008; Johnson 2010). Similarly, when educators and ABMS supporters Benjamin Wright and Jabali Sawicki praise boy-crisis pioneer Leonard Sax for recognizing that all boys need tactile, aggressive play in order to catch up academically with girls, they do so to buttress their own, more precise argument—that while all boys underachieve relative to girls, the achievement gap between black boys and black girls is particularly dire. Hence Sawicki's conclusion that educating black boys is "the new civil rights movement" (Weil 2008).

Embracing the idea of a transracial boy crisis allows black male supporters of ABMSs to advance a second, antifeminist argument—that single-gender schools are warranted because they help to address a key socioeconomic woe, fatherless households, that harms all boys, especially black boys, beyond and within the classroom. David Banks (2015) explains:

> [W]hile [the boy crisis] hits brown and black boys earliest and hardest, the underlying causes are increasingly shared by American boys of many backgrounds. . . . Years before [the] alarm was being sounded for men in general, I was aware that a large number of young men of color, including those in the South Bronx, where my school, Bronx Law, was located, were in serious

trouble. Even as I savored the success of our girls, I felt a strong desire to help those boys. . . . Nationwide, the percentage of children growing up without a father in the house has tripled from 11 percent in 1960 to 33 percent today. Among African-American families . . . in 1960 it was 20 percent. . . . Today it is 68 percent. (13–14)

Banks assumes that there is a universal boy crisis because boys of all races are "growing up without a father." Making this assumption enables him to legitimate the patriarchal, heteronormative claim that valid families, including black families, are composed of a mother and a father. What Banks fails to consider is that female-headed households are not inherently harmful to children's—including boys'—socioeconomic well-being. Instead, such households are often impoverished not because of women's innate inability to function as household heads but because gender and/or race discrimination in the labor-force depresses their wages relative to other social groups (Mink 2010). Furthermore, any blanket assertion that women-headed households are necessarily detrimental to their inhabitants obscures the reality that physical, sexual, and mental abuse can occur in two-parent households and, relatedly, that such households are less than ideal if and when they limit women's, including black women's, social and economic independence. In sum, "while it is possible to state that there is a rise in female-headed households . . . this rise cannot be discussed as a universal indicator of women's independence, nor can it be discussed as a universal indicator of women's impoverishment" (Mohanty 1984, 348).

Endangered Black Masculinity

My argument is not just that the notion of a boy crisis in education animates the discourse in favor of ABMSs in ways that are antifeminist. It is also that many of ABMSs' black male proponents articulate a politics that is antiracist. To understand this complicated, nuanced reality, we must turn our attention to how these advocates engage with another, older narrative—the ongoing conversation that constructs black men and black boys as endangered.

Specific concerns about black men's well-being have long informed conversations by and about black Americans—from Equiano's (1789) distress that he and other black male slaves were not real men because they were unable to defend the "virtue" of their female peers, to Ida B. Wells's (1892) postemancipation conclusion that white lynch mobs undermined black men's psychic as well as physical well-being, to sociologist Franklin E. Frazier's (1939) worry that "disorganized" black female-headed households exacerbate black boys' criminal delinquency. After World War II, these concerns gained a wider audience. Civil rights and black power leaders routinely couched the struggle against antiblack racism in masculine terms (Estes 2005). In addition, Daniel Moynihan (1965) and other commentators (Lewis 1967; Bernard 1966; Pettigrew 1964) penned widely disseminated texts that proclaimed that black female-headed households deny black men the opportunity to fulfill their supposedly natural role as breadwinners, husbands, and fathers of the race and, in the process, fuel these men's sense of hopelessness, high rates of criminal delinquency, as well as the broader "tangle of pathology" that purportedly plagues the entire black community.

The more contemporary narrative concerning black male endangerment, which emerged in the late 1970s, presumes that black men exist not on the margins of but well outside mainstream socioeconomic and political life. Gone is the time, many participants in this narrative contend, when factory work and other kinds of low-skill, low-wage employment were widely available to black men. Today's black men are, instead, "excess baggage" in a labor market that remains racist, that outsources low-skill jobs to low-cost foreign locales, and that requires education and technical skills to obtain high-paying jobs (Staples 1987; Jackson 2014). Others, convinced of black males' impending physical obsolescence, cite as evidence black men's and black boys' short life expectancy and high mortality rate relative to other groups (Floyd 2015). Also distressing for many is the number of black males who are politically obsolete or who cannot run for office or vote because of felony convictions meted out to them by the racist criminal justice system (Mack 2009; King and Mauer 2004).

Concrete expressions of this narrative include President Obama's 2014 My Brother's Keeper Initiative, which relies on corporate sponsors to provide mentorship and apprenticeship opportunities for boys of color, as well as the 1995 Million Man March, during which black men attempted to "atone" for their inability to function as patriarchs of the race. Several assumptions inform these and other expressions of the endangered-black-male narrative. One assumption is that black males are unemployed and underemployed at such high rates because black women are "twofers" whose hiring enables racist white employers to fulfill affirmative-action race and gender quotas (Mattox 1995; St. Jean and Feagin 2015). Participants in the narrative that depicts black males as endangered argue, too, that professional black women are better educated and more likely to obtain lucrative private-sector jobs because whites perceive them as less intimidating than black men (McAuliffe 2015; Mathis 2007). A last group of participants are equally convinced that black males are nearly obsolete in the labor market, the criminal justice system, and the family because black single mothers "raise their daughters" but either spoil or are inattentive to their sons (Milloy 1993; Squires 2012; Jones 2014).

Several supporters of ABMSs cast such schools as the best means of thwarting what they regard as endangered black males' impending obsolescence. Journalist Daryl Gale emphasizes that separate schools for black boys are key to ensuring that "thousands of young Black men [are] carrying books and headed for college rather than carrying guns and headed for prison" and, more broadly, to "reversing the tide of violence and despair that drowns [the black] community in broken lives" (Gale 2006). Scholars Thomas Midgette and Eddie Glenn (1993) are more blunt. They ask: "Why do we need African-American male academies?" The answer, they conclude, is that the "young, African-American man in America is endangered, embittered, and embattled" (69).

ABMSs and the Antifeminist Politics of Endangered Black Masculinity

I am especially concerned with how black male proponents of ABMSs employ the narrative on endangered black males for diverse political ends. Let me begin by detailing how these proponents use black males' supposedly endangered status in ways that ignore the severity of black women's and girls' own oppression within the classroom and elsewhere. I will then move on to demonstrate how these same advocates also deploy the discourse that casts black males as endangered for clear and important antiracist ends.

Consider, for a start, how Spencer Holland, an educator and one of the earliest proponents of ABMSs, attempts to make the case for such schools:

> I started looking for the reasons for the greater [black] female success—you know, what's getting the girls out of the ghetto while the boys stay? Something's happening in their early lives that makes [girls] see an alternative to the life Mama lives. You know what I think it is . . . [w]hat constitutes one of the most obvious deficits in the psycho-social environment of black inner-city boys? . . . Little girls come to school and are exposed to black women who have a little more on the ball. This offers an alternative, and for the girls that want it, these black women teachers will lead them out [of the inner city]. But the boys are overwhelmed by women . . . from preschool to late elementary or junior high, most are confronted with female teachers. (qtd. in Raspberry 1987)

Holland assumes that there are "obvious deficits in the psycho-social environment of black inner-city boys" that leave them increasingly endangered in the "ghetto" and that gender-segregated schools are the best way of remedying this troubling reality. He also takes it for granted that black boys' "deficits" are attributable to the ever-expanding cadre of professional black girls and women who are succeeding at black males' expense.

In doing so, in assuming that black females succeed because black males fail, Holland neglects to consider that black women teachers and other professional black women are paid less and are less likely to obtain tenure and promotion (in corporate management, academia, and elsewhere) relative to black men, despite their similar entry rates (Bell and Nkomo 2003; Pope and Joseph 1997; Soares et al. 2011; Shelby 2009). Holland's focus on black women's access to professional employment also obscures the harmful conditions of their employment, including their experience of being sexually harassed and stereotyped as combative in the workplace (Fordham 1993).[3]

Other black male advocates of ABMSs use the narrative that casts black men as endangered to validate an additional antifeminist argument—that successful black women teachers are traitors to the race who have little interest in improving the educational achievement of nearly obsolete black boys. Raymond Davies (2005), a chemistry teacher, argues in his aptly titled work, *The Extinction Coefficient: The Systematic Feminization of African American Males*, that black women teachers, like all "intelligent" black women, want "to be in control" and consequently "hate and distrust" black men and boys (9). A similar argument is that these teachers' "misandry and [f]eminist proclivities" mean that they "want the current situation" of near endangerment for "black male students" to continue ("Greg," qtd. in Martin 2011 [comments]). This stance—that black women teachers are not inclined to teach and mentor their "at risk" black male students—ignores data that indicates black women educators actually have the highest, most positive expectations of black boys when compared with teachers of other racial and gendered backgrounds (Gershenson, Holt, and Papageorge 2016).

Still other black male advocates of ABMSs direct their ire toward black single mothers, whom they cast as particularly detrimental to their endangered sons' poor educational outcomes (Pratt-Clarke 2010). David Banks, whom I quote earlier, is a case in point. So, too, is journalist Nick Chiles (2013b), who stresses that it is "single Black mothers" who are most often guilty of "saddling" their sons with "that most fatal of poisons: low expectations" (125). Psychologist Umar Johnson's (2014) rationale for attempting to establish a boarding school for black boys draws on a similar line of argument: "Why a residential academy? Black boys are disproportionately raised by single Black mothers, who . . . blinded by the influence of Eurocentric feminism . . . oftentimes struggle escorting their sons safely and successfully into manhood."

This attack on black single mothers' supposed educational malpractice rests on two flawed antifeminist assumptions—that educating children is women's primary responsibility and that ABMSs provide endangered black boys with a necessary respite from inherently dysfunctional matriarchal households (Pratt-Clarke 2010; hooks 1996; Williams 2004).

ABMSs' black male supporters use the narrative on endangered black males to advance a last, equally well-entrenched, antifeminist claim—that said males bear the greatest burden of and are charged with the greatest responsibility for resisting racism's harmful effects (Carbado 1999; Collins 2008; Crenshaw 1991; Crenshaw, Ocen, and Nanda 2015).[4] "Brothawolf" (2012), an online commentator, captures the first of these viewpoints when he proclaims: "With the state of the educational system the way it is today, especially in regards to black men, Urban Prep is sorely needed to uplift the minds and spirits of the disenfranchised males left out of the mainstream." Urban Prep head Tim King reflects the latter perspective when he equates endangered black boys' eventual freedom from oppression with that of all black people's: "You are not climbing by yourself. That's not what families do." This is the case, King concludes, because Urban Prep's students "choose a particular future" that is better for themselves, and by extension, for the entire race (qtd. in Lipman 2013, 142).

The troubling, antifeminist effects of casting ABMSs as the best way for black males to uplift other blacks are easy to discern. First, doing so validates the assumption that black males are, in fact, the "rightful" leaders of the race and the "natural" heads of black families (Smith 1985; Collins 2008; Crenshaw 1991; Carbado 1999). Second, reading racism and antiracist resistance as masculine phenomena encourages many black male supporters of ABMSs to perpetuate what I discuss earlier—the misguided belief that black schoolgirls are doing fine and are thus not in need of special attention (Pratt-Clarke 2010; Williams 2004). Third, positing ABMSs as key to enabling endangered black boys to uplift the entire race legitimizes the notion that even if black girls are not doing as well in school, their "needs must be subordinated to the needs of Black male adolescents" because the latter are "the members of the first sex who have the potential" to "become strong Black men" capable of "sav[ing] themselves and the Black community" (Carbado 1999, 7). This stance is especially egregious, given that privileging black boys' academic needs arguably exacerbates all black children's racist oppression. Verna Williams (2004), a law professor and a black feminist critic of ABMSs, explains:

> In today's world, the discourse around single-sex education focuses once again on making sure Black males learn how to become men, and, in a less direct way,

to ensure that Black females grow into "real women" who support their men. The goal essentially is to replicate the [gender] roles exemplified by whites and, in so doing, establish the "proper patriarchal balance" between Black women and Black men, without determining whether that goal is workable or desirable for African Americans. (68)

The Antiracist Politics of Endangered Black Masculinity

Black male advocates of ABMSs utilize the narrative on endangered black males to do far more than advance antifeminist politics. Constructing black males as nearly obsolete also provides these advocates with an important theoretical and material framework for understanding, articulating, and resisting the harmful consequences of racism in black schoolboys' lives.

THE THEORETICAL FRAMEWORK   Midgette and Glenn (1993) are key examples of ABMS supporters whose belief that black males are endangered leads them to challenge structural racism in the classroom. Both authors lament the "formidable systemic challenges" that young black males experience in school and are motivated to engage in this critique specifically because they believe the "considerable research and data [that] strongly indicate that the young African-American man is an endangered species" (69). Tony Laing (2010), an education professor, similarly critiques black males' status as "victims" of "poor education" on the assumption that "the urban black male" is an "endangered species" whose needs rarely take center stage in conversations about "education equality" (214).

For these and other supporters of ABMSs, including high-school principal Ilandus Hampton (2015), the idea that black males are nearly endangered is also a point of departure for identifying and critiquing more specific dimensions of structural racism in the classroom. Hampton explains that his quest to challenge racism in the classroom is a function of his deeply held assumption that "the country's social, political, and economic institutions have poised the African American male to become an 'endangered species' who has been systematically programmed for failure" (42). Hampton's quest reveals a number of important findings. These include the reality that black children, including black boys, are most likely to be taught by inexperienced teachers and the fact that poor, minority-dominated school districts often receive less government funding than those whose students are white and middle class (Hampton 2015).

The notion that black boys are endangered or that "plans for [the] destruction" of black males "have been a long time in the making" motivates Clifford Watson and Geneva Smitherman (1996, 1) to engage in their own, even more specific, antiracist critique of the nation's schools. Their point of departure is the continued presence of racist curricula and teaching materials or the:

> . . . blatant shortcomings and omissions in the core texts typically used in public schools throughout the country. Consider, for instance, the core science text [often] used at the fourth-grade level. This a book that contains over 300 pages, with no graphic or pictorial representations of African American scientists. Various sections of this core text provide biographic sketches of European scientists but neglect commensurate information about African American scientists who have made similar contributions. For example, there is a profile about Dr. Gladys Anderson, a European American nutritionist. . . . Here would have been an opportunity to include information on Dr. Lloyd Hall, an African American scientist, who developed innovative techniques for food preservation, and the refrigeration techniques for transporting food across the country. (61–62)

Jawanza Kunjufu (2005) similarly characterizes black males' purportedly endangered status as the motivating force for his own important critique of racist "special education" policies in the nation's schools. He begins by describing how and why black boys are endangered, referencing specifically the disproportionately large number of these boys who are placed in "special education" classes. Kunjufu then goes on to detail what this disturbing state of affairs means. The plain answer, he argues, is that "racism and discrimination," including but not limited to the "conspiracy" to "destroy" black boys, is alive and well in schools (vii, 19).

Numerous black male supporters of ABMSs are just as concerned about explaining how and why the racism that undergirds black schoolboys' endangered status has harmful effects well outside the classroom. Tony Laing (2010) notes that the black male's status as an "endangered species" means that he is caught up in a never-ending cycle of "gang fights/urban violence, being sent to the penal institutions . . . and other negative societal ills" associated with living in a structurally racist society (214). School principal Ilandus Hampton (2015) concurs that black boys who are endangered by structural racism in the classroom are more likely to "become involved with the juvenile and criminal justice systems" (30). Midgette and Glenn (1993) emphasize that dropping out of school or being otherwise endangered in structurally racist classrooms means that black boys are far more likely than other students to lack "the basic certificate or diploma necessary in our society for most entry-level jobs, apprenticeship programs, military service, or college" (71).

THE MATERIAL FRAMEWORK   The narrative on endangered black men and boys provides ABMSs' black male supporters with not only a theoretical but also a material framework for comprehending and communicating the reality of structural racism in the nation's classrooms. Key to this material framework is the veritable cottage industry on black male endangerment that has arisen since the 1990s (Butler 2013). Contemporary academic journals whose sole or primary focus is interrogating black males' marginal status include the *Journal of African American Men, Spectrum: A Journal on Black Men*, the *Journal of African American Males in Education*, and *Challenge: A Journal of Research on African-American Men*. The increasing amount of scholarship on black male endangerment is also made possible by Harvard University's TandemED Initiative for Black Male Achievement and Community Improvement, Morehouse College's Male Initiative, Ohio State University's Todd Anthony Bell National Resource Center on the African American Male, the University of Texas's African American Male Research Initiative, and the University of California–Los Angeles' Black Male Institute.

As is the case with all scholarship, this research does not pay for itself. Philanthropic groups, including the Bill and Melinda Gates Foundation, the Heinz Endowments, and the Knight Foundation sponsor scholarly research on black males. These and other philanthropies (Open Society Foundations, the Robert Wood Johnson and Skillman Foundations, the California Endowment, Casey Family Programs, Bloomberg Philanthropies) have also been keen to fund broader initiatives on or about black men and black boys. These initiatives include: the Campaign for Black Male Achievement, a nationwide membership network focused on strengthening the "'ground game' of local leaders and organizations devoted to improving the life outcomes of Black men and boys"; the 2025 Campaign for Black Men and Boys whose mission is "to collaboratively develop and implement an initiative for the educational, social, emotional, physical, spiritual, political and economic development and empowerment of Black men and boys" (Tsoi-A-Fatt 2010, iv); and New York City's Young Men's Initiative, which seeks to "tackle the broad disparities slowing the advancement of Black and Latino young men" (Harper 2014, 7). In 2012 alone, ninety-eight charitable organizations disbursed $64.6 million to these and other programs specifically designed to advance black men's and black boys' well-being. These same foundations have issued 1,791 grants and nearly $246 million for various black male initiatives since 2003 (Stiffman 2015; Shah and Soto 2015).

Some dimensions of the cottage industry on black male endangerment I describe above are certainly tantamount to "patriarchy masquerading as racial justice" (Butler 2013, 491). By this, I mean that the industry often serves to normalize the erroneous yet well-entrenched notion that black men and black boys bear the greatest burden of racism's harmful effects. It is also the case, however, that participating in this industry enables numerous black male advocates of ABMSs to provide important, cogent critiques of systemic racism in the classroom. Anthony Mitchell and James Stewart, for example, use their 2012 article, "The Effects of Culturally Responsive Mentoring on the High School to College Matriculation of Urban African American Males" to demonstrate that "school systems in the United States significantly diminish the humanity and potential of African American students," including but not limited to black male students (81).

Publications produced under the auspices of the University of California–Los Angeles' Black Male Institute include Tyrone Howard's *Black Male(d): Peril and Promise in the Education of African American Males* (2013), which argues for critical race theory in education or for scholarship that queries what "racism has to do with inequities in education" and that seeks to "challenge and dismantle prevailing notions of fairness, meritocracy, color-blindness, and neutrality in the education of racial minorities" (55). Just as important is the 2025 Campaign for Black Men and Boys's detailed critique of structural racism or the extent to which all blacks:

> continue to be gravely impeded in their climb toward economic prosperity and are unable to break the cycle of poverty. The cost of being Black and poor is tremendous. Poor Blacks pay more in money, time, stress and hazard. They pay more for food, housing, transportation and health care. While some transcend these obstacles, far more are unable to do so without supports that our nation is often reluctant to give (Tsoi-A-Fatt 2010, 8).

ABMSs and Urban Education

In the months preceding the 1991 establishment of the first ABMS, Detroit's Malcolm X Academy, many of the city's residents depicted their support for such schools as evidence of the depth and breadth of what ails urban classrooms. Implicit in these residents' claims was a core assumption that has long shaped understandings of urban education, both as an academic field of inquiry and in the everyday discourse of teachers, parents, and policymakers—that poor black students are warehoused in failing inner-city schools while their white middle-class peers thrive in academically successful suburban settings.[5] A typical example is former Detroit school superintendent Deborah McGriff's declaration: "I only want to be able to give parents (in Detroit) the same options that other parents have who are middle class" (qtd. in Pratt-Clarke 2010, 105). Detroit journalist Susan Watson (1991) similarly conjured up an educational system demarcated by race and space when she noted the "educational imbalances" inherent in the city's "90 percent black" schools and "overwhelmingly white . . . suburban districts" (3).

Toward Antiracist Urban Education

Clifford Watson, Malcom X Academy's first principal, echoed this notion of a two-tiered educational system when he described the push to open the Detroit-based ABMS as proof that black educators are "tired of attending seminars and workshops" that do nothing to challenge institutional racism in the city and are, instead, increasingly inclined to establish concrete institutions that can provide black boys with the same resources available in white, wealthy suburban schools ("Debate Surrounding Single-Sex Schools" 1992).

Watson's sentiments are firm evidence that, as is the case with many scholars of urban education (Ladson-Billings 1995; Fish and Rothchild 2010; Morris 2016), many supporters of ABMSs, including black male supporters, have long recognized and are critical of the systemic racism that often renders black urban schools academically subpar compared with their white suburban counterparts. Tony Laing (2010), exemplifies this critique when he proclaims: "The unfortunate reality is that the quality of education students of color receive varies" because "disparities exist in resources (financial, technical) available in many inner-city schools [when compared with] suburban schools" (221–22). Fellow scholar and ABMS advocate Nimrod Shabazz (1994) similarly bemoans the fact that "non-white pupils in urban areas" are more likely to "drop out of high school" and to earn lower grades "than their Euro-American contemporaries in the suburbs" (6).

Other black male supporters of ABMS embrace a specific, threefold antiracist critique that is present in much of the literature on urban education—that systemically biased decision-making procedures in these schools limit black parental involvement (Greene 2013; Ladson-Billings 1995), foster subpar teaching of black students (Emdin 2016; Tatum 2003), and perpetuate assessment and disciplinary policies that are biased against black students (Ravitch 2016; Morris 2016). ABMS proponents Marlon James and Clarence Terry echo the latter two critiques when they argue that black boys continue to underachieve in "urban schools" because of a lack of "systemic change" as evidenced by educators' continued ability to suspend and otherwise punish black boys at inexplicably high rates and to disseminate "Eurocentric standards, philosophies, [and] concepts" via curricula and pedagogy (James 2010, 168; Terry et al. 2013, 668, 683).

Watson and Smitherman (1996), Laing (2010), and Kunjufu (2002) contend that both "white-flight" from central cities and the increased outsourcing of living-wage jobs to suburban locations have skewed resource allocation and accumulation in urban communities in ways that ultimately diminish black people's, including black parents', material and political ability to resist systemic inequality in the classroom. Put more plainly, black parents who are unemployed, employed in low-wage work, and/or working multiple jobs to make ends meet often lack the money, time, and other resources to run for and sit on local school boards or to be active members of parent-teacher associations and other school-based entities. In positing this claim, these advocates conclude, as do numerous critics of urban education, not only that the political economy of the inner city, and by extension that of inner-city schools, is racist but also that it is racist in ways that disempower black parents (Massey and Denton 1993; Baronov 2006).

At the same time, some black male advocates of ABMSs express their concerns about urban/suburban inequities in schooling in ways that reinscribe rather than challenge black children's experience of race, gender, and other forms of systemic oppression in school. First, some of these supporters claim, as do several education scholars (Payne 2001; Bridges 2013; Duckworth 2016), that urban schools fail not because of structural inequalities but because of their students' cultural "deficits." Journalist and ABMS supporter James Causey (2010) argues that while "schools, teachers, the community, parents and students all share in the blame" for the academic failure of the city's black children, overly complacent black "communities" are most at fault because they refuse "to mobilize around education." The same assumption undergirds educator Renford Reese's (2004) conclusion that black children in urban schools underperform because both they and their parents have "embraced a culture of underachievement" (17).

A Patriarchal Vision of Urban Education

Other ABMS supporters' arguments about what ails urban schools also do little to challenge existing inequalities, particularly gendered inequalities, of power. Journalist Nick Chiles (2013a, 2013b) contends that many black boys in such schools underachieve because black mothers put a premium on their daughters' rather than their sons' learning and development. Chiles is not alone. Jabari, an ABMS student, also validates the flawed, patriarchal notion that urban schools fail because black parents refuse to act in ways that accord with conventional gender roles. I have in mind here Jabari's claim black boys "act up," get low grades, and are unmotivated to achieve in school because they lack dominant father figures who can and should serve as "positive male role models" (qtd. in Thomas-Whitfield

2011). Newspaper columnist William Raspberry (2005) strikes a similar chord when he castigates the black church for abandoning "its once stern sanctions against extramarital sex and childbirth." The supposed outcome "is a changed culture" of urban blackness in which "[f]ather absence is the bane of the black community, predisposing its children . . . to school failure, criminal behavior and economic hardship."

Even those black male proponents of ABMSs who embrace more structural explanations of failing urban schools sometimes do so in ways that tell a patriarchal, empirically flawed story about what racism looks like in the classroom. Simply put, some of these proponents argue not just that black children are racially oppressed in urban schools but also that black boys bear the greatest burden of systemic racism in inner-city classrooms. Absent from this analysis is what I discuss in the introduction to this book—that black girls also experience significant racism in school. Take, for example, scholar Spencer Holland's argument about why it is important to establish urban ABMSs: "I am not anti-integration, and I am definitely not anti-female. But I have to be pro-Black boy because he's the one this educational system in America has failed the most" (Holland, qtd. in Gilchrist 1991). Fellow academic Marlon James (2010) similarly cites not black children's but, rather, black boys' academic underachievement as the clearest evidence of the "total failure of the American education system" and, more specifically, of the nation's inability to "transform American urban education" (168, 186).

This same masculine-specific logic animates how ABMSs' black male supporters critique the political economy of urban schools. These advocates do not simply concur with scholars of urban education that "white flight" and the outsourcing of living-wage inner-city jobs have limited black people's power to resist oppression in the classroom and beyond. They go further and suggest—in ways that ignore the aforementioned dimensions of black females' own oppression—that it is "African Americans, particularly males" who are most harmed by this troubling socioeconomic reality as "America's industrial base declines and factories locate to parts of the world where wages are truly 'minimum'" (Kunjufu 1992; Laing 2010; Watson and Smitherman 1996, 8).

ABMSs and/as Neoliberal Educational Reform

My discussion thus far reveals that many advocates of ABMSs obscure black schoolgirls' oppression yet critique black boys' academic underachievement as an unacceptable, gender-specific manifestation of racism in urban schools.

A similar, normatively fluid politics informs these advocates' attitudes and orientations toward neoliberalism.[6] On the one hand, numerous black male advocates of ABMSs contend that neoliberal social and economic policies foster racism in the classroom. On the other hand, many of these same advocates also conclude that neoliberal inspired classrooms are important sites of liberation for oppressed black *boys*. The difficulty, as I make clear in the pages that follow, is that this latter stance ultimately exacerbates race-based as well as gender-based inequality in schools.

Defining Neoliberalism

Neoliberalism is both a political ideology and a type of political economy premised on the seemingly contradictory melding of liberal notions of individual choice, small government, and free markets with conservative principles such as social authoritarianism, nationalism, and "law and order" (Overbeek 1993; Gamble 2001). While the exact moment when "neo-liberalism" emerged is subject to debate,[7] it encompasses a specific discursive reality characterized, in part, by "new racism" or by whites' move from explicit acts of bias toward the (re)construction of seemingly egalitarian concepts such as "color blind" and "traditional way of life" in ways that delegitimize blacks' own collective demand for racial equality (Omi and Winant 2014; Bonilla-Silva 2013).

Neoliberalism also connotes a particular material reality in which free-market policies foster an increasingly deregulated, decentralized, competitive, and profit-maximizing business environment premised more on service-sector employment and less on manufacturing labor—all of which emboldens corporations to offer less rather than greater remuneration to workers, especially unskilled workers (Harvey 2007; Gamble 2001). Some observers praise this emphasis on free markets and a smaller state for fostering positive economic growth, enhancing municipalities' ability to manage their own affairs, and rightly rewarding workers according to their "marketable skills" (Friedman 2007; Giddens 1998; Ong 2006). Other observers (Stiglitz 2003; Fraser 2013; Wacquant 2009) are less enamored of neoliberalism's social and economic effects. Henry Giroux (2015), a scholar and a public intellectual, captures many of their concerns:

> Under neoliberalism, the state makes a grim alignment with corporate capital and transnational corporations. Gone are the days when the state 'assumed responsibility for a range of social needs'; instead, agencies of government now pursue a wide range of 'deregulations,' privatizations, and abdications of responsibility to the market and private philanthropy. (52)

Like neoliberalism itself, neoliberal educational reform is premised on "private-sector notions of accountability, worker flexibility, choice, standardization, incentives, and the free market" (Robert 2015, ix). Such reform began in the late 1970s and early 1980s or during a period marked by shrinking public-school budgets and by the growing belief, among many educators and lawmakers, that improving academic outcomes depends not on addressing systemic inequality in schools but on ensuring students' ability to participate in a technical and competitive job market and to make "choices" in an educational "marketplace" where schools function as efficient business entities that compete for "customers" (Williams 2006; Brathwaite 2016, 5–6).

President Ronald Reagan's 1980 election set the normative and administrative framework for comprehensive, nationwide neoliberal educational reform. "A Nation at Risk," a 1983 report published by the National Commission on Excellence in Education, posited a set of educational norms for schools across the country. Paramount among these was the four-pronged notion that all teachers should be held accountable for their students' academic performance, that student testing and learning should be standardized, that private-sector investment is crucial to improving public schools and, related to this third point, that education must contribute to the nation's economic interests (National Commission on Excellence in Education 1983). During the 1990s, the Clinton administration moved national neoliberal educational reform from theory to practice. The 1994 Goals 2000: Educate America Act allocated $15 million for school districts to open charter schools, established a federal-level agency to certify new state-level academic standards, and provided competitive funding to states willing to implement these standards (Wubbena 2016).

More recent efforts at neoliberal educational reform include the No Child Left Behind Act, which Congress approved with bipartisan support in 2001. The act encodes national educational standards and facilitates the establishment of nonprofit and for-profit charter schools that are exempt from many state and local regulations regarding staffing and curricula (Hursh 2007). These measures are ostensibly designed to facilitate parents' ability to make the best educational choices for their children as well as educators' capacity to more efficiently and fairly measure student outcomes. The 2004 federally funded school-voucher program and similar programs at the state and city levels provide students in underperforming schools with the choice to enroll in private schools of their choice (Lipman 2013). Changes to Title IX (legislation that bans gender-based discrimination in federally funded programs and entities) in 2006 also give public elementary and high schools greater freedom to segregate pupils by gender as long as the students in question receive a "substantially equal" education (U.S. Department of Education 2006). Finally, the federally funded Race to the Top initiative, implemented between 2009 and 2015, encouraged states to compete for funding to implement specific educational reforms, including linking teachers' assessment and pay to students' standardized test scores as well as shuttering underperforming public schools and transferring them to for-profit, privately managed organizations (U.S. Department of Education 2015b).

Reading Neoliberalism and Antiracism in Pro-ABMS Discourse

Some black male advocates of ABMSs critique neoliberalism in ways that clearly advance an antiracist political agenda. Sociologist Richard Majors and his co-author Janet Billson (1993) attribute 1980s-era increases in black children's academic failure, poverty, hunger, and homelessness to "institutional racism" as manifest in conservative politicians' quest for "small" government and corresponding cuts to social welfare programs. Jawanza Kunjufu (2008) similarly criticizes the fact that "between 1980 and 1993, Presidents Ronald Reagan and George Bush, Sr. cut federal spending on employment and training by nearly 50 percent" and increased spending on "corrections" or the criminal incarceration of Americans, particularly black men, to unprecedented levels (114). Reginald Hicks (2010), a high-school teacher, describes the "Ronald Reagan—George Bush—Newt Gingrich years" as a period of "Black-male bashing" during which politicians used stereotypes of black men as "derelict and lazy to justify the rolling back of civil rights and the slashing of social programs" (61).

Hicks, Kunjufu, Majors, and Billson echo the sentiments of Joy James (2014), Angela Davis (2000), and other black commentators who conclude that the neoliberal ethos of a minimal state, supply-side economics, and self-help has meant reduced state funding for inner-city public schools, public housing, healthcare, job training, and, in turn, growing black poverty and unemployment. Majors and Billson (1993) offer a particularly detailed critique of how neoliberal-inspired cuts in social spending have harmed black males since the 1980s:

> Although black poverty dropped slightly in 1984, the rate of 34 percent was still higher than it had been in any of the ten years preceding the Reagan Administration. That Administration's so-called recovery hardly made a dent in the average black male's chances of finding work. The 1990 rate was 31.9 percent. . . . Black unemployment and institutionalized racism have been further compounded by government cuts in federally sponsored programs . . . that serve children and young adults, including job training . . . [and] mental

health services. . . . The nation is apparently not yet prepared to ensure that black males are supported in their efforts to become strong men. (15, 25)

Another group of ABMSs' black male proponents, including journalist Ellis Cose (2015), emphasizes that the neoliberal ethos of "color-blindness" has, in fact, "dismantled virtually every obvious manifestation of racism without much alleviating the devastation that centuries of racism spawned." Cose highlights the fact that although Baltimore and other cities have black mayors and other high-level government officials, America remains "a society loath to give young black men the benefit of the doubt and which sees, in far too many of them, self-fulfilling portents of doom." Maulana Karenga, a prominent Africana Studies professor and supporter of ABMSs (see Wiley 1993, 21) historicizes and critiques color-blindness as whites' most recent attempt to camouflage the enduring, systemic antiblack racism that "lies below-the-surface" of American life:

> This recent bout of resurgent racism should surprise no one, for racism is an opportunistic social virus that often lies below-the-surface, deceptively dormant, waiting for the weakening of the will, strength and struggle of its chosen victims, peoples of color. . . . For whatever the U.S. imagines itself to be in its best moments—a democracy, a color-blind guardian and guarantor of equality, equal opportunity and justice under the law; it is not. Indeed, whenever it pretends to be color-blind, it is always to the disadvantage of the people of color. (Karenga 2007)

Both Cose and Karenga conclude, as do Omi and Winant (2014) and other left-of-center critics, that while neoliberalism's post-racial ethos seemingly connotes a willingness and desire not to discriminate based on race, any presumption that it is possible or even admirable to somehow see past race actually buttresses the continuing reality of structural racism—be it in the nation's classrooms or somewhere else—and undermines affirmative action and other efforts to ameliorate such racism.

Equally important, for my purposes, is that despite their broad antiracist critique of neoliberal social and economic policies, many of these same supporters of ABMSs cast neoliberalism as essential rather than detrimental to black people, including black males' academic and non-academic well-being. For example, while Ellis Cose critiques neoliberal-inspired "colorblindness" on the grounds that it does little to ameliorate structural racism, he also concludes that the "goal of race neutrality is one we cannot afford to abandon . . . if we wish to keep alive faith in the triumph of good ideas over bad" (Cose 1997, 244; see also Cose 2015). Reginald Hicks (2010), meanwhile, decries neoliberals' small government ethos as antithetical to black people's well-being but nevertheless posits a key neoliberal tenet—the need to transcend "the rhetoric of victimology"—as the best way for black boys to improve their socioeconomic standing. Rejecting such rhetoric, Hicks argues, allows black boys to move beyond the flawed assumption that "racial equality is an oxymoron and that racial rejection is inevitable" as well as the "blind tolerance for their own failure, lack of effort, and criminality" that undergirds this assumption (45).

Stated another way, Hicks, Cose, and many other black male proponents of ABMSs (Kunjufu 2007, 2011; Johnson 2012; Rollins and Hicks 2011) assume that neoliberal reforms, including but not limited to establishing charter schools, dissolving teachers' unions, and implementing school-choice vouchers, do, in fact, liberate educators as well as students, particularly black male students, from the purported bureaucratic burdens and inefficiencies—racist and otherwise—in traditional public schools. Tim King, whose union-busting efforts I describe at the beginning of this chapter, also typifies this mindset. So, too, does Kaleem Caire's affirmative stance on "the issue of vouchers" for black children (qtd. in Simmons 2011) as well as his view that:

> In public schools, you are so strapped by rules and regulations. If teachers work outside the rules of the union, they get slapped. . . . Education is not on the teachers union's agenda. . . . Their agenda is protecting the teachers. I understand that. But that doesn't fit with our agenda. . . . For one thing, we want a longer school day. This school would provide a lot of the family structure that some low-income mothers and fathers simply can't. We want a longer school year, too—at least 210 days, instead of the current 180. (Caire, qtd. in Schubert 2011)

Scholars Thomas Midgette and Eddie Glenn (1993) reach a strikingly similar conclusion—that deregulated, neoliberal-inspired classrooms, including all-black male urban classrooms, provide teachers, administrators, and students with the kind of educational and bureaucratic autonomy that is crucial for improving black boys' education:

> Congress and the U.S. Department of Education, recognizing that schools are controlled locally and seeing the need for pedagogical flexibility, have left schools with considerable discretion to decide which children to serve and how to serve them. . . . [L]ocal school districts can specify the setting for services, length of time for delivery of instruction, kind of personnel who must provide it, content or skills to be learned, and instructional materials to be used. Schools can experiment with varying pedagogies and academic services from school to school or from grade to grade. We must place African-American boys in [such] schools. (72)

Martin Luther King III is even more explicit. He characterizes charter schools, including Albany's Brighter Choice charter school for black boys, as a site of freedom from racial oppression: "Like the American Civil Rights Movement, [Brighter Choice's] efforts to educate . . . children . . . is about liberation— liberation from prejudice, liberation from socially imposed limitations, and liberation of the dignity, capabilities, and potential for excellence that dwells in the heart of *every* human being" (qtd. in Davis 2006 [original emphasis]).

King, Midgette, and other ABMS supporters' embrace of neoliberal educational reform is indicative of a broader "neoliberal turn" in black politics whereby "racial inequality is managed through black elite-promoted techniques designed to get black people to act according to market principles" (Dumas 2016; Spence 2012, 146). The black elites who administer these techniques do so in ways that encourage non-elite blacks "to govern themselves" or "to 'take control' of their own lives through technical modifications in their own behavior." These elites, most significantly, do so on the assumption that "neoliberal governmentality" is key to ameliorating black oppression. Such governmentality necessarily leaves "little role for the state except to facilitate the process whereby a professional-managerial class uses its technical knowledge and skills to bring about changes in individuals and communities" (Dumas 2016, 96).[8]

The difficulty with this "neoliberal turn," within the context of ABMSs and beyond, is that it actually does little to challenge racism. First, it mistakenly presumes that black boys' and other black people's liberation from racial oppression can be achieved by acquiring marketable skills and skills about the market rather than by organizing politically to challenge racist disciplinary practices, curricula, felony disenfranchisement laws, and other forms of systemic bias (Spence 2012; Dumas 2016). A typical example is Tim King, who suggests that under his leadership the Urban Prep Academies provide impoverished black boys with the technical skills, including the financial-management techniques, they need to succeed in the competitive, market-driven college-admission and labor markets:

> A lot of people criticize students about taking out loans to pay for education. I don't necessarily agree with this pattern of thought. . . . Education has deferred interest, but you're benefiting from it your entire life once you get the degree. . . . Students should make the connection with the student loan being an investment in yourself. The numbers show that people with degrees make more money on average than those who don't. . . . Students need to know what is needed to handle this responsibility. Don't waste the investment. As a student, you need to attend class and make good grades. Otherwise you've spent time and money for nothing. . . . We need to learn how to delay gratification. . . .

Remember, just because you want it now, doesn't mean you're being financially responsible. Save the money you would spend on one shirt, so one day you can buy two (qtd. in Jones 2015).

Second, ABMS supporters' embrace of neoliberal governmentality not only ignores but exacerbates black people's, including black schoolboys', racist oppression. I have in mind here some of these proponents' efforts to gauge black boys' acquisition of marketable academic and occupational skills via "measurable outcomes" or data-driven teaching, learning, and assessment. The result of these efforts is that, as is the case with other "choice" schools (Fergus et al. 2009; Lipman 2013; Potter 2008), ABMSs sometimes employ rigid disciplinary and learning techniques, fines, and other mechanisms that result in what so many of their black male supporters claim to oppose—the suspension and expulsion of black boys with below-average grades and standardized test scores (Mertz 2011; Fergus, Noguera, and Martin 2014).

ABMSs, Neoliberalism, and Antifeminist Politics

Just as troubling is that many of ABMSs' black male supporters also embrace neoliberal educational reform in antifeminist ways. To begin with, many of these proponents assert that black boys should be free to partake in the educational marketplace made possible by non-unionized teachers, charter schools, and vouchers primarily because this marketplace enables said boys to be taught in ways that are congruent with their purportedly gender-specific learning needs. A case in point is Jawanza Kunjufu's contention that so-called school-choice reforms, including the establishment of charter schools, are worth pursuing because they help create classrooms that are conducive to boys' "learning styles":

> We have seen a shift around the role of charter schools and their approach toward closing educational gaps for African American males. . . . [T]hese schools demonstrate and show that if you have high expectations, good classroom management, and a commitment toward understanding the various learning styles of males, then students will strive and surpass even our own high expectations. . . . This is not the case for public schools where there are a lot of ineffective teachers who are continuing to go through the system without being reprimanded for the moral harm that they are doing to our children. (qtd. in Johnson 2011, 142–43)

Missing from this analysis is any consideration that some boys, including black boys, might not have gender-specific "learning styles" or that these styles might be prevalent among black girls and other students. Instead,

Kunjufu makes the flawed, antifeminist assumption that black boys, like all boys, necessarily learn in ways that distinguish them from all girls.[9]

Many black male supporters of separate schools for black boys appropri-ate the rhetoric of educational choice to perpetuate another antifeminist perspective at the heart of the discourse in favor of ABMSs—that black girls are already succeeding in the classroom. Take, for example, David Hardy's rationale for founding a charter school for black boys, Boys Latin of Philadel-phia, despite having to do battle with the Education Law Center, the Public Interest Law Center of Philadelphia, and other organizations that are critical of charter schools and other efforts at neoliberal educational reform:

> [These organizations] lost because it is pretty hard for you to talk about Black boys being an advantage[d] population. . . . Twenty-five years ago, if you sepa-rated the sexes, the girls blossomed. Today, by separating the sexes, it's the boys who blossom. . . . These are city boys who are struggling and looking for a way out and they were standing in the way of that. There is no way to put a pretty face on that. (qtd. in Toomer 2007)

Hardy's argument in favor of giving black boys the choice to attend a charter school neither acknowledges the degree of black girls' own systemic disadvantage in the classroom nor contemplates the related possibility that these girls, like their black male peers, may need a variety of educational choices to improve their levels of educational attainment.

Still other black male advocates of ABMSs make use of neoliberal inspired educational "choice" to articulate a final antifeminist viewpoint—the notion that girls inevitably distract boys. David Banks embraces this logic when he argues not just that "single sex education should be part of a menu of choice" but also that such "choice" is critical for black boys who can only "open up" about and focus on their own hopes, fears, and dreams within "a single-sex environment" marked by "a spirit of brotherhood" and, by logical extension, the absence of sexually distracting girls (qtd. in Crellin 2004).

In casting girls, particularly black girls, as sexually distracting to black boys, ABMSs' black male advocates valorize not just a patriarchal worldview but also a racist kind of patriarchy that is especially harmful to black girls. I say this because central to many of these advocates' critique of black girls is the assumption that said girls are fundamentally unable to conduct themselves in the sexually chaste manner of "real" girls (read: white girls). According to this logic, black girls are, instead, imbued with an immoral, promiscuous sexual ethos that makes them forever willing and able to sexually service the males in their midst (Williams 2004).

Conclusion

This chapter further details the specific experiential claim that undergirds much of the discourse in favor of ABMSs—that black boys are oppressed because they are forced to learn in racist and overly-feminized classrooms. That this claim generally defies easy classification as either antifeminist or antiracist is far from natural or inevitable. Instead, the complex politics that underscores the effort to establish these schools emerges during a period marked by presumptions of a transracial crisis in boys' education, popular and scholarly discourse that constructs black men and black boys as nearly endangered, widespread concerns about urban education, and the proliferation of charter schools and other efforts at neoliberal educational reform.

I turn my attention in chapter 2 to demonstrating that these specific material and discursive forces do not wholly explain the often antifeminist as well as antiracist politics of ABMSs' black male supporters. Instead, any attempt to understand the complicated politics that informs these supporters' central experiential claim—that black boys are oppressed in racist, female-dominated classrooms—must also attend to another reality that is significant for feminists and for all of us interested in grasping the interplay of race and gender in the nation's schools. This reality is that social groups, including black males, can and do use the logic of intersectionality to advance multiple, diverse kinds of politics. Again, my specific aim is to elucidate what feminists acknowledge but do not fully clarify—that disadvantaged social groups' claims about their experience often defy simple categorization as either liberatory or oppressive.

2 Antiracist, Antifeminist Intersectionality

During the contentious 1991 court battle to determine the legality of Detroit's Malcolm X Academy, Clifford Watson, who would later become the academy's first principal, confronted Ruth Jones, a black woman lawyer with the National Organization of Women Legal Defense Fund and a critic of ABMSs, with the following accusation: "I wished I could have pulled you aside in the courtroom. . . . What you're doing to destroy Black boys in the city of Detroit clearly means that you're a woman first, working not for our interests but for the interests of women, in this case White women. . . . You're clearly the enemy" (qtd. in Pratt-Clarke 2010, 98). Twenty-three years later, Boyce Watkins, an economist and policy analyst, makes it clear that many black male supporters of ABMSs continue to believe that feminism, especially black feminism, is detrimental to black males' well-being:

> One thing that extreme black feminists and ignorant rappers have in common is that they've both been fueled by white corporate money to ignite a war against black people of the opposite gender. The black feminist who's been trained to emasculate black men is no better than the rapper who's been brainwashed into calling black women b*tches and hoes. As these political puppets are injected with these toxic messages, the greatest casualty in this plantation warfare is the black family in America. (Watkins 2014b)

Assumptions about the dangers of not only "feminized" classrooms but also feminist theory and practice clearly run deep in the worldview of several black male advocates of ABMSs. At the same time, Watkins's and Watson's antifeminist sentiments—as compelling or, better yet, jaw dropping as they are—do not tell the full story of the relationship between feminism and the discourse in favor of ABMSs. A more detailed examination reveals that while many black male supporters of these schools are clearly hostile to things feminist, their core claim—that black boys underachieve because they are forced to learn in racist, over-feminized classrooms—is actually premised on the black feminist-inspired, intersectional notion that race and gender-based oppression are mutually constructing. Indeed, Watson and Watkins suggest exactly this when they assert that racist whites—including white feminists and those with "white corporate money"—oppress black males not just because they are black but also because they are black *men*.

What sense are we to make of this complex, seemingly conflicting reality in which ABMSs' black male supporters use intersectionality—an analytical framework pioneered by black feminists—to critique white supremacy and to denigrate feminism, including black feminism, as harmful to black people's well-being? The answer is that while intersectional analysis highlights how racial, gendered, and other spheres of difference are co-constitutive, intersectionality's underlying logic does not prescribe which spheres are mutually constructing, who experiences oppression in the process, or how to relieve their oppression. Instead, these are context-specific, political decisions that are made by people who embrace intersectionality and not by intersectionality itself. As a result, social groups who engage in intersectional analysis can and do use it not to depict themselves as politically neutral but, rather, to make politically diverse arguments about their own and others' socioeconomic status. Within the parameters of the discourse in support of ABMSs, many black males use intersectionality to make a twofold, simultaneously antifeminist and antiracist argument—that black boys are oppressed because they are taught in racist classrooms that are "overly" feminized and that separate schools are the most appropriate means of remedying these boys' oppression.

Conceptualizing intersectionality in this manner, or as something other than a necessarily feminist or liberatory analytical framework, raises many questions. Are black male supporters of ABMSs the only social group who use intersectionality for emancipatory as well as oppressive ends? Does intersectionality, as I have reconceptualized it, inevitably silence women's, particularly black women's, experiences of oppression? If intersectionality can be used for antifeminist and other non-emancipatory ends, does this mean that it does little to make antifeminist, racist, heterosexist, and otherwise exclusionary social and political movements more inclusive?

The pages that immediately follow detail what it means to speak of intersectionality and to engage in intersectional analysis. I focus my discussion on intersectionality's status as a politically fluid heuristic. I then move on to explore how ABMSs' black male proponents use intersectionality, so defined, both to cast black boys as victims of masculinized racism and to posit separate schools as key to these boys' liberation from oppression. The remainder of the chapter reveals that conservative black Christians also use intersectionality for oppressive ends, that intersectionality is not a panacea for what ails exclusionary social movements, and that black women's voices are not necessarily silenced by intersectional analyses that focus on other social groups.

Historicizing and Contextualizing Intersectionality

While the concept of intersecting or interlocking oppressions has long been evident in the work of Anna Julia Cooper, Maria Stewart, and other historical black women thinkers and writers, contemporary intersectional scholarship emerged during the very period—the late 1970s and 1980s—when black women began to enter the academy in greater numbers (May 2015; Hancock 2016). This increase facilitated "a much broader range of voices and experiences to be articulated in academic scholarship." Not only that, their own experience of subordination in the academy meant that women of color had and continue to have "great stake in elucidating the social locations that [make] them more vulnerable to discrimination, isolation, and inequality both in the university setting" and farther afield (Manuel 2006, 179).

Intersectionality's contemporary emergence is also inextricably tied to the rise of black feminist activism in the United States. Intersectionality emerges during the same time, the late 1970s and early 1980s, when a series of events helped push a key black feminist concern—that black women's lived, daily reality is different from that of either black men's or white women's—to the forefront of academic and popular discourse. These events included: the Combahee River Collective's protest of twelve African American women's murders in Boston in 1983; the First National Conference on Third World Women and Violence in 1980; the establishment of Kitchen Table Women of Color Press in 1981; and the publication of popular and academic texts by black feminists, including Alice Walker's *The Color Purple* (1982), Michelle Wallace's *Black Macho and the Myth of the Black Superwoman* (1979), and Ntozake Shange's 1976 stage play, later published in paperback, "For Colored Girls Who Have Considered Suicide / When the Rainbow Is Enuf."

Many intersectional scholars examine how one social group is constituted at the junction of plural identities and across various social categories (Crenshaw 2000; Choo and Ferree 2010). Such an approach entails interrogating how, for example, black women's identities as "women" and as "blacks" are mutually constructing across the categories of "race" and "gender." Another intersectional approach involves capturing "the complexity of relationships among multiple social groups within and across analytical categories" (Yuval-Davis 2006; McCall 2005, 1786). Putting this approach into practice might involve illuminating how black women's subordination as "women" and as "blacks" gains meaning from white men's privilege as "whites" and as "men."

Intersectional theorizing also involves describing the relational process by which race, gender, class, sexual, and other social categories come to the fore. The focus here is not on a social group or groups but on illuminating mutually reinforcing processes of "gendering, racialization, ethnicization, culturaliza-tion, [and] sexualization" through which "subjectivities and social differences are produced" in relation to each other (Anthias 1998; Dhamoon 2011, 235). This approach does not deny the existence of categories of difference or the identities associated with these categories. It emphasizes, instead, that the "subjects" who occupy these categories do not merely "have identities" but are "socially produced as identities" within the context of specific institu-tions (the welfare state, the labor force, and so on) and systems of inequality (racism, classism, other -isms) (Dhamoon 2011, 235; Smith 1998).

While intersectional theorists vary in the extent to which they adopt a group- or process-centered approach, they have generally agreed, until quite recently, on intersectionality's normative orientation. Most of these theorists see intersectional analysis as part of a "liberation/political framework" in which gendered, racial, and other hierarchies of power are not only mutually constructing but also capable of being reordered in ways that are emancipa-tory (Jordan-Zachery 2007, 261). Members of the Combahee River Collective (1983) articulate this very assumption when they declare their dedication to "struggling against racial, sexual, heterosexual, and class oppression" and "see as [their] particular task the development of integrated analysis and practice based upon the fact that the major systems of oppression are interlocking." Members of the collective and many other black feminists conclude, too, that intersectionality is an explicitly black feminist analytical framework whose "single purpose" is to empower black women to assert their voices in a "racial discourse, where the subject is [traditionally] male; in a gendered discourse, where the subject is [almost always] white; and in a class discourse, where race [generally] has no place" (Mirza 1997, 4, 20). According to this reason-ing, "a black feminist ideology" necessarily "challenges the interstructure of the oppressions of racism, sexism, and classism both in the dominant society and within movements for liberation" (King 1988, 72; Smith 1985).

Political scientist Ange-Marie Hancock (2007b) contends that intersec-tionality is part of a movement for social change that does not necessarily privilege black women as its primary subjects. This is so, according to Hancock, because intersectional analysis not only illuminates how "gender, class, and sexual orientation . . . are mutually constitutive at both the individual and institutional levels," it also does so in ways that foster "political change" for multiple social groups[1] (2007a, 252). Another explanation is that intersectionality fosters emancipatory social change because it deconstructs the myth of universal subjectivity or undermines the notion, for instance, that the social category "woman" is "homogenous" and unchanging and, in doing so, "disrupts a calcified and definitive way of understanding difference, subjects, and subjectivity" (Brah and Phoenix 2004; Dhamoon 2011, 239). In other words, because it is the very "social fictio[n]" of "woman," "black," and so on that generates inequality, it thus follows that to destabilize the notion of a homogenous, "self-referencing, unified subject" is to challenge hierarchies of power (McCall 2005, 1773).

Other intersectional scholarship suggests another, starkly different reality—that social and political conservatives are increasingly appropriating intersectionality for antifeminist, racist, and heterosexist ends. Michelle Fine, in this vein, notes the media's use of statistics disaggregated by race, ethnicity, gender, class, and so on to illuminate higher rates of sexually transmitted disease among black teenage girls versus their white peers. The problem with this approach, Fine explains, is that it obscures the underlying structural factors—racial imbalances in access to healthcare, and so on—that explain the disparity between the two groups. Put another way, journalists mistakenly fail to consider the role of socioeconomic structures and institutions when contemplating the interaction between race, gender, and other terrains of difference. The result, on Fine's account, is a profoundly conservative kind of intersectional analysis that presumes that mutually constructing racial, gendered, and class disparities among social groups stem from "culture or genetics, rather than [the] systematic effects of cumulative oppression" (qtd. in Berger and Guidroz 2009, 70).

Kimberlé Crenshaw also critiques the "flattening" of intersectionality, or the process whereby scholars provide "just a listing of people and a description" of their "particular conditions." This kind of intersectional approach, Crenshaw asserts, is "just another form of identity politics"—in this case—one premised on simply "multiplying identity categories." Such an approach, she goes on to explain, is flawed because it provides little in the way of "structural analysis," "political critique," or, more concretely, of how and why particular social groups "are located within structures of power" (qtd. in Berger and Guidroz 2009, 70).

In describing this same "flattening," Patricia Hill Collins (2006) singles out for criticism "privileged academics [who] feel free to claim a bit of oppression for themselves" on the grounds that "if all oppressions mutually construct one another, then we are all oppressed in some way by something." While Collins does not explicitly describe these academics' use of intersectionality as "conservative," she does suggest that such use is complicit with a conservative agenda or is "oppression talk [that] obscures actual unjust power relations" (212).

The first explanation of why intersectionality can be used for oppressive or potentially oppressive ends is that intersectionality itself is "a result of the discursive environment through which [intersectional] ideas travel rather than a reflection of inherent deficiencies in [the] ideas themselves" (Crenshaw 2016, 223). This discursive context, Kimberlé Crenshaw explains, is a legal and academic one in which black women's experiences are regarded as too specific to constitute valid truth. Put more explicitly:

> While black feminism figures as the widely acknowledged generative source of intersectionality, somewhat conversely, the role of black women has sometimes troubled those seeking to grow intersectionality beyond its discursive origins. The fact that questions about whether intersectionality is "just" about black women are still voiced despite the contributions of many scholars . . . who deploy intersectionality to analyse a plethora of issues, contexts and groups, seems to reflect a deeper anxiety about the constitutive role of race in intersectionality and of black women in particular. . . . In the same way that courts saw the specific pleadings of black women as setting forth a particularity that disqualified them as representatives of the universal experience of sex discrimination, some theorists taking up intersectionality intimate a certain parochialism in its origins that compromises its theoretical comprehensiveness. There is a sense that efforts to repackage intersectionality for universal consumption require a re-marginalizing of black women. (2016, 224)

In other words, understanding why intersectionality is used for conservative ends requires us to examine how it is "adapted, disciplined and deployed" within and across specific legal, academic, and other "borders" (Crenshaw 2016, 223). A related explanation is that intersectionality is more than a means of describing "complex identities." It is also a "strategic politics" whose specific goal is "invalidating" the perspectives of some while validating the viewpoints, including the conservative viewpoints, of others (Williams 2016, 79).

A third explanation of intersectionality's conservative cooptation is that many who embrace it subscribe to a "myth of equivalent oppressions" or the flawed assumption that the interaction of race, gender, and other social categories and the identities associated with these categories generate the same results for all disadvantaged groups. Collins (1998) contends that this myth, or the dangerous tendency to obscure the very real differences in power that exist among social groups, is made possible by intersectionality's status as a "heuristic device" or as that which "describe[s] what kinds of things to consider" rather than "any actual patterns of social organization" (208). What Collins means is that while "intersectionality provides an interpretive framework for thinking through how intersections of race and class, or race and gender, or sexuality and class, for example, shape any group's experience across specific social contexts" (208), this does not signify that social groups understand these intersecting systems of oppression in ways that are necessarily liberatory. On the contrary, some groups mistakenly presume that "to be a Black woman" is the same as being a "White gay man or a working-class Latino." The more nuanced reality, Collins concludes, is that while "these experiences are all connected, they are not equivalent" precisely because "intersecting systems of power" have "differential effects" on various groups (211).

Conceptualizing Intersectionality as a Heuristic

I contend that intersectionality can be used for conservative ends because it is a heuristic that guides us to ask and clarify a particular question—How do multiple identities, social categories, or processes of identification and categorization gain meaning from each other? Intersectionality, as I conceptualize it, is not imbued with a fixed or stable orientation, progressive or otherwise, toward the social world. Instead, intersectionality's adherents use a variety of ideological perspectives to analyze how identities, social categories, or processes of identification and categorization gain meaning from each other, and to arrive at normatively diverse conclusions based on their analyses.

Intersectionality, so (re)defined, is not politically neutral. In fact, it is difficult, if not impossible, to think of intersectional analysis as such, given that its very reason for being is to determine the effects of hierarchical systems on people situated in and at different interstices. Indeed, as Cooper (1892), Crenshaw (2000), and other feminist theorists of intersectionality powerfully illuminate, intersectionality is, at its most fundamental, a tool for conceptualizing the machinations of power. What can and does happen is that intersectionality's practitioners bring their own, often diverse, politics to bear when contemplating who is oppressed and how to challenge their oppression. Most important, as the ensuing discussion illustrates, intersectional analysis is a normatively malleable endeavor not just because many of the conservatives who currently embrace it do so in ways that corrupt its fundamentally feminist orientation but also because its underlying orientation or logic is not necessarily a feminist one.

Put more specifically, understanding intersectionality as a normatively malleable heuristic means querying the notion that we should read its use for conservative ends only as a function of the neoliberalism of the 1980s and beyond. While chapter 1 clearly demonstrates that this is so—that many supporters of ABMSs cast black boys as victims of masculinized racism in "overly" feminized classrooms during the very period in which neoliberal educational reform comes to the fore—intersectionality's status as a heuristic also suggests that it can possibly be used to advance conservative sentiment in any socioeconomic context. My aim is not to endorse particular uses of intersectionality and especially not to endorse conservative uses of it. It is, rather, to posit intersectionality's insufficiency as a means of *necessarily* emancipatory social critique and to suggest that those of us who want to engage in such critique need to do more than invoke "intersectionality" to make our arguments compelling.

This perspective rejects conventional understandings of intersectionality as an always-liberatory analytical framework in favor of Collins's suggestion that intersectionality's use for antiprogressive ends is made possible by its status as a heuristic.[2] However, unlike Collins, I detail *why* intersectionality's standing as a heuristic makes it normatively or politically flexible. This is the case—or intersectionality can be used to advance racist, heterosexist, and antifeminist arguments—because it does not specify which identities, social categories, or processes of identification and categorization are co-constitutive or with what effect. Furthermore, I fully embrace the implications of recognizing intersectionality as a heuristic, the most important of which is understanding that intersectionality has a normative core, but that this core is malleable. In other words, my analysis moves away from Collins's suggestion that intersectionality's inability to prescribe particular "patterns of social organization" is evidence of its own shortcomings or, more specifically, of intersectional scholars' failure to fully develop and articulate its underlying feminist core. I make this move to resist the notion that intersectionality has a stable, normative center or foundation that scholars can, in fact, better elucidate.

My argument also aligns with Juliet Williams's (2016) suggestion that supporters of ABMSs can and do use intersectionality to strategically advance an "unapologetically antifeminist" agenda (78). I argue, as does Williams, that many advocates of these schools use an intersectional framework to erroneously depict feminists, including black feminists, as "uncompromising

ideological extremists" who do not have black boys' best interests at heart
(79). Unlike Williams, I emphasize that this antifeminist agenda is made
possible by intersectionality's status as a heuristic.

Let me start with my first claim, that intersectionality is a heuristic that
guides us to consider how identities, categories, or processes of identification
and categorization are mutually constructing. Using this logic, theorists who
embrace a single-group approach to intersectionality might argue that the
racial identity "black" and the gendered identity "woman" can and do enter
into a relationship with each other, and when they do, each identity is rede-
fined such that "woman" takes on new racialized qualities and "black" takes
on new gendered characteristics. By this reasoning, "black woman" is more
than "black" plus "woman" because a black woman's experience of "blackness"
is feminized in ways that a black man's is not. Meanwhile, her experience of
being a woman is racialized in ways that a white woman's is not.

Proponents of a multi-group approach might use intersectionality to argue
that white men's status as "men" and as "whites" gains meaning from black
women's status as "women" and as "blacks." According to such reasoning, it
is not merely the case that white men's experience of masculinity is a function of their whiteness and that how they experience whiteness is shaped by
their masculinity. The group "white men" also exists in hierarchal relation to
the group "black women" to the extent that the former is widely presumed
to be the antithesis of the latter. For instance, to be a white man (supposedly
rational, virtuous, responsible) is not to be what a black woman is (ostensibly
irrational, immoral, irresponsible). The idea here is that the intersectional
status of a social group (for example, heterosexual middle-class white men),
within and across racial, sexual, gendered and other categories of difference,
is a function of another or other groups' intersectional status or the absence
thereof (for example, working-class black lesbians). Lastly, scholars who
contend that intersectionality enables us to understand how racialization,
gendering, and other processes of inequality are organized in relation to
each other might use intersectionality to demonstrate how the public-school
system generates and sustains mutually constructing experiences of race and
gender through institutional regulations and customs. These customs and
practices include using textbooks and other curricular materials that cast
hypersexual, violent sexual predators as male and nonwhite.

While intersectionality illuminates how identities, categories, or processes
of identification and categorization gain meaning from each other, it does not
specify which identities, categories, or processes of inequality are most important to analyze. As a result, intersectional theorists can advance very different
understandings about who is intersectionally disadvantaged and what to do

about their disadvantage. I do not deny that intersectional theorists have long identified specific dimensions of social life as mutually constructing. What I want to emphasize is that while feminist theorists of intersectionality have traditionally focused on the co-constitutive relationship between race, gender, and sexuality, there is nothing in the logic of intersectionality that mandates a focus on these particular categories. Instead, those who use intersectionality can and do argue that any number of other categories, including age, religion, and ethnicity, gain meaning from each other.

Furthermore, even when intersectionality's adherents are attentive to the "traditional" triad of race, gender, and sexuality, an intersectional framework does not dictate the content or the specific identities associated with these social categories. The result is that those who use an intersectional framework can designate "black," "man," and "heterosexual," and any other combination of identities associated with the categories "race," "gender," and "sexuality," as mutually constructing. Similarly, intersectionality does not mandate a focus on some mutually constructing processes of identification and categorization over others. This is so because these processes are co-constitutive in contexts that organize privilege and power inequitably. As a result, whether we focus our attention on intersection of race and gender versus, say, the intersection of gender and sexuality is not preordained. Instead, it is a function of our historically specific knowledge systems and structures. Persons who embrace intersectionality are thus free to posit anything from the racialization of the welfare state to secularization in the classroom to the feminization of the labor force as co-constitutive.

Intersectionality's Value Fluidity

Intersectionality's inability to prescribe which identities, social categories, or processes of identification and categorization are mutually constructing is ultimately a function of its value fluidity. This term has several meanings. To begin with, intersectionality does not determine the socioeconomic status of persons associated with a given identity (for example, black), social category (such as race), or social process (like racialization).[3] Intersectionality's practitioners can thus conceivably contend, for example, that white men are victims of systematic racial and gendered oppression.[4] Furthermore, there is little in the logic of intersectionality that guides those who utilize it to privilege a given identity, social category, or social process as normatively ideal. Intersectionality's practitioners are consequently free to determine, for instance, that "woman" is an identity to be reviled, celebrated, or some combination thereof.

Finally, intersectionality's value fluidity means that it does not prescribe to those who embrace it how best to remedy the status of the intersectionally oppressed. This claim might seem surprising, given the arguments and orientations of intersectionality's black feminist pioneers. Intersectional pioneer Deborah King (1988) argues that intersectionality "fundamentally challenges the interstructure of the oppressions of racism, sexism, and classism both in the dominant society and within movements for liberation. It is in confrontation with multiple jeopardy that black women define and sustain a multiple consciousness essential for our liberation" (72). Fellow pioneer Assata Zerai (2000) similarly describes intersectionality as premised on an "activist research agenda" that aims to "make scholarly work relevant to the people in the trenches" by "making social change happen" (212). According to this reasoning, the relationship between intersectional scholarship and activism is not a unidirectional one in which academicians bestow their supposed wisdom upon those in the field. Instead, women's "concrete experiences" or "day-to-day work in the trenches" (213) is the necessary basis for insightful, relevant intersectional theorizing as well as "the acts of resistance than can follow" (Brewer, Conrad, and King 2002; Collins 2008, 33). In short, a true intersectional approach is achieved "when abstract thought is joined with pragmatic action" (Collins 2008, 34).[5]

Yet there is little in the intersectional literature that reveals either what kinds of knowledge and action are required to effectively challenge intersectional oppression or if some combinations of knowledge and action are better than others. Indeed, beyond requiring practitioners to produce knowledge that empowers the oppressed to challenge their subordination, intersectionality allows for fairly broad interpretations of what constitutes emancipatory knowledge and action. Feminist theorists of intersectionality consequently emphasize the importance of melding "thought and actions" to foster subsequent resistance without specifying which types of knowledge/action dyads, if any, are superior to others (Collins 2008, 33, 38).

Instead, these theorists present a range of knowledge/action dyads as ideal. Claudette Williams (1993) encourages all black women to "evolve and mould our experiences into useful knowledge to advance our understanding . . . sharpen our analysis, [and] to forward our struggle" (163). Rose Brewer, Celia Conrad, and Mary King (2002) note the need for a specific group of women— "Black feminist intellectuals"—to "retain this notion of agency/activism largely by incorporating resistance into their analyses and by participating in social-change struggles at the university and community levels" (6). Jennifer Fish and Jennifer Rothchild (2010) caution that melding intersectional thought and action requires scholars to reflect on and articulate how their own interactions in the "field" often perpetuate the same gendered, classed, and other inequalities of power they claim to oppose. Patricia Clough and Michelle Fine (2007) argue, in contrast, that intersectional scholars should focus less on producing "critical self-reflective scholarship" and more on "studying, learning, and teaching" on the applied "plane of policy, program, and legislative reform." This focus is warranted, they conclude, not because contemporary reform-oriented politics is more "aimed at radical change" but because it is not and is thus in need of the kind of intellectual intervention that can help make such change possible (272).

Practicing Intersectionality as a Heuristic

When Rhonda Tsoi-a-Fatt (2010), a public-policy analyst, declares that the "precarious situation of our nation's Black men and boys" stems from the "complex intersection of race, class, structural/institutional racism, personal responsibility, and lack of equal access to opportunity," she provides tangible evidence that ABMSs' supporters subscribe to the logic of intersectionality (3). Fellow legal scholar and ABMSs advocate, Miriam Gladden (2013), concurs that "boys seem to suffer specific discrimination because they are both Black and male" (266). So, too, does Pamela Smith (1992), a law professor, who cites research by Kimberlé Crenshaw, Angela Davis, and other feminist theorists of intersectionality to make the case that "for the African-American male, his gender is as much a part of his oppression as [the African-American female's] gender is a part of hers" (2032). Sociologist Tyrone Howard (2013), another proponent of ABMSs, is equally forthright in embracing intersectionality:

> The intersectionality of race, class, and gender, and other identity markers, is fundamentally critical in research concerned with young Black males, as in the case of any subgroup. Each marker, in its own way, profoundly influences identity construction, self-concept, interactions with the world, and meaning-making. Black males possess multiple identities that are profoundly shaped by race, socioeconomic status, and gender in all of their complex manifestations. (18)

Other black male supporters of ABMSs posit a more implicit, perhaps unconscious, but plainly evident intersectional logic. These supporters do not use terms like *intersectional* or *intersectionality*. Instead, they privilege intersectionality's key tenet—that race, gender, sexuality, and other kinds of disadvantage are mutually constructing—in their analyses. For example, scholar Tony Laing (2010) claims that "race and gender define the experience of black boys in the classroom and that these defining characteristics work to their detriment" (212). Anthony Mitchell and James Stewart (2013) articulate a similar, indirect embrace of intersectionality when they assert that "racial, class, and gender hierarchies in school . . . undergird the past and current educational under-achievement of African American males" (386). Jawanza Kunjufu (2014) like-wise declares: "We talk about racism in America and throughout the world, but we should not assume that it affects Black boys and Black girls similarly. Though we talk about sexism, we should not assume that White girls and Black girls experience sexism in the same manner" (1).

Understanding Black Boys as Victims of Masculinized Racism

Most noteworthy for this project is that numerous black male proponents of ABMSs use an intersectional framework to detail why black boys are op-pressed, how they are oppressed, and who is responsible for their oppression. A case in point is the following declaration from sociologist Nathan Hare and his co-author Julia Hare (1991) regarding why black males are disadvan-taged: "In patriarchal racism, it is the male who poses the primary threat to the ruling male, who in his mind can take his place in the bedroom and the boardroom. Hence a white oppressor must take special pains to suppress the black male" (9). These authors make two important points. First, it is black males, rather than black females, who can usurp white male patriar-chal power. Second, this is the case because black males possess inherent qualities—including an ability and desire to sexually dominate women and a capacity and yearning to exert financial dominance over men and women alike—that threaten white males' power and privilege.

Nathan Hare and Julia Hare further emphasize that black males possess these fearsome qualities not because they are black or because they are male but because they are black males. The idea here is that white men do not fear black males simply because they are black. If this were the case, the authors explain, white male patriarchs would be equally intent on oppressing black females as well as black males. Instead, these patriarchs supposedly focus their energies on containing black males whose antiwhite animus is mascu-linized or marked by an aggressive yearning for privilege and power that is both "natural" and threatening. Furthermore, these same patriarchs focus on oppressing black males (and not men of all races) because black males' "natural" masculine yearning for privilege and power is racialized—that is, intensified by their being victims of antiblack racism. Again, the logic here is that black males are victims of intersecting race- and gender-based op-pression or, more particularly, of masculinized racism.

Clifford Watson and Geneva Smitherman (1996) echo this view—that white men have long oppressed black males not because they are black or are male but because they are black males who are endowed with a physical willingness and ability to resist racism as well as a psychological yearning for and capacity to exercise patriarchal power:

> During the seventeenth century, when Europeans were preoccupied with ravaging the land that would become the United States, they lived in constant fear of Indian and African males. . . . In the case of Black males, the Europeans' fear was not only related to the possibility of physical and violent resistance against them, but also to the economic threat posed by Black men who deployed their West African entrepreneurial skills throughout Britain's North American colonies. (1)

On this account, white men rightly recognize that it is black men, not black women and black girls, who pose the most serious threat to white male patriarchy. This threat, according to Watson and Smitherman, stems from a complex intersectional reality—black males' dual capacity to physically resist racism and to economically undermine white male privilege.

Ronnie Hopkins (1997) offers a less abstract but equally potent explanation of why black boys experience gender-specific racism at school. He argues that the contemporary American classroom reflects a "biosocial reality" in which antiblack racism is "most often targeted at African American males" because whites assume that black boys, rather than black girls, are unacceptably "tough" and thus in need of containment and degradation (100–101). Another, related explanation is that whites' widespread assumption about "tough" black boys is actually symptomatic of their profound fear of these boys' distinctly masculine way of being in the world. Psychiatrist Alvin Poussaint (1996) explains: "In a lot of school systems, it's anecdotally reported over and over again that schoolteachers are afraid of young black males, afraid of their aggression, and have stereotypes about them. These factors don't carry over in the same way to black females." This gender-specific fear, education professor Harry Morgan further explains, is deeply emotive and often expressed via white teachers' literal, tangible dread of black male bodies: "There's often an undercurrent of fear or tension between black male students and many white teachers. . . . This fear can be triggered over something as minor as a black boy walking around the room. On some subliminal level, the teacher is afraid to have even a very young black male defy the simplest rule" (qtd. in Fremon and Renfrow 1997).

Numerous black male advocates of ABMSs also offer an intersectionally informed explanation of who oppresses black schoolboys. This task, according to these advocates, is one that white men delegate to white women. In conveying this viewpoint, teacher Reginald Hicks (2010) asserts, in a somewhat conspiratorial tone, that it is not "sheer coincidence" that "the lowest achieving students (black males)" are taught almost exclusively by "White female teachers" (57). Jawanza Kunjufu (2015) pointedly asks:

> Can you imagine [that] African Americans may be the only group expecting someone else to educate their children? White female teachers constitute 83 percent of the U.S. elementary teaching force. . . . Unfortunately, African American males constitute only 1 percent of the teaching population. . . . I often wonder [if] the reason White girls are placed in special education the least and African American males the greatest, [is] based on the race and gender of the teacher?

Boyce Watkins (2014a) is more succinct, concluding that black boys are "poisoned" by the "white female teacher from the suburbs" more than any other social group.

David Banks (2014), head of the Eagle Academies, exemplifies this assumption, albeit in a less hostile tone, when he discusses his brother Philip:

> The majority of teachers in this country are white and female, and their personal experiences have given them little in common with boys like Philip. When they were young girls, they probably liked school. Teachers approved of their behavior. They did well. For all these reasons, they may have been inspired to become teachers themselves, but the very strengths that qualified them to be teachers mean that they probably lacked the personal context for understanding a boy like Philip—either why he was so unhappy in the classroom or how his feelings could provoke him to behave in disruptive ways. (4)

Black schoolboys fail, Banks suggests, because their racist teachers have had few "personal experiences" with racial minorities and because these teachers practice their subsequent racism in gender-specific ways that involve ignoring why black boys, like Philip, might be inclined to be "disruptive" in class. Or, put another way, black boys underachieve not only because of systemic racism or because of an antimasculine bias in the nation's schools but because of both or, more concretely, because they are forever engaged in a losing battle or "power struggle" with the vast majority of elementary schoolteachers who are not just white but who are also white women (Kunjufu 2005, v, 97).

What motivates white women to carry out this task of (mis)educating black boys? One explanation, espoused by Nathan Hare and Julia Hare (1984), is that although white women and white men are "comrades" who enjoy the same racial privileges, it is also the case that white men exercise patriarchal power over their white female peers. The supposed result is that white women are white men's "comrades sans arms" and are, thus, compelled to do the latter's racist bidding regardless of their own racial attitudes and orientations (28). What this means in the context of America's classrooms is that stymieing black boys' ability to achieve in school is an important reflection of white women teachers' racially privileged but gender-subordinate role in the white patriarchal order.

Another explanation is that white women can only maintain their racial privilege if they reproduce or have children with their white male peers. Put another way, "the umbilical cord of biology itself" means that white women and white men are equally committed to sustaining their shared racial privilege (Hare and Hare 1984, 94). It thus follows that white women are racists who also want what racist white men desire (Watkins 2014a). And white men's central desire, according to Hare and Hare, Hopkins, and many other advocates of ABMSs, is to perpetuate white supremacy by thwarting black males' supposed willingness and capacity for patriarchal power. Hence, Umar Johnson's suggestion that "it is the job of the White middle-class teacher to break the Black male's spirit; to psychologically emasculate him so that he simply acquiesces into the oppression that the society has in store for him" (qtd. in Raton 2012).

Other black male advocates of ABMSs emphasize that white men use relatively subtle practices to help ensure that white women, including white women teachers, oppress black boys. Chief among these is normalizing gendered identities and identifications that emphasize that "true" white women support white supremacy by helping white men to oppress black males. Reginald Hicks (2010), in articulating this perspective, suggests that white women teachers are beholden to "socially and psychologically constructed . . . identity orientations" that lead them to believe that it is their moral duty to ensure that black boys remain the nation's "lowest achieving students" (57, 60). In short, the very notion of respectable white womanhood is inextricably linked to legitimizing and sustaining white supremacy.

While black male supporters of ABMSs debate whether white women teachers want to harm black boys or if they are simply doing so at white men's bidding, what these supporters do agree on is how or the means by which said teachers render black boys victims of masculinized racism. These means, ABMSs' black male advocates explain, include curricular, pedagogical, and disciplinary tools, such as suspensions and special-education placements, that oppress black boys at the intersection of race and gender. Nick Chiles (2014) and Reginald Hicks (2010) contend, for example, that "fearful" white women teachers frequently assume not only that their black male students, like all blacks, are socially and intellectually inferior to whites. These teachers also take it for granted that black male boys' racially derived social and intellectual deviance is manifest through their masculinity or via violent, hyperaggressive, and otherwise inappropriate classroom behavior. It comes as little surprise, then, as Hicks concludes, that black boys are more likely than all other students to be expelled or suspended from school and that many of these boys ultimately "reject academic success" on grounds that it is "mainly a 'feminine' endeavor" (36). In sum, Chiles and Hicks encourage us to consider that the "factors that contribute to the disproportionate number of African American males in special education exceed racism" and that "sexism," including gender bias against males, is "part of it" (Kunjufu 2004, 25).

Fellow ABMS supporter Spencer Holland's point of reference is "time-outs," which, he argues, are a key disciplinary technique that white women teachers use to harm those black boys who have not (yet) been officially pushed out of the classroom:

> We're talking about first graders, and here you got grown women saying, "I can't handle these little boys." And I say to them all the time, "You're thirty-two and he's six. This is on you. This is not on him. He's not going to rape you!" There's not a six-year-old boy in this world that I would let intimidate me. But this is a lot of what's happening, the adultification of boys. Black boys, just sitting in the corners. Go in inner-city classrooms, you'll find almost a boy in every corner . . . [in] isolation away from the group. (qtd. in Hopkins 1997, 101)

White female teachers, according to this reasoning, frequently presume that black boys' racial inferiority is manifest not only via inappropriate aggression but also through something else—(hetero)sexually predatory behavior that, if left unchecked, undermines the moral fiber of all children.

Let me end this section by emphasizing that Hopkins, Hare and Hare, and other black male advocates of ABMSs are quite right to suggest that white women teachers exercise discriminatory power over their black students, including their black male students.[6] Said teachers are more likely than their black female counterparts to discipline black boys and are also more likely to regard black boys as less intelligent than other groups of students (Lindsay and Hart 2017; Ferguson 2001; Warren 2012). There is evidence, too, that white women teachers base their interactions with black boys on the racist, psychosocial assumption that their blackness renders them both sexually desirable and repulsive (Murrell 1993; Coffee et al., 2017).

Furthermore, as numerous black male supporters of ABMSs argue, the power that white women teachers exercise over many of their pupils is inter-sectional. By intersectional, I mean that these teachers' mutually constructing status as whites, women, and/or members of the middle class underscores both their desire and ability to negatively stereotype or otherwise harm students of color, including black boys. ABMS supporters Nathan Hare and Julia Hare, whom I discuss earlier, allude to this reality when they depict white women as complicit in white male supremacy. Decoteau Irby (2014), an educational policy studies professor, makes a strikingly similar point—that white women teachers who stereotype black boys as hypersexual deviants often do so by voluntarily positioning their own "white female bodies" not just as vulnerable but also as in need of protection from black males by white males. The goal of such positioning, Irby emphasizes, is the normalization and sustenance of white privilege and power.

Irene Yoon (2016), an educational leadership and policy professor, further details how and why embracing "middle-class White womanhood" is tantamount to "tak[ing] part in the injustice of seeing students and families of color not as people or learners but as tropes of delinquency or pathology" (3). Yoon's point of reference is the many white women teachers who mistakenly assume that they are necessarily wise and insightful educators because they are white, middle-class women whose "knowledge about motherhood" gives them a "superior understanding of how to monitor children's activities" and whose middle-class whiteness gives them license to "collectively describe" both the "parenting" and the "studen[t] school behaviors" of nonwhites as "pathological" (32).

Where Hopkins, Holland, and other black male advocates of ABMSs err is in presuming that white women teachers' status as women or, more specifically, as leaders of "overly" feminized classrooms explains why black boys academically underachieve.[7] Such a stance obscures the fact that while white women teachers and other white women frequently yearn for the same degree of power as their white male counterparts, they generally do not achieve this goal. White women teachers' continued underrepresentation as superintendents and in other senior educational administrative positions, combined with their low pay relative to their male peers, is firm evidence of this reality. Put more succinctly, white women's unequal partnership with white men means that they have limited ability to exercise *gender-based* power over their black male pupils (Gammill and Vaughn 2011; Hegewisch, Williams, and Harbin 2012).

Furthermore, focusing on "overly" feminized classrooms as the key culprit in black boys' underachievement places too much emphasis on the psychosocial biases of a specific social group—white women teachers—and not enough attention on how racism, classism, and other intersecting forms of structural or systemic oppression harm black boys. Finally, in casting white women teachers as a key source of black boys' academic underachievement,

ABMSs' black male supporters overlook research that suggests that "feminized" classrooms are not necessarily and always harmful to black boys if they are led by white women who acknowledge and address the reality of racism, who have high expectations for black boys, and who forge empathetic and trusting bonds with their black male students (Hardy 2010; Warren 2015). This insight is especially important given that many of the teachers employed by at least two ABMSs are white women (Williams 2013; Oeur 2012).[8]

Casting ABMSs as Liberation from Intersectional Oppression

Spencer Holland, Ronnie Hopkins, and other black male supporters of ABMSs make it clear that they view black schoolboys as victims of masculinized racism. Less obvious is what leads these supporters to regard ABMSs as the ideal means of ameliorating such oppression. One possible explanation is that these black male proponents mistakenly "cherry pick" the existing data in ways that minimize the well-documented limitations of these schools. And, indeed, it is possible to selectively focus on data that suggests that ABMSs are bearing fruit. Education professor Marquis Dwarte (2014) reports that black boys' reading achievement levels improved after they were enrolled in single-sex schools. Other scholars (Clarence Terry et al. 2014) note that ABMSs increase students' "academic focus," ability to understand and respond to racism, and opportunities to forge meaningful, mentoring relationships with teachers of color. Finally, two of the largest networks of ABMSs—Urban Preparatory Academies and the Eagle Academies—report high college acceptance rates (100 percent and 98 percent, respectively) ("They Did It Again!" 2016; Sommerfledt and Otis 2016).

There are difficulties, however, with these findings. For instance, while Dwarte reports that enrolling in ABMSs improves black boys' reading scores, he finds that their scores actually remain below those of their peers in coeducational schools. Furthermore, even those ABMSs with high college-acceptance rates are struggling in other important areas related to test scores and college readiness.[9] Not only that, even if we accept that test scores and college readiness do not tell the whole story of any schools' success or failure, qualitative measures reveal other limitations of ABMSs. Researchers have found, for example, that teachers and administrators at many of these schools "lack a clear sense of how to approach their work" and that they often approach teaching in ways that are grounded neither in "evidence-based theory" nor "substantive planning" (Noguera 2012, 11; Terry et al. 2014).

Black male advocates of ABMSs who embrace intersectionality are, nevertheless, free to ignore the less-than-positive reality of these schools described above. This is because of what I discuss earlier—that intersectionality guides those who embrace it to meld thought and action toward remedying the plight of the oppressed without specifying exactly what the emancipatory melding of knowledge and action looks like. As a result, there is little in the logic of intersectionality that encourages ABMSs' black male supporters to embrace another, more emancipatory means of challenging black boys' subordination in the classroom.

This lack of specificity ultimately means two things within the parameters of the discourse that promotes ABMSs. On the one hand, many black male supporters of these schools assume, as do feminist theorists of intersectionality, that blending thought and action is the best means of challenging oppression at the crossroads of race, gender, and other hierarchies of power. Ron Walker, the executive director of the Coalition of Schools Educating Boys of Color (COSEBOC), encourages his members to challenge the confluence of racial/ethnic- and gender-based oppression in black boys' lives by "merging" existing ideas or "what is known about promising practices for boys of color" with actual "research on effective schools" (COSEBOC 2015, 5). Other supporters of ABMSs similarly conclude that the best way to challenge black boys' status as an oppressed "race/gender subgroup" is by "balancing" the knowledge gained from educators' reasonable "sense of urgency" with an active "research and intervention focus" (Terry et al. 2014, 693–94; 668–69).

On the other hand, because intersectionality offers an expansive understanding of what constitutes an emancipatory blend of knowledge and action, it can inspire very different understandings of how to address the needs of the intersectionally oppressed. Many black male advocates of ABMSs and feminist theorists of intersectionality are particularly far apart in this regard. The activist research agenda of the former draws on academics, policymakers, community activists, and the popular press to host conferences, write popular and scholarly articles, obtain grant funds, and pass legislation—all to help legitimize a model of education that propagates the seeds of antiracism and antifeminism in the classroom.

Intersectionality's feminist pioneers meld scholarship and activism in different ways. These include thinking critically about how to minimize the exploitative dimensions of their own scholarship as well as agitating for policy reforms that address racism, patriarchy, and other sorts of subordination in the criminal justice system, immigration law, and elsewhere. Accompanying actions include everything from establishing college degree programs in women's prisons to hosting town hall meetings—with policymakers, students, scholars, and others—that aim to critically interrogate systemic racism and gender-based discrimination in the classroom (Clough and Fine 2007; Crenshaw 2015).

Lessons about Intersectionality

Black male proponents of ABMSs are not alone in embracing intersectionality for a kind of politics that its feminist pioneers did not intend. Some conservative black Christian[10] critics of gay marriage use intersectionality to argue that blacks' "true" experience of oppression is one of co-constructing racism, heterophobia, and anti-Christian bias, and that the needs of blacks who are not disadvantaged in this manner are secondary (Lindsay 2013). In doing so, these commentators provide additional evidence—as do many critics of affirmative action and supporters of Donald Trump[11]—that intersectionality is a politically fluid heuristic that reveals how identities, social categories, and processes of inequality are co-constitutive but that does not reveal who is disadvantaged as a result or how best to remedy their disadvantage.

Many black Christians communicate and cultivate their opposition to gay marriage through a variety of legislative, judicial, and other advocacy-related activities, including lawsuits, educational programs, and political lobbying.[12] The rhetoric they typically use to oppose gay marriage is both similar to and different from that used by other opponents. Like white evangelicals, some black Christians justify their opposition to gay marriage via "fate-linking" or by suggesting that other groups subordinated by mutually constructing racial, religious, and other types of systemic oppression share their views. Unlike white evangelicals and other critics of gay marriage, conservative black Christians rarely suggest that gay marriage is unconstitutional (Wadsworth 2011).

These black Christians' specific argument is that gay marriage undermines blacks' explicitly Christian religious traditions and, in the process, thwarts their successful use of these traditions to challenge racism. According to this logic, gay marriage's supposedly harmful racial and religious effects are mutually reinforcing in ways that deepen blacks' systemic subordination. Reverend Clenard Childress (2009), a senior pastor at the New Calvary Baptist Church in Montclair, New Jersey, perhaps captures this sentiment best:

> Equating the [civil rights struggle to the] current same-sex marriage effort being waged by gays and lesbians and their supporters is, quite frankly, insulting to most African-Americans and . . . trivializes our long and painful struggle . . . through a bloody civil war, the enactment of four separate amendments to our federal Constitution, thousands of federal court decisions and millions of hours at the "back of the bus". . . . [I]f you are to better understand the nature of African-American opposition to same-sex marriage [you must] also understand that our faith and our civic duty are intertwined. "Separation of church and state" arguments do not hold water in the black community. We understand that

if not for the strength of leaders like the Rev. Martin Luther King Jr., Malcolm X, Adam Clayton Powell Jr. and scores of others, our struggle would have been longer and more painful.

According to Childress's reasoning, gay marriage undermines blacks' religious traditions and in doing so thwarts their successful use of these traditions to challenge racism. In short, gay marriage's supposedly harmful racial and religious effects mutually construct each other.

Some conservative black Christians also contend that gay marriage exacerbates their intersecting sexual and religious subordination. The founders of BlacksForMarriage.org (2011), an online information portal, explain:

> BlacksForMarriage.org was founded with the mission to stem the tide of homosexuality, homosexual marriage, and broken families across America, and in the black community of America in particular. . . . In 2009, Christian leaders and individuals took part in signing a document called the Manhattan Declaration . . . "born out of an urgent concern about growing efforts to marginalize the Christian voice in the public square, to redefine marriage, and to move away from the biblical view of the sanctity of life." We at BlacksForMarriage.org wholeheartedly agree with this important document. . . . we stand for marriage between a man and a woman. . . . Now, more than ever before, traditional marriage has come under attack and it will be up to us as Christians to counter that attack with the uncompromising Word of God. (BlacksForMarriage.org 2011)

Two simultaneously antiracist and heterosexist assumptions are at work in conservative black Christians' critique of gay marriage. The first is that heterosexual black Christians are disadvantaged by the reality that so many of the "efforts to marginalize the Christian voice in the public square" come in the form of assaults on the supposed pillar of heterosexual family life, "marriage between a man and a woman." According to this argument, heterosexual black Christians' experience of anti-Christian bigotry is (hetero)sexualized. The second assumption is that heterosexual black Christians are also oppressed in a social context in which it is acceptable to "attack" heterosexual family life and to do so by denigrating Christians' "biblical view" that marriage is between men and women. In short, if you are a heterosexual black Christian, your experience of heterophobia is heavily informed by anti-Christian bias.

In-Group Policing

Conservative black Christians' critique of gay marriage offers further evidence that intersectional analysis can be used to advance a range of ideological agendas. Their critique is also important because it suggests, as does the push for ABMSs, that intersectionality and "in-group" policing may not be mutually exclusive phenomena. Scholars of ethnic conflict define such policing as the "formal or informal administration of sanctions, even violent sanctions, within a group so as to enforce a certain line of action vis-à-vis outsiders (who may be defined not only in ethnic terms but in religious, ideological, class, or any other terms)" (Brubaker 2004, 99; see also Fearon and Laitin 1996). Enforcing this "line of action" usually involves reining in group members who are offensive to other social groups or compelling group members to attack or otherwise challenge other social groups (Bhavnani and Backer 2000; Fearon and Laitin 1996).

Many observers of racial, gendered, sexual, and interest-group politics similarly contend that social groups practice in-group policing either to mitigate or to encourage conflict with other social groups. However, these authors emphasize that in-group policing is often less about physical violence and more about articulating which group members are "truly" disadvantaged. Cathy Cohen (1999) argues that blacks exclude homophobia from their "real" experience of oppression to help render the race "normal" and to ultimately diminish whites' rationale for practicing antiblack racism. Shane Phelan (1994) notes that white feminists routinely reject racism as central to women's "true" experience of oppression because they assume that positing women's disadvantage as purely gendered is key to challenging patriarchal power.

Many of these same scholars also conclude that in-group policing occurs when social groups are inattentive to intersectionality. Cohen (1999) asserts that many blacks do not count homosexuals or women among "truly" disadvantaged members of the race precisely because they suppose that black oppression occurs along the "single dimension" of racism. Ian Barnard (2004) and Nikki Sullivan (2003) contend that because gay white men take it for granted that homosexuals are defined by one "marginalized subjectivity (i.e., gayness)," they routinely construct lesbians' and black men's experiences of gender-based oppression and/or racism as "irrelevant and divisive" or as something other than "real" homophobia (Barnard 2004, 4).

Dara Strolovitch (2007) develops a similar perspective in her nuanced account of how race, class, and gender inform interest-group politics. She carefully analyzes the different advocacy claims advanced by interest groups purporting to represent subaltern interests and in doing so demonstrates the insufficiently intersectional character of these claims. Strolovitch thus concludes that social groups and the advocacy organizations that claim to speak on their behalf "are traditionally organized around single axes of discrimination" and that they, consequently, regard as secondary the concerns of members who are "caught at the crossroad of multiple forms of disadvantage" (23). They way forward, Strolovitch concludes, is for these organizations to become more intersectional in their orientation by "framing disadvantaged-subgroup issues broadly and in ways that emphasize their connections to advantaged ones" or by fostering "intersectionally linked fate on behalf of disadvantaged groups" (211).

This line of reasoning—that to embrace intersectionality is to mobilize on behalf of greater inclusion and equality not only among but also within social groups—is present in the literature on black males and schooling. Paul Butler (2013), a legal scholar and critic of the narrative that constructs black males as endangered in the classroom, posits an "intersectionalist Black male intervention strategy" as the best way to ensure that foundations and government officials eschew "traditional ideas" about blackness as a masculine phenomenon that often lead them to devote more resources to male-centered versus female-centered "racial justice" initiatives (507). Fellow critic Menah Pratt-Clarke (2010) argues that paying more attention to "intersecting race and gender identity" is central to valuing and improving the "educational performance" of black boys and black girls (161).

My argument is that social groups can and do embrace intersectional logic on behalf of or in pursuit of exclusionary politics. In making this claim, I reject the common, abovementioned presumption that in-group policing occurs when social groups are inattentive to intersectionality. To be clear, I also value a less policed, more inclusive understanding of blackness in relation to ABMSs and beyond. The difficulty is that, contrary to what Butler, Pratt-Clark, and other commentators suggest, engaging in intersectional analysis is not necessarily a means of achieving this vision. That conservative black Christian critics of gay marriage can use the logic of intersectionality to police the boundaries of blackness or to cast themselves, rather than other blacks, as the "true" victims of oppression at the crossroads of race, religion, and sexual orientation is a prime example of this troubling reality. So, too, are the many supporters of ABMSs who assume that black males are more oppressed than black females not just because they are black or because they are male but because they are black males whose "inherent" willingness and capacity, as such, to usurp white male patriarchy makes them particularly threatening to the powers that be. These same supporters also construct blacks' antiracist resistance as an inherently masculine phenomenon when they cast black males, and black males only, as the "rightful" leaders of the race. Again, they do so not by eschewing but by embracing the logic of intersectionality on behalf of or in pursuit of exclusionary politics.

Black Women's Voices

There is another way in which redefining intersectionality as an ideologically fluid analytical framework potentially fosters a politics of exclusion. As I allude to earlier, disentangling intersectional analysis from its black feminist origins arguably erases black women's voices both as theorists and as a social group positioned at or near the bottom of economic, gendered, racial, and sexual hierarchies of power. As a reminder, the concern here is that redirecting intersectionality's lens away from black women promotes a misguided equivalence of oppressions that silences black women's experiences and in so doing hides the very real differences in power between them and other social groups (May 2015; Collins and Bilge 2016; Berger and Guidroz 2009).

Many feminists are also worried that there is a broader "omission project occurring in published political science research generally and within intersectionality research specifically" whereby "Black women as research subjects are being omitted" (Jordan-Zachery 2014, 22). For Crenshaw (2016), whom I cite earlier, this omission of black women from the intersectional literature stems from the flawed assumption that black women's experiences of oppression are not "universal" enough to constitute valid truths for anyone other than themselves. Other theorists argue that this omission occurs when European scholars use intersectionality to facilitate their own desire to talk less about racism and more about ethnicity, gender, class, and other kinds of inequality as they are manifest outside North America (Bilge 2013; Petzen 2012). As Nikol Alexander-Floyd (2012) eloquently argues, the result is arguably that:

> Barely a decade into the new millennium, a new wave of raced-gendered occultic commodification is afoot, one focusing not on black female subjectivity per se, but on the concept of intersectionality. . . . Although the recent enthusiasm about intersectionality should ostensibly promise a broadening of research based on black feminist insights, as a practical matter the various interpretations . . . disarticulate intersectionality from its theoretical, political, and methodological roots. . . . [T]he voices, intellectual contributions, and political projects of black feminists magically disappear or are supplanted by post-black feminist readings of intersectionality. (2, 18–19)

These are valid and important concerns given the myriad ways black women's voices continue to be silenced in antiracist and feminist activism as well as the extent to which black feminist theorizing remains marginalized within the academy. However, suggesting that intersectional analysis can be informed by less-than-emancipatory political agendas, including antifeminist ones, may not be as worrying as the reasoning above suggests. This is so because intersectionality is not a zero-sum phenomenon in which identifying the mutually constructing oppressions that shape one group necessarily nullifies the intersectional reality of other groups. Instead, the logic of intersectionality allows us to do the opposite—to interrogate how the intersectional subjectivity of one social group gains meaning from the intersectional status, or the lack thereof, of one or more other groups. What this means, in practice, is that feminists, including black feminists, can and should use the patriarchal, antiracist politics so central to the discourse in support of ABMSs to better identify and challenge the processes, norms, and values that enable educators, lawmakers, and others to ignore black women's and girls' intersectional oppression in the classroom and elsewhere.

To this end, some feminists might interrogate many black men's deeply held, co-constitutive racial and gendered reasoning—that a black woman's place in the struggle against white supremacy is as literal reproducers of the race—to better understand black women's absence at the forefront of the black power and Civil Rights Movements. Other feminists might query the historical absence of black women as formal church leaders by highlighting many black men's intersecting racial and gendered assumption that black women's ideal position in uplifting the race is not in the pulpit but, rather, at home or in the church kitchen. Of course, if the black women in question are gay, they are also deemed inimical to the home or to "authentic" black family life. Both lines of inquiry are key to understanding how and why black women are intersectionally oppressed.

Put another way, using intersectionality to explore black men's location at the crossroads of racial, gendered, and other systems of power can deepen understandings of black women's own intersectional oppression—often at the hands of black men. Equally important is that nothing in this kind of intersectional analysis promotes what Collins (2006) rightly warns about— namely, a dangerous "myth of equivalent oppressions" that denies the reality of sharp social and economic inequalities between black women and other social groups. On the contrary, the intersectional analysis I describe above does the opposite by highlighting the complicated sexual and other inequalities that prevail between black women and black men.

Conclusion

In the end, there is much to criticize about how black male proponents of ABMSs use intersectionality for antifeminist, heterosexist, and other conservative ends. Foremost among these criticisms is that in casting black boys as the only true victims of intersectional, systemic bias in the nation's schools, these proponents deny women and girls, particularly black women's and black girls' own intersectionally informed underachievement in the classroom. These proponents do so in two ways. They claim that black boys underachieve not because they are black or because they are males but, rather, because they are intersectionally oppressed black males who are made to learn in racist, female-dominated schools that impede their academic success and their concomitant ability to undermine white male patriarchy. In addition, unlike intersectionality's pioneers who strive to merge black feminist theory and activism, ABMSs' black male supporters argue that melding patriarchal antiracist theory and practice is the best way to challenge black males' oppression at the crossroads of race and gender.

The effort to establish ABMSs is evidence, in sum, that while intersectionality enables those who embrace it to discern that race, gender, and other hierarchies of power are mutually constructing, who is consequently oppressed, why, and what should be done about it are political matters that are not decided or preordained by intersectionality itself. The result is that intersectionality can illuminate, at the same time that it obscures, inequality among black women, black men, and other social groups. Or, put more precisely, while intersectionality is always political, its potential to foster more rather than less policing of social groups' real and imagined boundaries means that its politics is not always emancipatory.

3 The Double Dialectic between Experience and Politics

Governments that consist of very few women have hurried to recognize as women men who believe that they are women and have had themselves castrated to prove it. . . . The insistence that manmade women be accepted as women is the institutional expression of the mistaken conviction that women are defective males.

—Germaine Greer, 1999

Radical feminist Germaine Greer has faced an avalanche of adulation as well as condemnation since she proclaimed these words in her book, *The Whole Woman*. Some feminists have praised her for validating the lived experiences and oppressions of "real" women or those for whom gender identity is supposedly not a choice (L. Green 2015; Nott 2015). Many feminist, gay, lesbian, and transgender rights groups have condemned Greer's obvious disdain for transwomen and have accused her of encouraging discrimination and violence against all transpeople (Penny 2009; Sergent-Shadbolt 2015).

Germaine Greer's simultaneously feminist and transphobic politics tells us much about the black-male-led campaign to open separate schools for black boys. Her words are further evidence that black male supporters of these schools are not alone in articulating experiential claims that trouble the boundary between liberatory and oppressive politics. Greer's sentiments also suggest new evidence of why this is so—namely, because there is a *dialectical* relationship between making an experiential claim and espousing a particular kind of politics. Experiencing patriarchal oppression arguably motivates Greer to make the antifeminist claim that women are not "defective males" or somehow inferior to men. At the same time, patriarchy's very ubiquity means that when Greer resists it, she does so by reproducing a key patriarchal assumption—that the world is divided into "men" and "women" or into two fixed and immutable genders whose boundaries can never and should never be transgressed.

"Dialectic" is, of course, a term with a long history in philosophy and political theory that reaches back to Plato and that is prominently and variably featured in the thought of a diverse group of thinkers. Karl Marx (1867) articulates a dialectic between labor and capital or a contradictory state of affairs in which members of the working class are unable to afford the value of the commodities, including the food, clothing, and other life-preserving goods, that they produce. A hundred years later, Shulamith Firestone (1970) posits a "family-based" dialectic in which being relegated to reproductive labor (breastfeeding, childbirth, and so on) is both the cause of and an effect of women's patriarchal subordination. Frantz Fanon (1967) makes the case for a "master-slave" dialectic in which colonialized people are free from oppression when their colonizers recognize them as full-fledged humans. The difficulty, Fanon explains, is that no such recognition is possible because to be colonized is, by definition, to be subhuman.

I take "dialectical," as its most basic, to describe the tension that arises from the presence of opposing thoughts and ideas. In many ways, this core understanding of dialectics—as that which describes the connection between a given ideological, discursive, and/or material force and the strains that arise from this force—is central to my reading, thus far, of the discourse in favor of ABMSs. In chapter 1, I draw on the dialectical, *ontological* presumption that specific historical conditions foster contradictory socioeconomic and political realities. The historically specific condition that animates much of my analysis is neoliberalism. My analysis reveals, more specifically, that many blacks enthusiastically embrace a neoliberal social, political, and economic order that posits equality of opportunity, a color-blind legal system, and privatized public schools as pathways to middle-class life for individual blacks who work hard and play by the "rules." At the same time, these neoliberal social and economic policies actually deepen black oppression by privileging privatized public schools that surveil and punish rather than foster black students' individual talents and by promoting a rhetoric of individual "choice" that legitimizes antifeminist efforts to exclude "distracting" black girls from the classroom. This gap—between what neoliberalism promises blacks and what it actually delivers—ultimately fosters a kind of ideological befuddlement that leads many black males to misread ABMSs as the solution to black boys' experience of oppression.[1]

My ultimate goal, however, is not only to use dialectics to make a context-specific or historically grounded claim about the tensions that structure black people's lives under neoliberal conditions. I want also to illuminate what this ontological reality—that the social and political world is contradictory—reveals about what we can and cannot know about our own and others' appeals to experience. To this end, I use the first section of this chapter to make a dialectically informed *epistemological* claim—that it is impossible to articulate a politically unmediated grasp or knowledge of experience. This is so, I argue, à la Hegel, because the ideological bewilderment that neoliberalism and other systems of oppression engender means that perception is misperception (Theron 2013). Put more precisely, what people who exist under historically specific, contradictory socioeconomic conditions regard as their "experience" is not the thing in itself but, rather, a notion of it that is politically mediated both by dominant racist, gender-biased, and other harmful constructs and by their desire to resist these constructs. What this means, within the confines of the discourse in support of ABMSs, is that when black male supporters of these schools make claims about their own and other black males' experience of oppression, they do in ways that advance antiracist politics and are informed by antifeminist politics.

This chapter goes on to describe how numerous feminist theorists—from Sandra Harding to Joan Scott—gesture toward this complicated reality. I focus my analysis on these theorists' suggestion that women's appeals to experience motivate feminist and other politics of resistance and that these appeals are informed by patriarchy, heterosexism, and other existing hierarchies of oppression. I conclude this discussion by drawing on black feminist historian E. Frances White's (1990) more precise conceptualization of "discursive dialectics." White convincingly argues that in order to understand why women, black men, and other social groups' appeals to experience are associated with emancipatory and oppressive politics, we must accept the fact that "counter and dominant discourses contest the same ideological ground" (84).

As I make clear, this epistemological reality, in which social groups' appeals to experience inform and are informed by politics, ultimately offers an important lesson for feminist theorists of experience. Simply put, the fact that experiential claims are mediated by politics makes it difficult, if not impossible, to posit any kind of ideal or unmediated experiential claim about black boys or other disadvantaged social groups. This is nevertheless the approach that undergirds Gayatri Spivak's argument that "strategic essentialism" and Iris Young's contention that "seriality" are the best means, respectively, of ensuring that women can enjoy the advantages without becoming mired in the disadvantages of their experiential claims. I conclude the chapter by demonstrating that such well-intentioned efforts to craft a more ideal appeal to experience are limited, at best, given that social groups' assertions about their experience both engender emancipatory politics and are informed by oppressive politics.

Pro-ABMS Discourse and the Dialectic
between Experience and Politics

> With an overwhelmingly white female teaching force across the country, many
> Black boys encounter instructors who are not entirely comfortable with their
> presence. This has a severe impact on their academic fortunes. . . . Black boys
> are less likely to be placed in advanced-placement classes . . . much more likely
> than other students to be placed in special education classes and labeled men-
> tally retarded . . . [and] are three times more likely to be suspended or expelled
> from school than their white peers. (Chiles 2014)

With these words, journalist Nick Chiles offers a potent reminder that
many black male advocates of ABMSs articulate an experience-based politics that defies simple, neat classification as either antifeminist or antiracist.
These advocates are able to do so, as chapter 2 makes clear, because they
embrace a politically fluid intersectional logic. This, however, is only part of
the story regarding how and why so many black male advocates of ABMSs
make experiential claims that both foster and inhibit a politics of resistance.
The other equally important explanation is that there is a dialectical relationship between how black male proponents of these schools understand
and articulate black boys' experience of oppression and these proponents'
political attitudes and orientations.

Experience as the Motive Force of Emancipatory Politics

On the one hand, identifying and articulating black boys' experience of racism motivates the antiracist politics of ABMSs' black male advocates. Mark,
an eleventh-grade student at an ABMS, suggests exactly this when he makes
a link between his own firsthand experience of oppression as "a Black male"
and his recognition that systemic racism unfairly protects many "Caucasian"
students from, among other things, life in violent, crime-ridden neighborhoods:

> Honestly, being a Black male is really important to my experience. I've been
> exposed to a lot of things that have affected me and how I see things. I live
> in a neighborhood where I've been exposed to a lot of violence. This is not a
> good thing, but it has helped me in certain situations. I know what to do and
> what not to do, or how to react and how not to react when confronted with
> violence. I feel like if I were a Caucasian, I wouldn't have been exposed to so
> much. I wouldn't have these "bells on my back" that force me to be aware of
> what's going on around me. . . . [W]hat I've been through and what I've seen

throughout my life, has made me stronger. It made me realize that I have to get out of here if I want to be successful . . . so I won't have to live those things in the future. (qtd. in Fergus, Noguera, and Martin 2014, 145)

Kaleem Caire strikes a similar note. He draws on his experience as a student—at Madison's Cherokee Middle School, where students "voluntarily segregated themselves" by race, and then at the city's West High School, where he was "totally uncomfortable" in "a sea of white kids"—to identify and critique what structural racism looks like in the classroom. Caire contends, more specifically, that:

> Before [attending Cherokee Middle School], I knew I was black . . . but I never felt like it was something that other people didn't value. . . . Madison schools don't know how to educate African Americans. . . . It's not that they can't. Most of the teachers could, and some do, valiantly. But the system is not designed for that to happen. (qtd. in Ginsberg-Schutz 2010)

Kevin Brown (1993), a law professor and proponent of ABMSs, likewise concludes: "Every time I think about public education, my own experience during the 1960s and the early 1970s is never far from my mind." Brown cites as an example his white female English teacher's "dispassionate" insistence that he read a racially derogatory text because it is "one of the great literary classics of all time" (814, 816).

Another black male proponent of ABMSs, community activist Anthony Samad (2009), emphasizes that his antiracist politics is valid specifically because it arises from his direct knowledge of racism not only as a student but also as an educator: "For the past 15 years, I've taught at the college and community college levels where over 3,000 students have taken my classes. I am in the classroom. I witness first-hand, on a daily basis, the largely under-prepared product of LAUSD [the Los Angeles Unified School District]." Craige Thomas, a high school teacher and fellow advocate of ABMSs, focuses less on the fact that experiencing racism motivates his antiracist claims and more on what animates or makes this relationship possible. The answer, he explains, is that he and other black males have "double-vision" or the capacity to grasp reality both from their own disadvantaged perspective and from the perspective of those, including women teachers, who disadvantage them:

> Teachers don't have that sixth sense of reading a child. They say kids don't read, I say, "There's a lot of reading that you missing too, girlfriend," especially when it come to the Black male. A lot of them have the attitude that "My kid's in private school, so I'm just here to make a paycheck." So they developed an apathetic approach to teaching. And the kids know when you're being apathetic towards

them, when you really don't give a shit. Don't give a shit! They can sense it; and
with you not giving a shit, they don't give a shit. (qtd. in Hopkins 1997, 97–99)

On Thomas's reading, being marginalized as hyper-aggressive, immoral
deviants gives young black males a distinct perspective on or a twofold vision of the world that allows them to understand reality not only from their
own but also from the flawed perspective of their oppressors—a perspective
that constructs black men as necessarily and always "under the 'element of
suspicion'" (qtd. in Gause 2008, 132). What this means in more concrete
terms is that black boys know what it is like to be unfairly disadvantaged in
classrooms that are inimical to their needs *and* they understand their teachers'
antithetical view of them as subhumans who are socially and intellectually
unworthy of care and attention.

There are obvious similarities here with Du Bois's notion that black people
have a "double consciousness" or "sense of always looking at one's self through
the eyes of others, of measuring one's soul by the tape of a world that looks
on in amused contempt and pity" (Du Bois (1997 [1903]), 38). Thomas and
other like-minded commentators' reading of black boys' "double vision"
as a source of political resistance also brings to mind Paget Henry's (2005)
concept of "potentiated double consciousness" or idea that the oppressed
see the world from their own and their oppressors' perspective *and* use this
"double" vision to critique the very reality of a stratified social world in which
groups are either privileged or oppressed.

Most important, several supporters of ABMSs assert, is what this distinctive perspective or double vision engenders—namely, black boys' and
black men's collective recognition that their own liberation from oppression
rests on resisting the worldview of those who exercise power over them.
Sociologists Richard Majors, Janet Billson, and Theodore Ransaw argue,
on this note, that black boys often enact a "cool pose," premised on certain
attention-getting behaviors, which reflect their collective recognition that
they are marginalized and that their oppressors are wrong to regard them
as innately inferior and thus worthy of subordination (Ransaw, Majors, and
Moss 2016; Majors and Billson 1993). Put more tangibly:

> By acting calm, emotionless, fearless, aloof, and tough, the African-American
> male strives to offset an externally imposed "zero" image. Being cool shows both
> the dominant culture and the black male himself that he is strong and proud.
> He is somebody. He is a survivor, in spite of the systematic harm done by the
> legacy of slavery and the realities of racial oppression, in spite of the centuries
> of hardship and mistrust. (Majors and Billson 1993, 5)

Majors and Billson assume that the conditions of young black males' oppression motivate them to make antiracist claims that challenge their subordination. This is the case not merely because black boys necessarily see the world from two perspectives but also because doing so enables them to critique the unjust disparity between their own lives and those of their oppressors. In sum, black boys who develop a "third eye" or "cool pose" are not just reacting against racism—they are also performing a prescriptive act whose very existence indicates that they see themselves through their own as well as their oppressors' eyes and thus have the wherewithal to critique the oppressors' perspective.

The A Priori, Anti-Emancipatory Politics of Experience

It is not adequate to simply conclude that the conditions of their oppression or, more specifically, identifying and articulating their experience of oppression leads disadvantaged black males to embrace antiracist and other kinds of emancipatory politics. I say this because the push for ABMSs suggests another kind of dialectical relationship between experience and politics—one in which proponents' understanding of why black schoolboys experience oppression is itself a function of an antifeminist politics that casts girls and women as necessarily complicit in black boys' oppression. Take, for example, what I mentioned earlier—the many proponents of ABMSs who argue that black boys underachieve in the nation's coeducational schools because they are sexually distracted by black girls. This argument only makes sense if we already assume, as do many black male advocates of these schools, that young black women are primarily (hetero)sexual beings who serve as dangerous, "forbidden fruit" for otherwise upstanding young black men.

Cleve Warren, co-founder of an ABMS, Valor Academy of Leadership for Boys, makes exactly this assumption when he declares that taking "girls out of the picture" or creating "gender-based" schooling seems to work best because the "competition between boys for girls" is a "significant distraction" for the nation's black boys (Warren, qtd. in Amos 2014). The same flawed assumption—that black girls' sheer physical presence is to blame for derailing black boys' academic progress—undergirds eighth-grade student Elijah Landsman's assertion that life at an ABMS is better specifically because "there is less distraction" from black girls (qtd. in Matthews 2013, 54). Another ABMS student concurs not only that black girls are, by definition, sexual objects for male conquest but also that their status as such is what harms the black schoolboys in their midst:

If there were girls here, I think it would be even worse. There would have been a lot of fights between boys trying to get girls or whatever. At my old school, people were showing off for girls and trying to start fights just to get the attention of a girl. They might try to put someone else down to make themselves look better than they really are. (qtd. in Fergus, Noguera, and Martin 2014, 160)

Of course, in casting black girls as sexually distracting to black boys, black male advocates of ABMSs ultimately perpetuate rather than challenge a key tenet of masculinized racism. I have in mind here the gender-specific, racist notion that black males are hypersexual savages who, unlike their more "civilized" white male peers, cannot control their violent sexual impulses. Depicting black girls as sexual temptresses also leads black male proponents of ABMSs to reinforce a racially specific, gender-biased notion that is especially harmful to black girls. Put more specifically, central to many of these advocates' rhetoric about "distracting" black girls, is the co-constitutive antifeminist and racist assumption that black females' inferiority to whites is manifest in their "failed" gender performance or in their inability to conduct themselves in the sexually chaste manner of "real" women and girls—in other words, white women and white girls. According to this reasoning, black women and black girls are, instead, imbued with an immoral sexual ethos that makes them forever willing and able to sexually service the males in their midst (Williams 2004).

Other kinds of a priori, antifeminist politics inform how supporters of ABMSs conceptualize the reasons for black boys' experience of oppression. Key among these is the oft-repeated notion that white female teachers' status, as women, plays an important role in black boys' underachievement in traditional schools. The following declaration from Umar Johnson, a psychologist, is an important reminder of what this assumption looks like in practice. On Johnson's account, white women teachers oppress black boys because they are racist whites and because they are women intent on not only racialized but also gender-based warfare. Hence, Johnson's use of the term "emasculate" to describe the harm that these teachers inflict upon their black male students:

The first stage in the psycho-academic holocaust against Black boys is miseducation. Mis-education . . . teach[es] the Black male child to hate himself. That's most important. [Then it] teach[es] the Black boy to love White culture. . . . It is the job of the White middle-class teacher to break the Black male's spirit; to psychologically emasculate him so that he simply acquiesces into the oppression that the society has in store for him. . . . [I]f the White middle-class female is unsuccessful in breaking the spirit of the Black boy, she then turns to the psycho-tropic drug cartel to induce the submission psychologically . . .

[via] psycho-tropic medication. If the Black boy still is a "man child" and ha[s] not been broken through mis-education and schooling, you now go to juvenile incarceration. (qtd in Raton 2012)

Jawanza Kunjufu (2004) is even more clear about the explicitly gendered as well as racialized harm wrought upon black boys by their white women teachers. He argues that "[f]emale teachers, especially White ones, are integral" to black boys' academic failure—because these teachers inevitably transfer their own flawed presumption that all males are "sexist" to the black boys in their charge. Again, the assumption here is that white women teachers harm black boys not only because the teachers are white but also because they are women:

> Do you really believe that the way female teachers feel about themselves, men and sexism can be left at home and not enter the classroom? . . . For White women it becomes more complex, because their Black students may be the first Black males with whom they have ever had direct contact. This amazes me. How can you teach a child who you do not know or understand . . . [when] in an insecure world, most people equate differences with deficiencies? (84)

Fellow supporter of ABMSs Reginald Hicks (2010) emphasizes, finally, that when white women teachers emasculate their black male students the damaging outcome is more than a racialized one in which black boys are "made to feel inadequate, inferior, and self-conscious about their own 'blackness' through a constant barrage of low expectations," including "reaction and response," which suggests "that their dialect, attitudes, and clothing styles are culturally illegitimate." Equally disturbing, Hicks contends, is that white women teachers' emasculation of black boys also has a racially informed gendered effect—one in which young black males "write off academic achievement" not just as a "white" phenomenon but "as a *white, feminine thing.*" There are few other explanations, Hicks concludes, of why so many black boys ultimately shun all things academic and instead "pursue unrealistic nonacademic goals, like professional sports and entertainment" (71).

As chapter 2 makes clear, Johnson, Hicks, and Kunjufu, and other black male advocates of ABMSs are right to suggest that white women teachers, like their white male peers, exercise racial privilege and power over black male students. Indeed, as I detail earlier, there is ample evidence from the sociological and psychological literature that this is the case. My claim, rather, is that these advocates' presumption that black boys underachieve because they are necessarily harmed by white women's status as *women* is antifeminist and, as such, evidence of an important dialectical reality—that a priori, patriarchal politics shape these supporters' very understanding of why black boys experience oppression. The final outcome, again, is a knotty reality in which black male advocates of these schools make experiential claims that are difficult to predict specifically because they resist easy classification as either liberatory or oppressive.

Feminism and the Contradictory Politics of Experience

My wider aim is to illuminate what the antiracist and antifeminist ethos of the discourse in favor of ABMSs reveals about the perils and promise of experience-based politics—including the possibility of articulating an ideal experiential claim. I accomplish this goal, in part, by expanding upon what numerous feminists gesture toward but do not fully elucidate—exactly how the contradictory politics of experience is manifest in social groups' discourse on or about concrete public policy. At first blush, this expansion is difficult to achieve because much of the feminist conversation about "experience" and its political implications appears to be mired in a kind of binary reasoning that leaves little space for consensus. Sharon Willis (1996) alludes to this seemingly stagnant state of affairs when she describes "ongoing debates" about "the politics of experience" as part of the "large, amorphous categories" that feminists have "set up as antagonisms struggling around a phantasmatic borderline" (76). Feminist historian Joan Sangster (2011) likewise notes that "debates about experience" may very well be "ubiquitous, unsolvable, and always with us" (356).

Psychotherapists Luise Eichenbaum and Susie Orbach (1982) capture one side of this apparent debate when they suggest that feminist consciousness-raising groups have long used "the nuts and bolts of [women's] individual life experience" to "challeng[e] previous understanding of the social, economic and political basis of society" (12). Standpoint theorist Nancy Hartsock (1983b) agrees that there are "liberatory possibilities present in experience" or that being concentrated in unpaid or low-wage work can foster a distinct "feminist standpoint" among women that allows them to critique the "perverse" world that "men have constructed" (259, 303).[2] Other participants in the feminist conversation about experience, which was especially pronounced in the 1980s and 1990s but continues today, appear to reach a different conclusion—that groups frequently read their "personal experience" through "the filter of prior political and philosophical assumptions" that are far from emancipatory (Willis 1984, 94). Chandra Mohanty (2003) argues that one such assumption—that all women have a shared, universal experience of oppression—rests on a racist, colonial politics that denies important class, sexual, and other differences among women. Historian Joan Scott (1991) concludes, more broadly, that "[w]hat counts as experience is neither self-evident nor straightforward; it is always contested, and always therefore political" in ways that are decidedly antiprogressive (797). Donna Haraway (1990) is even more direct: "This [women's] experience is a fiction and a fact of the most political kind" (191).

Beyond the Binary of Experience and Politics

A more nuanced reading suggests that this feminist debate about the politics of experience—which is part of broader conversations about identity politics that also peaked in the 1980s and 1990s[3]—is not as contentious as first glance suggests. Patricia Hill Collins (2008), for example, contends that black women occupy "group standpoints" that can challenge inequalities of power, and that these same "standpoints" are "situated in, reflect, and help shape unjust power relations." The supposed outcome is that "while common experiences may predispose Black women to develop a distinctive group consciousness, they guarantee neither that such a consciousness will develop among all women nor that it will be articulated as such by the group" (28). Collins presumes, in short, that black women's experiential claims are mediated by diverse politics and thus defy easy classification as emancipatory or oppressive.

Sandra Harding (1991), a fellow standpoint feminist, concurs that while making claims about their experience of oppression often engenders women's feminist politics, doing so is not a necessary condition for generating feminist knowledge" because how women comprehend and convey their experience, including their experience of oppression, can be just as "distorted" and "narrow" as those of "men in the dominant groups" (127–28). This is so, Harding concludes, because women's belief system is rooted, in part, on social arrangements that "have been created and made to appear natural by the power of the dominant group" (287). The result is that women often make "misogynist statements, illogical arguments . . . racist, class-biased and heterosexist claims" (123). Put another way, women can achieve a feminist standpoint when they think critically about their experience of oppression but they often fail to do so because their very vision of why they are oppressed reflects patriarchal and other oppressive power relations.

Sonia Kruks (2001) concurs that "experience can serve as both a point of origin and as the object of an explanation" (138). Her conclusion has two meanings. The first is that although social groups' experiential claims are "discursively constructed" by racism, patriarchy, and other hierarchies of power, they still function "as a point of 'origin,' or even a 'foundation,' from which to work" for liberatory ends. The second meaning is that while experience-based claims provide a "foundation" to do feminist and other kinds of political "work," said claims are also "objects" that are shaped or explained by racist, gender-biased, and other kinds of oppressive discourses (138–139, 144). Both interpretations rest on the same assumption—that social groups' experiential claims can be and often are tied to a politics that is both harmful and emancipatory.

This same dialectical logic also undergirds some postmodern feminist theorizing. Judith Butler and Joan Scott (1992), for instance, not only conclude that claims about "women's" collective experience are "already an interpretation" or function of a patriarchal, heterosexist, and racist politics that recognizes only two genders and that strives to "erase and exclude" lesbians, blacks, and other women from "the notion of 'community' all together" (xiv; see also Scott 1999, Butler 1990). Butler (1988) also embraces a "politics of performative gender acts" in which feminists use their knowledge of harmful, traditional gender categories to fashion a "prescriptive view about the kind of gender reality there ought to be" (530). Scott (1999) concludes that "experience is not a word we can do without" because she understands that the same essentialist and ahistorical categories of difference that oppress women also create the conditions for a novel kind of political resistance premised on historicizing and critically analyzing why certain people come to occupy the category "woman" in the first place (37–38).

More recent feminist efforts to articulate the relationship between experience and politics similarly gesture toward a comparable dialectical logic. Diane Perpich (2010) emphasizes that black women who make claims about their shared oppression as "black women" often do so in ways that are essentialist and thus oppressive. Yet Perpich also recognizes that "[a]ppealing to and building on [their] personal experience" is a key means by which black women have "actualized themselves as full subjects, claimed authority for their voices and perspectives, [and] created solidarity among themselves and with other groups and movements" (23). Johanna Oksala (2014) argues that postmodern feminists rightly conclude that how women conceive of, communicate, and resist their experience of oppression is "constructed" via patriarchal and other kinds of oppressive discourses. Oksala concludes, too, that it is possible to "hold onto experience as an important resource for contesting sexist discourses and oppressive conceptual schema" without perpetuating "metaphysical or epistemological foundationalism" (388).

"Discursive Dialectics"

I am particularly beholden to historian E. Frances White's (1990) effort to make sense of this contradictory reality in which social groups' appeals to experience are mired in politics that is both emancipatory and oppressive. My reasons are twofold. First, White illuminates what the "inseparably intertwined nature" of social groups' "hegemonic and oppositional discursive practices" looks like not only in theory but also in practice or, more specifically, in the concrete context of many black people's social and political discourse (84). Second, unlike many other feminist commentators on the politics of experience, White focuses most, though not all,[4] of her analysis on how and with what effect black males make simultaneously liberatory and oppressive claims regarding their experience of oppression. In addition, while other black feminists engage in dialectical analyses (see May 2012), White is the only one who emphasizes that the conditions of social groups' oppression enable and encourage them to practice a politics of resistance *and* shape, in often harmful ways, their very understanding of *why* they experience oppression in the first place.[5]

White's point of departure is many black men's embrace, rhetorical and otherwise, of the "Afrocentric paradigms that support [black] nationalist discourse on gender and the African past" (1990, 73). While the meaning of Afrocentricism is far from settled,[6] it is generally regarded as "a consciousness, quality of thought, mode of analysis, and an actionable perspective" whose raison d'être is validating black people's "subject place within the context of African history" (Asante 2007, 16–17) or engaging in thought and action that mirrors and serves "the cultural image and human interests of African Americans" (Karenga 1990, 1). Concrete manifestations of Afrocentrism include everything from rewriting American history textbooks to creating "rites of passage" programs for black males, to establishing Kwanzaa, the first U.S. holiday designed to celebrate black culture and history.

White, like other black women scholars (Hudson-Weems 2004; Collins 1998), explores whether Afrocentrism, so defined, provides a cohesive sociocultural and political framework within which black people can collectively resist racism or if this framework is, instead, a masculine-centered one that silences black women's specific experiences of oppression. She pays special attention to many black male Afrocentric thinkers' key experience-based claim—namely, that blacks are oppressed because they fail to embrace and celebrate their African origins. White emphasizes that this claim often engenders a "radical and progressive" politics that undermine[s] racist paradigms" and challenges "racist images" about people of African descent. She observes: "African-American nationalists have taken the lead in resurrecting and inventing African models for the African diaspora in the United States. They recognize that dominant, negative images of Africa have justified black enslavement, segregation, and continuing impoverishment" (74, 77). Just as important, White emphasizes, is that black male Afrocentrists who engage in this kind of nationalist discourse do so without "access to state power," which gives their "Afrocentric ideology" a "progressive, radical edge [that] ultimately distinguishes it from European and Euro-American bourgeois nationalism" (76).

At the same time, White argues, Afrocentric thinkers who attribute blacks' oppression to their own failure to embrace and celebrate their African ancestry often do so on the flawed assumption that ancient African cultures are worth celebrating only when they approximate European standards of "civilization." As an example, she points to the many black male Afrocentrists who praise ancient Egypt as a "real" African civilization because its social structures presumably resemble those of Europe at the same time that they view "the majority of Africans who lived in stateless societies" as "primitives" (74). To make matters worse, White argues, many of these same thinkers believe that certain African cultures are worth celebrating and emulating because they adhere to "traditional" African gendered and sexual relations that assign black men and women "separate tasks and unequal power" and "link homosexuality with betrayal of the race" (75, 86, 75). The two-pronged result of this perverse, "Eurocentric" black nationalism and Afrocentrism is, according to White, a flawed binary worldview that assumes men and women have different and unequal roles as well as a "conservative agenda on gender and sexuality" that "excludes feminists, lesbians, and gay men" from "true" blackness (75).[7]

Put more expansively, White guides us to consider that it is not merely the case that black men's experiential claims motivate a politics of resistance or that "the very nature of dominant discourse leads it to be contested by subordinate groups whose daily experiences help penetrate and demystify its hegemony" (79). It is also true that black men often understand their experience of oppression according to the same "conservative agendas on gender and sexuality" that racist whites subscribe to (94). Most valuable, for my aims, is White's conclusion—that this "search for a glorious African past" on or according to "dominant European notions of what that past should look like" (74)—is not an aberration that is specific to black nationalism and Afrocentrism and that can thus be explained away. On the contrary, this quest is, as White persuasively demonstrates, solid evidence of the "dialectics of discursive struggle" or the fact that "*all* oppositional discourses," including black peoples', inhabit a "contested terrain" (82, emphasis added) that inevitably "links their work both to dominant discourse" and to "competing oppositional voices" (93). The discourse in support of ABMSs is no exception. Black male proponents of these schools challenge "zero tolerance" and other manifestations of structural racism in the classroom *and* do so in ways that perpetuate the flawed patriarchal assumption that varying aspects of black schoolgirls' as well as white women teachers' femininity are crucial factors in the academic failure of black boys.

Toward an Ideal Experiential Claim?

One way of responding to this reality—that making experiential claims enables social groups to resist their subordination and leads them to do so in ways that reinscribe inequalities of power—is to conceptualize a new, more ideal kind of experiential claim. This is the approach that undergirds Gayatri Spivak's embrace of "strategic essentialism" and Iris Young's advocacy of "seriality" as important points of departure for conceptualizing how social groups can enjoy the advantages without becoming mired in the disadvantages of laying claim to an experience of oppression. Other feminist theorists, including Wendy Brown (1995) and Johanna Oksala (2014), also attempt to fashion a middle ground or a better kind of experiential claim (Hekman 2013).[8] However, Spivak's and Young's attempts to do so are especially widely known and influential. I therefore concentrate my analysis on their efforts as I explore whether such a claim does, in fact, exist.

My conclusion, which I articulate in the following pages, is that the possibility of making problem-free experiential claims is limited, at best. In positing this argument, I am less interested in identifying flaws, if any, in Spivak's and Young's theorizing and more interested in demonstrating that the dialectical relationship between experience and politics means that appeals to experience—no matter how insightful—are enmeshed in multiple, ideologically diverse agendas that are anything but necessarily emancipatory.

Theorizing Seriality as an Ideal Experiential Claim

It is possible, Iris Young (1994) contends, to regard women as members of a "series" or as "a reasonable social category expressing a certain kind of social unity" and to do so in ways that "avoi[d] the problems that emerge from saying that women are a single group" (728). The series *women*, on Young's account, describes the "structured social relations positioning all biologically sexed females" (736). Young argues, more particularly, that members of the series *women* are united by the fact that patriarchal structures, like compulsory heterosexuality and the gendered division of labor, put them into contact with the same "practico-inert objects" that include everything from the social etiquette associated with menstruation, to washing machines, to public bathrooms, and so on.

What is not the same, Young emphasizes, is how women orient themselves around these objects. Some individuals in the series *women* might regard washing machines as a liberating invention that spares them from the time-consuming, arduous task of hand-washing clothes. Other members might understand washing machines and the feminized, unpaid domestic work associated with these machines as evidence that women are oppressed and need to resist their oppression. A "series," in sum, is a means of conceptualizing and articulating women's status as a disadvantaged collective without claiming that all women have the same characteristics or political dispositions.

How are we to understand Young's comprehension of seriality? The answer is that it reflects rather than transcends the dialectic relationship between experience and politics. To recap, this dialectic is one in which the systems of inequality that oppress us also create the conditions that allow us to make experiential claims that challenge our oppression. The second part of this dialectic occurs when these same, systemically derived conditions shape how we understand or interpret our experience of oppression.

Young lends credence to the first half of this dialectic when she emphasizes the possibility of women "actively and reconstituting the gendered structures that have passively unified them" (736). Young cites as an example "women supporters" of Shirley Wright, a local school-board candidate. When Wright speaks of her "women" supporters, she is referring, Young explains, to disadvantaged people or to members of a "gender series" in which "woman" describes a "position in the division of labor that tends to be specifically related to schools" and that exists "outside authority structures" (736). At the same time, Young argues, the very existence of the disadvantaged series women makes it possible for Wright and many of her followers to form a group of women who are willing and able to make experiential claims that challenge their oppression. Or, put more plainly, while Wright may or may not use her speeches to critique or "politicize" gender-based oppression, the fact remains that the patriarchally derived "serial structure"—*women*—is what enables her and her supporters to do so if and when they choose (736).

The second half of the "double" dialectic between experience and politics is evident in Young's depiction of a social world necessarily divided into one of two gendered series—women or men. Young's presumption of such a world is evidence that systemically derived conditions inform her and other women's understanding of how and why they are oppressed. Chief among these conditions, as Young herself admits, is the sexual division of labor that shapes at the same time that it "constrains" both her own and others' understanding of and action in the world:

> What usually structures the gendered relation of these practico-inert objects is a sexual division of labor. Though their content varies with each social system, a division of at least some tasks and activities by sex appears as a felt necessity. The division between caring for babies and bodies, and not doing so, is the most common sexual division of labor, over which many other labor divisions are layered in social specific ways . . . The sexual division of labor both enables [individuals] to gain [a] living and constrains their manner of doing so by ruling out or making difficult some possibilities of action. The bathroom [similarly] enables me to relieve myself, and its gender-marked door constrains the space in which I do it and next to whom. (730)

Let me add two points to Young's insightful analysis. The first point is that the sexual division of labor makes gender-based oppression visible and thus particularly available for her to challenge. It is hardly surprising, then, that the obvious, hierarchical relegation of men and women into different roles in the home, the workplace, and elsewhere is the motive force of Young's feminist critique. Of course, it is quite possible for members of disadvantaged groups not to recognize oppression, especially in contexts in which its manifestations are obscured by color-blind and/or post-feminist rhetoric (Bonilla-Silva 2013). The point nevertheless remains that many effects of past and present oppression are *not* hidden and thus serve as important points of departure from which members of oppressed groups can contemplate and critique their status or the lack thereof. Linda Alcoff (2005) concurs, albeit more abstractly, when she notes, "Visibility is both the means of segregating and oppressing human groups and the means of manifesting unity and resistance" (7).[9]

The second point is that the seeming obviousness or visibility of patriarchally defined sex categories, in the labor market and elsewhere, also constrains Young's ability to imagine the possibility that not everyone in the contemporary social and economic world, including the labor market, have a biological sex that aligns with their gender identity. This includes women who are *not*, as Young describes them, "biologically sexed females"—a reality that Young does not explore (736). Her failure to interrogate this reality is not unexpected, given that she conceived of "seriality" some twenty-three years ago, when transpolitics and transidentity were not nearly as prominent in popular and academic discourse as they are today. Most important for my immediate argument is that what Young posits as a new or ideal experiential claim, seriality, is less than ideal because while it motivates her and presumably other women's feminist critique of patriarchal oppression, it also rests on the flawed, patriarchal presumption that the contemporary social world is divisible into and understandable, in large part, according to biological sex categories.[10]

Beyond Spivak's Strategic Essentialist Ideal

The dialectic between experience and politics similarly curtails Gayatri Spivak's (1988b) effort to cast strategic essentialism as a reference point for making problem-free or ideal experiential claims. Central to Spivak's call for strategic essentialism is the notion that social groups can and should engage in the "strategic use of positivist essentialism in a scrupulously visible political interest" (205). Spivak has in mind here the effort of the Subaltern Studies Group to empower the socially and economically dispossessed of postcolonial India. Spivak argues that the group rightly recognizes that India's subalterns can exercise agency or effectively resist their subordination only by articulating their shared experience of oppression. According to this reasoning, "strategically adhering to the essentialist notion of consciousness" or to a politics born from collective experience is the only means of ensuring a positive outcome for the subaltern (206–7). Such a position, Spivak contends, allows India's subalterns to function as agents rather than as mere victims of history. Spivak also suggests that women, more generally, can and should embrace this kind of essentialist politics. Hence her claim that it is possible to use "an essence" for successful "political mobilization" (1993b, 4). In sum, Spivak presumes that shared "experience makes the strongest bond" precisely because it is instrumental in bringing about radical political change (1993b, 12).

At the same time, Spivak recognizes the limitations of such experience-based politics. She argues that attempting to improve the status of subalterns, in India and beyond, by constructing them as having a collective consciousness mistakenly assumes that "the personal is political"—or that positing essential, homogenous categories such as "woman" or "subaltern" is always an emancipatory act (1993b, 4). Spivak suggests that this position is flawed in two regards. First, it rests on the erroneous, "logocentric" assumption that women and other heterogeneous groups are somehow socially and culturally cohesive. Second, this error often leads the most privileged group members to unacceptably silence the voices of other group members who are more disadvantaged. Specific examples of the latter include the failure of India's male anticolonial leaders to hear and respond to Indian women's gender-specific experience of colonial oppression, as well as white women's long suppression of black women's voices in the feminist movement.

Spivak concludes that social groups must embrace their collective subaltern experience but also recognize that articulating said "experience" is only effective when done as tactical fiction. Or, put another way, Spivak's strategic essentialism presumes that women and members of other social groups can and should embrace the traditional or "old" politics and "carve out a representative essentialist position" from which to articulate their oppression and then (in the words of fellow feminist theorist Diane Fuss) "deconstruct these spaces [or positions] to keep them from solidifying" (Spivak and Harasym 1990, 45; Fuss 1989, 118).

The difficulty with Spivak's theorizing is not only that it ignores the dangers of secondary marginalization and of vanguardist politics[11]; it is also that her analysis fails to consider how the dialectical relationship between experience and politics makes it difficult, if not impossible, to ensure that strategic essentialism will not be used for harmful ends. On the one hand, Spivak is right to suggest that Jim Crow, banning same-sex marriage, and other expressions of "politics, according to the old rules" cultivate the conditions that make strategically essentialist claims possible (Spivak and Harasym 1990, 45). This is so because "old" politics, which presumes that disadvantaged groups are relatively homogenous, provides a clear reference point from which members of these same groups can communicate and resist their experience of subordination. On the other hand, Spivak is inattentive to how "old" politics not only creates the conditions that allow social groups to make strategically essentialist experiential claims that challenge their oppression but also influences women and other social groups' very understanding of *why* they experience oppression. The all-too-common result is not that these groups are well positioned to "deconstruct" the strategic fiction of their collective experience; it is, rather, that they often end up reinscribing existing inequalities of power.

India's "subaltern" are hardly alone. The status of refugee women in contemporary Europe and the politics of intimate-partner violence both serve as tangible examples of why strategically essentialist claims are far from ideal. Women asylum seekers who strategically reconstruct their experiences of oppression to match Western officials' understandings of what "real" refugees look like—namely, that they are solely oppressed as "women," as "Christians," and so on—often succeed in gaining the right to stay in Europe and, in so doing, flee war and other oppressive conditions in their countries. Yet these same asylum seekers often achieve these important social and political gains by validating a key assumption in patriarchy, racism, and other systems of oppression—that some people's experiential claims are more authentic or valid than others. Pretending to be a victim of female genital cutting instead of, say, religious discrimination because genital mutilation is what immigration officials regard as the true problem facing Somali girls, invalidates the claims of Somali girls who are, in fact, victims of religious bias. In addition, women and girls who experience female genital cutting may eventually come to perceive themselves and to be perceived by others as the sole representatives of "authentic" Somali womanhood within Western asylum courts and beyond (Hajdukowski-Ahmed 2013).

Some of the literature on intimate-partner violence similarly highlights the less-than-ideal politics of strategic essentialism. It is true, as law professor Elizabeth Schneider explains, that although women experience intimate-partner violence differently according to their race, sexual orientation, and class, it is also the case that highlighting their "shared experience" of "physical abuse and pain provides a concrete basis for the commonality of woman battering" (qtd. in Gordon 1988, 254). Put another way, the very visibility of such violence and its manifestation on women's bodies creates the circumstances that enable feminists to make broad, politically palatable claims about women's shared experience of oppression. However, such claims also reproduce racist, patriarchal, and other oppressive understandings of how and why women experience such violence in the first place. We thus see anti–domestic violence campaigns that claim to speak for all women but do so by drawing on the narratives of white women, middle- and upper-class women, cisgendered women, and heterosexual women (Goodmark 2012, 143). Furthermore, members of feminist advocacy groups who favor such narratives often do so because they presume that the best way to enact legislation against intimate-partner violence is to focus on women who are privileged except for their gender. The result is the reproduction of the same single-axis approach to discrimination responsible for women's oppression in the legal system and elsewhere (Crenshaw 1991).

Conclusion

Because the dialectic between experience and politics ensures that social groups' experiential claims are frequently enmeshed in liberatory and oppressive politics, little is gained by trying to conceptualize new, more ideal terrains—be it strategic essentialism or seriality—from which to make such claims. One need look no further than how I began this chapter, by describing Germaine Greer's transphobic feminism, for proof of this dispiriting reality. Finding a better approach rests on answering the following questions. In what circumstances, if any, are disadvantaged social groups most likely to acknowledge that their experiential claims both resist and perpetuate gendered and other forms of oppression? Once they recognize the political diversity of their experiential claims, can these groups build explicitly feminist and antiracist coalitions? And what might such coalitions look like?

Chapter 4 makes use of a third understanding of dialectics—as a method of inquiry—to answer these questions. Taking Plato and Aristotle as archetypes,[12] this definition of dialectics is less concerned with providing an ontological understanding of the socioeconomic contradictions that shape black people's lives under neoliberalism or an epistemological reading of why it is impossible to realize an ideal, liberatory perspective of one's own or others' experiences of oppression. Understanding dialectics as a method of inquiry makes it possible to do something else—to highlight how or the specific means by which social groups, including black male supporters of ABMSs, can interrogate the political assumptions and political demands that underlie their own experiential claims; survey and assess the veracity of the assumptions and demands associated with others' appeal to experience; and, through intensive interrogation, arrive at a more nuanced grasp of the social world. Supporters of ABMSs who utilize this dialectical method are well positioned to forge antiracist, feminist coalitions whose members understand that what unites them with their critics is not a shared experience of oppression but the shared challenge of how to enjoy most of the advantages without succumbing to all of the disadvantages that come with experience-based politics.

4 Building Progressive Coalitions around Experience-Based Politics

In 1992 four panelists and a moderator gathered to discuss the effort to open ABMSs. At the time of the roundtable—officially titled "African American Male Immersion Schools: Segregation? Separation? or Innovation?" (AMIS)—parents, educators, and government officials had established or were in the process of proposing numerous publicly funded ABMSs, including Detroit's Malcolm X Academy, Milwaukee's African-American Immersion Schools, and New York City's Ujamaa Institute (Whitaker 1991; Watson and Smitherman 1996). The official summary of the roundtable suggests that its co-sponsors, the National Urban League (NUL) and the Carnegie Corporation of New York (CCNY), were very much aware of this context:

> The purpose of this roundtable is to provide educators and professionals . . . an opportunity to explore the background of educational initiatives for Black males. These gender and race specific academic programs represent efforts to meet the academic and cultural needs of African American males. The [round-table] also examines the controversy surrounding the development of these schools and recent judicial decisions that have ruled against these models or caused them to be modified. Roundtable panelists examine a school model which many feel can have a significant impact on the positive development of school age African American males. A second goal of this roundtable is to present a balanced perspective on these school models and provide the opportunity for the viewer to make informed decisions on immersion school proposals. (NUL 1992, iii)

While it might seem counterintuitive to focus on a roundtable that occurred so early in the history of ABMSs—just a year after the first such school opened in Detroit—doing so is useful and relevant on a number of other fronts. The AMIS roundtable is one of the earliest and remains one of the few public venues in which black male supporters and feminist critics of ABMSs have met to discuss the perils and promise of such schools.[1] Its duration (the typed transcript runs twenty-five pages) and relatively small number of participants also give it a depth and scope that is uncommon in other gatherings about ABMSs. Furthermore, unlike other workshops, panels, and forums about separate schools for black boys, participants in the AMIS roundtable are evenly split between supporters and critics. As a result, they do not express concerns about being outnumbered or about the objectivity of the proceedings. Nor is there any opportunity for those with the majority view to engage only with each other. And last, participants in the roundtable reflect the diversity of the educators, lawmakers, advocacy groups, and civil rights organizations, such as the National Urban League, the American Civil Liberties Union, and the National Organization of Women Legal Defense and Education Fund, that have been active, from the very beginning, in the ongoing debate about single-gender schooling for black boys.

Most important, the AMIS roundtable provides a point of departure for envisioning the circumstances in which black male supporters of ABMSs might help to forge antiracist as well as feminist coalitions among black men, black women, and other social groups. Of course, any suggestion that black male proponents of these schools can progressively coalesce with or build coalitions with other groups might initially seem farfetched because, as we have seen, many of these proponents attribute black boys' experience of oppression to classrooms that are not only racist but that are also "overly" feminized. As a consequence, these supporters rarely acknowledge or challenge how patriarchy harms women and girls, including black women and black girls, inside and outside of the nation's schools.

However, black male proponents of ABMSs are not as averse to forging worthwhile political coalitions with other groups as first glance suggests. First, as I describe in the pages that follow, some of these proponents, including but not limited to those on the AMIS roundtable, subscribe to a normative-critical understanding of power that presumes, in part, that domination necessarily has harmful outcomes. Second, embracing power, so defined, makes several black male supporters of ABMSs willing and able to interrogate the political assumptions and political demands associated with both their own and their feminist critics' appeals to experience. Such interrogation, in turn, leads numerous black male advocates of separate schools for black boys to recognize two important realities. One reality is that both they and their feminist critics make simultaneously emancipatory and harmful experience-based claims about black girls as well as black boys. The other reality is that what consequently unites them with these critics is the shared challenge of obtaining as many of the benefits without succumbing to all the limitations of their respective claims.

This chapter first situates what I term a normative-critical theory of power within its origins in the Frankfurt School and beyond. I then demonstrate how black male advocates of ABMSs—on the AMIS roundtable and elsewhere—use this particular understanding of power to interrogate the political assumptions and political demands associated with their own and with their feminist challengers' central claims. The penultimate section of the chapter explores what these supporters' interrogation ultimately reveals. The answer is that both they and their feminist critics make experiential claims regarding ABMSs that advance as well as hinder a politics of resistance. I end the chapter by emphasizing what it looks like, in concrete terms, for black male advocates of ABMSs to maximize the liberatory potential of their own, specific appeals to experience. Plainly put, these advocates do so if and when they recognize that improving black boys' educational outcomes, whatever the means, necessarily involves striving to do the same for black girls.

Toward a Normative-Critical Theory of Power

Normative-critical theory is a specific mode of thought that has its origins in the Frankfurt School of Western European philosophy and whose adherents include, among others, Max Horkheimer and Theodor Adorno (2002), Herbert Marcuse ([1937] 1989) and, more recently, Jürgen Habermas (1996) and Axel Honneth (1999). Critical thinkers reject what they describe as "traditional" understandings of theory or efforts to unearth the truth by way of universal laws and empirical verification. These thinkers argue, instead, that the goal of social and political theory is to challenge social, political, and economic hierarchies of power by being normatively suspicious of the harm—be it the unequal distribution of material goods and resources, the absence of self-determination, or the impossibility of freedom and/or justice—that results from domination (Bronner 2011). Horkeimer's assertion that to engage in critical theory is to seek "emancipation from slavery" and to "create a world which satisfies the needs" of all human beings is typical of these theorists (Horkheimer 1972, 246). So, too, is Honneth's "suspicion" that a profound "social pathology" underlies "capitalist society as a whole" and his concomitant desire to unearth and critique how capitalist labor markets engender workers' experiences of isolation and disintegration (Honneth 1999, 249).

To engage in critical theory is, more specifically, to embrace a normative-critical understanding of power that presumes that domination necessarily has negative consequences. Some critical theorists characterize such harm as "the institutional constraint on self-determination" (Lovett 2010, viii). Others, including Ian Shapiro, emphasize the harm that arises when people are unable to obtain "the security, nutrition, health, and education" or the "basic interests" and "capacities" they need not just to survive but also to thrive in a democratic society (Shapiro 2012, 293). Still other critical theorists emphasize that the harm arising from domination is indefensible. Philip Pettit (1999) contends, for example, that acts of domination are the antithesis of "what is reasonable to expect of a decent state and a decent civil society" (4).

That reflexivity plays a key role in challenging dominative harm is equally central to a normative-critical theory of power. Herbert Marcuse explains: "Critical theory is, last but not least, critical of itself and of the social forces that make up its own basis" (Marcuse 1989, 72). It thus follows that to be a critical theorist is to be "intrinsically open to development and revision" of others' as well as one's own thoughts and perspectives (Bronner and Kellner 1989, 2). The assumption here is not only that critical theorists necessarily take "interest in the way one's history and biography has expressed itself in the way one sees oneself, one's roles and social expectations" (Mezirow 1981, 5), but also that theorists who fail to do so—to engage in this kind of self-reflection—often end up perpetuating the very dominative harm to which they are opposed (hooks 2004).

At the same time, closely aligning a normative-critical understanding of power with past and present members of the Frankfurt School obscures the extent to which power so defined informs and is informed by social groups other than white men. These groups include black feminist theorists. One such theorist is bell hooks (2000), who proclaims that "whenever domination is present love is lacking" or, more specifically, that in a "culture of domination" the privileged "maintain power by the threat (acted upon or not) that abusive punishment, physical or psychological, will be used whenever the hierarchal structures in place are threatened" (77, 64). Many black feminists also agree, as do critical theorists more generally, that the harm that comes from domination is indefensible. Audre Lorde's (1984) famous assertion that "the master's tools will never dismantle the master's house"—that it is impossible to successfully use the tools of domination to fight domination—is a prime example (110). As is the case with other critical theorists, Lorde assumes that to defend domination is to foster societies that lack nurturing, interdependence, and, ultimately, any basic capacity for humans to survive, much less thrive.

Other black feminists embrace the normative-critical dictum that self-reflection plays a key role in challenging dominative harm. Members of the Combahee River Collective (1983) assert: "We are committed to a continual examination of our politics as they develop through criticism and self-criticism as an essential aspect of our practice." They also emphasize that this commitment stems from their realization that to do otherwise is to risk falling prey to or perpetuating a politics that is anything but liberatory. In the collective's own words: "In the practice of our politics we do not believe that the end always justifies the means. Many reactionary and destructive acts have been done in the name of achieving 'correct' political goals. As feminists we do not want to mess over people in the name of politics."

Black feminists, finally and perhaps quite obviously, also shed intersectional light on why it is often so easy for social groups to reinscribe dominative harm. These feminists argue that such harm is more persistent when social groups fail to realize not just that there are multiple, interconnected systems of oppression but also that these interconnections make it difficult to challenge any one form of subordination without challenging the others (Collins 2008; Crenshaw 2000; King 1988). Crenshaw's (2000) now classic depiction of intersectional oppression aptly captures this perspective:

> Consider an analogy to traffic in an intersection. . . . Discrimination, like traffic through an intersection, may flow in one direction, and it may flow in another. If an accident happens in an intersection, it can be caused by cars traveling from any number of directions and, sometimes, from all of them. Similarly, if a Black woman is harmed because she is in the intersection, her injury could result from sex discrimination or race discrimination. (216)

Normative-Critical Power in Pro-ABMS Discourse

A Public Debate on ABMSs

I am particularly interested in using the abovementioned AMIS roundtable to understand how another social group, black males, use a normative-critical theory of power to examine the key assumptions and demands that inform the discourse in support of ABMSs. A preliminary reading suggests that such an understanding is hard to come by. I say this because the roundtables' participants, including its black male participants, seem to do little more than reflect established arguments regarding the merits, or the lack thereof, of ABMSs. Consider the following declaration from participant Michael Webb, who served as the director of education and career development at the National Urban League during the 1990s:

> I think that as a people, African Americans have been put in a position of having low self-esteem. Our history is often begun with slavery. . . . We don't feel, as a people, that we have a history that is rooted as rich[ly] in terms of accomplishments in many different fields; science, history. We think of our history in terms of a few inventors because that is what we are taught. The schools traditionally have not been able to portray the contributions of African Americans in an appropriate light. (NUL 1992, 7)

Fellow participant Roger Green—a former public-school teacher and a New York State Assembly member at the time of the AMIS roundtable—concurs that educational institutions have failed to ensure that "the African and African American experience" is included in "textbooks," "syllabi," and "teaching methodologies" (6). This notion, that white educators in traditional schools are too wedded to Eurocentric curricula, echoes what many other black male supporters of ABMSs conclude—that black boys underachieve because they are forced to learn in racist classrooms.

Green is equally adamant that black boys are disadvantaged because they are taught in female-dominated classrooms, as is made clear in his exchange with Richard Brown regarding recruiting black male teachers for a New York City–based ABMS. Brown is the AMIS moderator and the former head of the NUL's National African American Adolescent Male Development Center:

> BROWN: . . . Given the minimum numbers of African American teachers nationally, and that no time soon will there ever be sufficient to be teachers in all of the classrooms in the country or in predominately African American schools, systemically what needs to be done in order to meet that need? [. . .]
> GREEN: Well, I was going to say when the [ABMS] that we propose—one of the reasons that we've linked it to Medgar Evers College is because it has an education department and it is our hope that we can develop an affirmative action program that would attract more African American males to this profession. . . . [O]ne of the main reasons that this hasn't occurred is also cultural and because of stereotypes. Because the teaching profession is defined as essentially a nurturing profession. And so it is one of the areas of—a profession that's engaged in socialization of children that again has been stereotyped as being segmented for women only. (20–21)

The other participants—Walteen Truely (director of the Project on Equal Education Rights at the National Organization of Women's Legal Defense Fund at the time of the roundtable) and Jacqueline Berrien (former staff

counsel for the American Civil Liberties Union's Women's Rights Division)
take a sharply different stance. Like many other black feminist critics, they
emphasize that the push for ABMSs is flawed because it obscures black girls'
own oppression in the classroom. Berrien explains:

> By defining the issue as one of [masculine] gender I think that we are disre-
> garding about half of the problem. While it is true, that for example, there are
> more Black men in prison than there are in college, it is also true that since
> 1980 overall Black college enrollment has declined precipitously. . . . So, I believe
> that we need to define the issue as one of the crisis or the crises facing African
> American youth. And while there may be different manifestations in some ways
> between male and female youth, for example teen pregnancy rates for young
> women as opposed to incarceration rates for young men, I think that we do
> have to define the issue comprehensively. (3)

Truely goes on to suggest that ABMSs actually exacerbate girls' oppression.
She points to research that indicates that while some boys do well in single-
gender schools many also develop "anti-female attitudes" that are actually
encouraged" by "their adult male teachers" (15).

In crafting the claim that ABMSs harm black girls' social and academic
well-being, Truely assumes, as do other black feminist critics, that the effort
to establish such schools not only disadvantages black women and black girls
but also does so at the crossroads of race and gender. Indeed, on Truely's
reading, the push to establish ABMSs is just the latest example of how black
women's gender-based oppression is racialized:

> I think that the points that we have been discussing around the table with regard
> to the history of racism in the U.S. society and the history of the struggle for
> gender equality are very important. . . . I often point out to my colleagues in
> the Women's Movement that it was only with the passage of the Voting Rights
> Act in 1965 that [gendered] political equality was acknowledged for African
> American women. . . . [O]ur struggle for equality within the African American
> race is taking place in some ways in a whole different cycle than the fight for
> equality by white women. (10)

Berrien worries, too, that ABMSs—particularly those that embrace Afrocentrism—prevent white children from getting a much-needed education
about black history and culture. In her own words: "I would say I certainly
want to see my children be educated about their people and their heritage,
but quite frankly I also think it is important that their peers and colleagues,
whatever race should get that same education" (9). Truely articulates a more
expansive critique of Afrocentric ABMSs—namely, that their theoretical
underpinnings and practical implementation are often flawed:

> I guess for me what is of particular concern in our discussions about this Immer-
> sion School concept is what notions of Afrocentrism guide the development of
> these schools. And I have a deep concern both because of personal experience
> in living in Africa for a number of years and recognizing that there is tremen-
> dous diversity among African peoples on a number of questions including the
> question of the role of women in society. And I am deeply concerned about
> how in our haste to I think rightly understand our own history that we may
> grasp for romanticized notions about an African past which may or may not
> have existed and may or may not exist today. (10–11)

Given these sentiments, it is unsurprising that both Truely and Berrien make a specific demand—an end to gender-segregated schooling for black boys. Berrien favorably notes the "court finding invalidating" Detroit's attempt to establish an AMBS on the basis that attempting "to make pupil assignments based on sex" "is a violation of Federal, Constitutional and Statutory Law" (8). Truely rejects the push for ABMSs on the twofold grounds that "Black girls are in crisis, as well as Black boys" and that any valid "curriculum and [s]chool strategy—an educational strategy, should really address both genders" (10).

Dominative Harm, Intersectionality, and Reflexivity

Simply concluding that members of the AMIS roundtable echo ongoing conversations about single-gender schools for black boys is inadequate. For doing so obscures the extent to which the roundtable's black male participants use a normative-critical theory of power to do something else—to interrogate both their own and their feminist critics' claims about black children's underachievement in school. When I say that these participants embrace key tenets of a normative-critical understanding of power, I mean, first, that they regard dominative harm as indefensible. One need look no further than Roger Green's call, in very global terms, to protect children from maltreatment. "We need," he explains, "an arc of protection around our children and youth. . . . [A]ll governments regardless of whether they are in a surplus economy or a deficit economy should [thus] provide for the basic survival, protection and development of children and youth" (25).

Michael Webb assumes, as do other normative-critical theorists, that the interconnections among various systems of oppressions make it impossible to challenge one form of domination without challenging others. His specific argument is that it is impossible to understand why black boys are in "crisis" if we ignore the reality of masculinized racism and the gender-specific ways in which race and racism "have impacted on young African American males" (18). Green concludes, on a similar, intersectionally informed note, that black males' experience of racism and classism is masculinized or that living in "economically disadvantaged areas that are predominately populated by people of color" leads to outcomes that are "unique" or different for "young men" versus "young women" (16).

Webb goes further and embraces a third and final tenet long associated with a normative-critical understanding of power—that self-reflexivity is key to challenging dominative harm. I have in mind his insistence that he and other blacks can defeat antiblack racism only when they acknowledge and challenge the fact that they have internalized white supremacist presumptions about their own supposed racial inferiority:

> So there is a question of having a feeling about ourselves that we come from a people who have achieved and still achieve . . . feelings of almost—almost being anchorless, of floating without this link to our past. This link to something we can feel good about, I think is an issue that impacts in a negative way on our ability to first of all as individuals, achieve and also in our interpersonal relationships, among ourselves and with other groups. (7)

According to this logic, black people need to wage not only socioeconomic but also self-reflective psychological warfare in order to effectively resist antiblack racism.

Green and Webb are not outliers. Other black male supporters of ABMSs, on and beyond the AMIS panel, embrace key elements of a normative-critical understanding of power. Jawanza Kunjufu (2005) suggests that enacting dominative harm is inexcusable. In his own words: "Children, like adults, believe in fairness. Black boys want to be treated fairly. Public schools are breaking the spirit of African American males. How do you think a Black boy feels when he sees White children receiving warnings while he receives special education placement, suspension, or expulsion for behaving in similar ways?" (35). Nimrod Shabazz (1994), a spoken-word artist, concludes that the intersecting nature of race and gender-based oppression means that it is difficult to resist either kind of disadvantage without resisting the others. Shabazz's specific argument is that because "the patriarchal structure of Euro-America dictates that Black males are to be prime targets for White racism," it stands to reason that antiracist politics must be masculinized or "directly aimed at the Black male" (9, 15).

The additional normative-critical notion—that engaging in self-reflection challenges oppression—is also present in the broader discourse in favor of ABMSs. Consider how Chezare Warren, a former Urban Prep teacher, contemplates his own preconceived notions about what constitutes a "good" student:

> There was a lot I didn't know that, at times, put me at odds with the youth who sat in my Algebra I course. My upbringing was very different from my students and the knowledge I had of them was constructed as an outsider. . . . I had been trained to create boxes for which to place my students, because after all, good students look one particular way, or so I thought. I learned to value the reflexivity of knowledge, which meant that I couldn't always be in control. I learned to treat students as cultural experts and the lessons they shared with me were invaluable to the maturity of my urban pedagogy. (Warren 2012, 11)

Yet, even if we acknowledge that other black male supporters of ABMSs subscribe to key tenets of a normative-critical understanding of power, an important question remains: Why is it significant that they do so? I argue, in the ensuing discussion, that subscribing to this specific reading of power means that these supporters are *able* to critically interrogate the political assumptions and political demands associated with their own and with their feminist challengers' experience-based claims. For starters, to embrace a normative-critical theory of power is, by definition, to adhere to a wide but tangible set of guidelines regarding the parameters of dominative harm. These guidelines, in turn, make it possible for black male advocates of ABMSs to distinguish if and when they and their feminist critics make assumptions and demands that harm and/or help black children. Second, to subscribe to a normative-critical theory of power is to guard against one's own as well as others' complicity in perpetuating dominative harm. It thus follows that black male proponents of ABMSs are not only able but are also *willing* to interrogate whether their own or others' political demands and political assumptions perpetuate such harm.

Self-reflectivity, another dimension of a normative-critical understanding of power, further explains why black male supporters of ABMSs are both willing and able to critically interrogate the assumptions and demands associated with their own and with their feminist critics' appeals to experience. Being self-reflective makes these supporters amenable to the notion that black boys' experience of oppression can be improved by learning from the experiences of others. Roger Green is an example. He directly calls on other black male advocates of ABMSs, including Webb, to join him in a "critical analysis of our history" that involves understanding the activism of not only fellow black male leaders but also of their female peers, including Ella Baker and Fannie Lou Hamer (NUL 1992, 12). Green notes, moreover, that such reflexivity is ultimately the motive force of critical thought. Hence, his assertion that black students are well situated to engage in such critical thought when they are primed with the "understanding that though there are some good things in our cultural [lexicon], there are also some questionable things" that warrant serious interrogation (12).

Agyei Tyehimba (2015), an author, educator, and fellow black male advocate of ABMSs, takes this same logic—that there is a link between being self-reflective, learning from others, and fostering a politics of resistance—even further:

> Before you mistake me as some highly evolved brother on LGBT issues, I must say that I **still** struggle with this issue. I still cringe or shake my head when I see a transgendered person. I still get that WTF look on my face when I encounter a "flamboyant" gay man, or a lesbian couple kissing. (And like many of you reading this) I still occasionally wonder if there is a multimedia conspiracy to endorse and promote LGBT lifestyles. But while I won't march in a gay parade, or consider myself an activist or spokesperson on those issues, I do understand that people have the right to choose and exercise their own sexual lifestyle. Such people should not face discrimination, brutality or ridicule for doing so. . . . To the degree that I've become more sensitive to this issue, I've done so from taking classes, reading, and having my thoughts challenged by members of the LGBT community. . . . I believe EVERYONE should face legitimate criticism, especially those of us who are leaders, activists and problem-solvers. (2015)

Tyehimba contends, in sum, that while he still harbors significant antigay sentiments, his views are changing as he is more exposed to and learns more about gay people's lives. His comments are part of his larger, twofold argument that while all injustice, including homophobia and racism, must be challenged, it is also the case that ABMSs are worth supporting even when they are spearheaded by black males whose critical views on gay rights have yet to change.

Critiquing the Political Assumptions and Political Demands of Pro-ABMS Discourse

There is solid evidence that black male supporters of ABMSs—on and beyond the AMIS roundtable—do, in fact, identify and critique the political assumptions that precede and the political demands that arise when they cast black schoolboys as victims of gendered racism. Paramount among these assumptions is, of course, the notion that black males are in crisis in the classroom and elsewhere. Webb brings to mind this view when he declares that "there is a tremendous crisis that faces our young males, African American males." Webb's reference point is the notion that there are more black males "in prison than there are in college" (NUL 1992, 3). As is the case with other, similarly minded black male commentators, both Webb and Green also demand that the state establish single-gender schools to ameliorate this crisis. Green, in fact, posits ABMSs as the only way to cure what ails black boys as well as all males of color:

> [O]ne of the things that we needed to focus on . . . [is] the crisis that we [find] African American males in. . . . [A]ll of the empirical evidence demonstrate[s] that our young men [are] in severe crisis; . . . increasing numbers of them [drop] out of the public school system particularly at the age of sixteen. The largest concentration of those who are incarcerated in our local and state correction facilities are in fact African American and Latino males. (1)

Most significantly, while they never waver from their core experiential claim that black boys are victims of racist, female-dominated classrooms, Webb and Green not only identify but also interrogate the political assumptions and political demands that come with this claim. Green's critical interrogation leads him to conclude that he and other black male supporters of ABMSs make the case for such schools on an oversimplified understanding of black males' status. Green's particular argument is that too many black male sup-porters of ABMSs mistakenly assume that disadvantaged black males cannot oppress women and girls. The more complicated reality, he explains, is that "when we look at the dissolution of our family structure . . . [m]uch of it is directly related to the questions of sexism, machismo—that have [yet] to be overcome." Black male educators, Green emphasizes, are not immune. They too, unfortunately, "come to many school[s] with certain contradictions" still in place. Green suggests that these "contradictions" have to do with the reality that black men can and do oppress women and girls at the same time that they themselves are victims of masculinized racism. Hence his insistence that the best way forward for black male teachers who want to "confront" their gender bias is "[to work] with the Center for Women's Development [at Medgar Evers College] and several other women's groups" (17).

Webb, for his part, devotes much of his critical energy to exploring his and other black males' demand for the establishment of separate schools for black boys. Webb's critical interrogation leads him to deduce that this demand is premised on an undertheorized understanding of what constitutes good schooling in general and good single-gender schooling in particular. Like Green, Webb does not renounce his support of ABMSs, but his critical analysis does encourage fellow supporters of such institutions to consider that single-gender schools for black boys may not be worth demanding if they are premised on inappropriate and harmful teaching and disciplinary practices:

> I would hope that even the issue of the single gender school would be looked at in terms of the [pedagogy]. . . . [I]t is not enough for me that kids are in an

all male or all female class or that there's an afrocentric, whatever that means curriculum. To me, the issue is what is the quality of learning? What are the opportunities for young people to develop the kinds of skills that we need now and that increasingly we are told we are going to need? What are the facilities and resources? Do the teachers care about the students? Are the teachers prepared to go in the classroom and work with the students to help them develop skills? These are the issues to me that are [of] paramount importance . . . when I think that the single gender school and the Immersion School is an approach [that] under certain circumstances can be an effective approach. I think the more reasonable question to ask is what kind of instruction—what kind of learning opportunities are our kids going to receive in the classroom. (23)

Such critical analysis raises the possibility that far from being a necessarily liberatory act, there are circumstances in which demanding ABMSs may, instead, harm black boys' educational outcomes.

As is the case with their embrace of key dimensions of a normative-critical theory of power, Webb's and Green's effort to interrogate the assumptions and demands at work in the discourse in support of ABMSs echoes that of other black male supporters of such schools. In his more recent writings, for instance, Jawanza Kunjufu (2014), critically explores his and other supporters' oft-repeated assumption that black girls are always academic achievers. Kunjufu's self-described "research" or exploration leads him to chastise himself and other proponents of ABMSs for ignoring an important reality—that "[w]hile our boys may be on life support, our girls are in critical condition" with "special challenges and needs, independent of their brothers, that would greatly benefit from national attention" (1). In other words, what Kunjufu discovers when he explores racial and gendered hierarchies of power in the classroom encourages him to challenge other ABMS advocates' erroneous assumption that black girls always succeed in school. While these findings do not motivate Kunjufu to conclude that black girls are as oppressed as black boys, they do lead him to embrace a new viewpoint—that black schoolgirls' oppression does, in fact, warrant special attention and concern.

Like Webb and Green, other black male supporters of ABMSs also see fit to substantively interrogate the merits of their political demand for separate schools for black boys. One such supporter is Maulana Karenga, who implores fellow black male proponents of such schools to regard them as a "transitional arrangement" within a larger project whose ultimate end is equipping black males to succeed in race- and gender-integrated classrooms (qtd. in Wiley 1993, 21). Karenga pushes back against other advocates of ABMSs who often see these schools as the dawn of a permanent, hard-won reality in which black boys can shed their protective armor against the masculinized racism they experience in traditional schools, and firmly renounce the kind of "soft bigotry" that privileges proximity to whites as the definitive barometer of black achievement (McWhorter 2014; Maxwell 2013; Chiles 2014). Karenga's analysis leads him to a sharply different conclusion—that to think of ABMSs as something other than a means to the larger end of racially integrated schooling is to validate the racist assumption that black boys are either unwilling or unable to learn alongside whites.

Interrogating the Feminist Critique of ABMSs

Webb, Green, and other black male advocates of ABMSs are not merely content to examine their own political assumptions and political demands. They are equally keen, if not more so, to cast a critical eye on the assumptions and demands associated with their *feminist critics'* chief experiential claim—that ABMSs harm black girls' well-being. One of these assumptions, which I allude to earlier, is that the curricula of many ABMSs is premised on an Afrocentrism that is antithetical to black girls' intellectual and psychological development. As a reminder, this assumption, as articulated by Walteen Truely of the AMIS roundtable (NUL 1992), is as follows:

> I guess I would simply like to say that in talking with some of the key writers on the concept of Afrocentrism about this point, about the role of women in an Afrocentric approach to teaching, I have not heard responses which reassure me about how questions of gender and family would be discussed. I think we need a lot more discussion of that particular point in addressing the curriculum [of ABMSs] in context. (11)

A preliminary glance suggests that the roundtable's participants in support of ABMSs summarily dismiss Truely's assumption that Afrocentrism is antithetical to gender equality. Webb, for instance, counter-argues that Afrocentrism is "invaluable" to the "self-esteem" and "positive sense of identity" of all black children (8). He also suggests, more broadly, that Truely and other feminists are wedded to a rigid, overly negative understanding of Afrocentrism that reflects their broader failure to grasp that the push for ABMSs rests on a progressive, presumably antipatriarchal politics, that is good for black girls:

> I think it is important, to further complicate the discussion,—by saying that there are various kinds of approaches used in these programs. There is no class called an Afrocentric or a male immersion [class]. . . . [I]f you look at what Detroit is doing, you look here at what is going on in New York, you look at Tampa, Atlanta, Baltimore you find different elements. And one of the issues

in trying to understand how these schools work and the impact that these schools have on kids is that we don't know because there is no class of schools with common characteristics. What one person means by Afrocentric may not be the same as another. So we have to understand that there is diversity even in the Movement. (12–13)

Michael Green is not as quick, however, to reject feminist assumptions about Afrocentrism. His response to Truely's concerns about "the role of women in an Afrocentric approach to teaching" exemplifies this point:

> I agree with her. I want to be clear that one of the reasons that we were determined to name the school that we're going to open up in September, Ujamaa—was because we thought it had the broadest kind of definition and that it stood for familihood. It would, in fact, reflect our desire to create a school that would be co-educational, though it would also have some gender specific programming in it. When we spoke to the importance of gender specific programming we felt that this program had to be aggressively anti-sexist. (11)

In the end, Green and Webb's critical insights do not repudiate Truely's black-feminist-inspired concerns about Afrocentric ABMSs. Instead, both commentators guide Truely to acknowledge the nuanced, complicated reality that numerous other black feminists, including Frances E. White, have long recognized—namely, that Afrocentrism, in the classroom or elsewhere, defies easy classification as either a liberatory or an oppressive phenomenon.[2]

Webb and Green also direct a final, interrogative eye on Berrien, Truely, and other feminists' political demand for an end to ABMSs. Their critical interrogation leads them to determine, quite predictably, that Berrien's and Truely's call for an end to ABMSs is flawed. Webb contends that such schools are actually key not only to saving black boys but also to "reclaiming our communities and saving our families," and, by extension, the black women and girls in these communities and families (18). Green's own critical rumination similarly leads him to conclude that ABMSs are justified because of "the whole question of choice" and because blacks, like "all people have the right to uplift and celebrate the contributions that they have made to society" (16, 5).

Again, Webb's and Green's sentiments are not unique. When Agyei Tyehimba, a fellow advocate of ABMSs, casts a critical eye on the feminist demand for an end to gender-segregated schooling for black boys, he also determines that the advantages of such schools outweigh the disadvantages. Tyehimba's (2015) specific claim is that while all schools are unfortunately gender biased and homophobic, ABMSs do what no other school can—provide black male students with the antiracist "academic, cultural and professional" characteristics they need to succeed in the classroom and elsewhere:

> If we as Nationalists and Pan Africanists call for "Black unity," we can't advo-
> cate for, educate, and defend only heterosexual Blacks or those that subscribe
> to traditional notions of gender. At the same time, our boys (and girls) do
> need proper academic, cultural and professional preparation and they will
> only receive that in independent Black-centered institutions. . . . And all of us
> who graduated from elementary, middle, or high school and college need to
> remember that many of those institutions were created and staffed by white
> folk, some of whom were racist, sexist, **and** had issues with the LGBT lifestyle.

Tyehimba concludes that while feminists are right that gender and sexual
bias is a disconcerting reality in the nation's schools, their demand for an end
to ABMSs is flawed because it ultimately perpetuates the status quo of systemic racism in the classroom. To be clear, there is little evidence to support
this conclusion—namely, that gender-based discrimination and homophobia
in ABMSs is unfortunate but acceptable since such attitudes are also the norm
at educational institutions that enroll boys and girls. Nor, for that matter, is
there any conclusive data to corroborate Green's abovementioned determi-
nation that ABMSs are the best "choice" for blacks, or Webb's more specific
assertion that such schools somehow empower black *women* and black *girls*.

This lack of evidence or data regarding the merits of ABMSs should not,
however, blind us to the fact that there is merit in how Webb, Green, and
Tyehimba critically interrogate feminist critics' demand for an end to separate schools for black boys. Put more succinctly, while their critique does
not lead them to accept this particular feminist demand, it does guide them
to recognize that what motivates the demand in the first place—the reality
that women and girls are also oppressed in the classroom—has merit and is
worthy of further attention. It is hardly surprising, then, that Webb praises
feminists who use Title IX legislation (which bans gender-based discrimination in federally funded educational programs) to justify single-gender
colleges and, more broadly, to help provide women with less patriarchal
educational spaces:

> Well, I just wanted to say that even Title IX does affirm that there is a value to
> single sex institutions and does affirm their right to existence, even though it
> puts them in a historical context. In other words, if these are historically single
> gender institutions . . . there's some validity to that. There is some affirmation
> in law—that there is a value for single gender institutions. (NUL 1992, 17)

Of course, the content of the education that Webb thinks young women
should be exposed to and his reasons for promoting their education may not
be what Berrien, Truely, and other feminists have in mind.[3] The fact nevertheless remains that critically interrogating Berrien's and Truely's demand for
a moratorium on ABMSs positions Webb closer to, rather than away from,

a viewpoint that many feminists actually share. Furthermore, while Green dismisses feminist calls to end ABMSs as an affront to blacks' ability to make their own educational choices, he nevertheless concludes that it *is* appropriate to have "gender specific programming," including not only courses on "family life skills" but also on black women's history and activism in order to tackle the "necessity of addressing" the concerns of black girls and other particular "populations" (16).

In stating the case for all-female educational "programming" and "institutions" Green and Webb not only suggest that girls, including black girls' education, warrants focused attention; both men end up validating many of the same arguments put forward by feminist supporters of all-girls schools. These feminist supporters include scholars like Susan Estrich (1998), Rosemary Salomone (2003), Makiko Yamaguchi (2014), as well as organizations such as Girls Incorporated. Estrich captures much of the feminist case for all-girls schools when she asks:

> What is so sinister and frightening about allowing public schools an option to provide single-sex classrooms and schools, provided there are comparable opportunities for both sexes? . . . Without boys in the classroom, researchers have found, girls speak up more, take more science and math, and end up getting more Ph.D.s, and serve on more corporate boards. (B-11)

I do not cite Estrich because I necessarily espouse her perspective. My aim, rather, is to demonstrate that when Roger Green and Michael Webb critically analyze feminist demands for a moratorium on ABMSs, they actually end up embracing what is a feminist view in many quarters—that single-gender schools are worth pursuing because they are beneficial to *girls*.[4]

From Critical Interrogation to Coalitional Practice

The depth and breadth of Webb's and Green's interrogation of their own and their feminist challengers' appeals to experience, allows them to reach two broad conclusions. The first conclusion is that they and their feminist detractors alike make experiential claims that trouble the boundary between emancipatory and oppressive politics. Within the specific context of the AMIS roundtable, Webb's and Green's critical interrogation enables them to discover that while they and many other black male supporters of ABMSs rightly critique systemic racism in the classroom, they also erroneously assume that racially oppressed black males are incapable of perpetuating oppression, including gender-based oppression, against black girls and black women. Webb's and Green's analysis also reveals that while Berrien and Truely correctly conclude that black males oppress their female peers and that Afrocentrism often celebrates flawed, patriarchal understandings of life in the African diaspora, these feminist critics also ignore the possibility that an Afrocentric curriculum need not be detrimental to black women's and black girls' efforts to challenge their oppression, be it racial, gendered, and otherwise.

The second conclusion is that what consequently unites black male advocates and feminist critics of ABMSs is not a shared experience of oppression per se but a shared conundrum—how to manage the simultaneous advantages and disadvantages associated with their respective experiential claims regarding how and why black boys and black girls are oppressed in the nation's schools. Or, put more crudely, black male supporters of ABMSs understand that they and their feminist detractors exist in a state of mutual dependence in which they are held hostage (and, by extension, the children about whom they are concerned are held hostage) by each other's insightful but also flawed appeals to experience.

This mutual dependence is more than an abstract concept. There is tangible proof that black male advocates of ABMSs are aware of and concerned about its existence. Consider Green's realization that when black males demean and otherwise oppress black girls and black women, what results is unacceptable for all black people. Chief among these results, Green explains, is the diminished ability of black men and black women, past and present, to work together by, among other things, collectively "struggl[ing] to maintain" black family life in the face of white supremacy (11–12). In short Green recognizes that black males' "sexist" treatment of their black female peers undermines *both* genders' capacity to fight systemic racism in the classroom and beyond.

Webb and Green suggest that the solution or right way forward for black male advocates of ABMSs involves embracing concrete policies and programs that challenge the harmful dimensions of their own and their feminist critics' experiential claims. In doing so, Webb and Green not only conclude that helping black boys necessarily depends on also helping black girls, they also echo black feminist Anna Julia Cooper's (1892) recognition, one hundred years earlier, that improving educational opportunities for black women also benefits black men. Webb, in concretizing this view, posits more flexible teacher certification programs as an important means of challenging black men's and black women's experience of structural racism in the classroom. Webb, most significantly, makes this proposal in dialogue with Berrien and Truely. That he does so is proof of his recognition that "we are a people, a people comprising of males and females. And the issues that are important for males are equally important for females . . . in the African American community" (23).

Equally important, as the following exchange reveals, is that how Webb makes this proposal challenges a key assumption in the discourse in favor of ABMSs—that black women and black girls are already wildly successful in the classroom and thus in need of little assistance, be it state-led or otherwise.

> BERRIEN: Exactly. The access to higher education by Black students male and female has plummeted over the last decade. And the Urban League in *The State of Black America* has reported on that trend annually. And without that access to higher education, the opportunity to increase the numbers of Black men in the teaching profession is greatly minimized. And we really have to address that as a public policy issue.
>
> BROWN: I would agree. Michael, you had a comment.
>
> WEBB: I was just going to say that I think that the certification of teachers that's in place right now serves more of a gatekeeping function to keep many people out. And there is no evidence, there's no research that I know of that conclusively shows that passing the NTE or the Teachers' Certification Examination creates a better classroom teacher. Yet and still there are many people with a variety of skills that have been proven in the workplace. People have worked as professors, as doctors, as lawyers as every other profession as well, who are excluded from teaching because they have not taken a course leading to the National Teachers Examination.
>
> TRUELY: That's an excellent point. (22)

Green's plan of action is more detailed and comprehensive. It involves establishing an ABMS that is both "anti-sexist" and Afrocentric or creating educational "programming that is gender specific and is also clearly not sexist in its approach" (16). Green argues that such an approach will "confront" and remedy what too many black male supporters of ABMSs deny—that black men are victims of masculinized racism and perpetrators of gender-based discrimination (17). He also suggests that his approach crucially highlights what feminist critics fail to recognize—that Afrocentric ABMSs can improve girls' well-being. What Green has in mind involves using "historical memory" to tackle "questions of sexism that our young men and young women must face in this generation" (6). In more concrete terms, this means making black women's history and activism a central part of the curricula at ABMSs, including Green's own proposed Ujamaa Institute:

> When we look at African American history, one of the things that we would focus on, particularly during the period of enslavement . . . [a]re some customs that we had such as jumping the broom. Young men and young women in spite of laws that forbade them from being married, locked arms together and they jumped the broom. We wanted to talk about that within the context of

our curriculum. . . . And again focusing on the question of sexism. One of the things that we've determined to do is through the development of the extended school year . . . to have a summer academy program that would be named after Sister Ella Baker. And to talk about the role that Fanny Lou Hamer played and Septima Clark and Daisy Bates in the formulation of the struggle for civil rights during the 1960s. And we felt that that's critical and that we would do this aggressively. (11–12)

Green clearly has an ideal vision of Afrocentrism that he wants to see realized—one in which Afrocentric feminist schooling highlights the interconnection between racism and gender-based discrimination in black girls' lives and provides these girls with a culturally relevant way of challenging their intersectional oppression. At the same time, Green is careful to emphasize that black boys, too, will benefit when this vision is achieved; this is so, he explains, because it stands to reason that black women and black girls who are freed from the yoke of black males' gender bias will be more interested in and able to work with their male peers to create a more "socially responsible" society. Or, as Green surmises: "[I]t is important for our young men, and even our young women, to be placed in some programs in which they're encouraged to bond together as young women and as young men. For the purpose of coming back out into the larger society and working together in a way that is socially responsible" (17).

Conclusion

Embracing key dimensions of a normative-critical theory of power encourages and enables black male advocates of ABMSs to critically interrogate the political assumptions and political demands associated with their own and with their feminist critics' appeals to experience. Engaging in this kind of interrogation is important because it leads these supporters to discover that they, like their feminist detractors, make experience-based claims that help as well as harm black boys and black girls. What this means, in more tangible terms, is that many black male proponents of ABMSs understand that while there is much that they and their feminist critics get right, it is also true that their respective experiential claims are sometimes premised on erroneous assumptions and demands. One example is ABMS supporters' assumption that black men and black boys cannot and do not exercise gendered privilege and power. Another example is some feminist critics' demand for a moratorium on ABMSs on the grounds that these institutions' often-Afrocentric ethos necessarily harms black girls.

Of greatest importance is that in highlighting the complicated normative strains associated with their own and with their feminist critics' claims,
Webb and Green reveal what they have in common with these critics. What
unites them is that they both make experiential claims whose political underpinnings are not always neatly classifiable as liberatory or oppressive. As
a result, these claims harm as well as help black boys and black girls. Or, put
another way, black male supporters and feminist critics of ABMSs face a
shared conundrum—how to enjoy as many of the advantages without falling
prey to all of the disadvantages that accompany their particular experiential
claims. Green and Webb attempt to resolve this difficulty by pragmatic but
nevertheless emancipatory means or, more specifically, by taking concrete
steps to remedy what they get wrong when they claim that black schoolboys
are victims of masculinized racism, as well as what feminist critics get wrong
when they respond to this claim. This approach takes it for granted that improving black schoolboys' well-being is not separate from but intrinsically
linked to doing the same for black girls.

Conclusion

A New Politics of Experience

As I was writing the final chapter of this book, I came across a newspaper article with a provocative title—"Black Babies Matter" (Cunningham 2015). The article, which appeared in the right-leaning *Washington Examiner*, described the efforts of black anti-abortion activists to get the message out that black women abort their babies at a much higher rate than other women and that this "horrific" reality is part of a racist, genocidal conspiracy to eliminate blacks from the national landscape. These activists' claims foster and stymie a politics of resistance. By depicting state-sanctioned abortion as an immoral act, they perpetuate the flawed, patriarchal argument that women, including black women, do not have the right to make their own reproductive choices. At the same time, these anti-abortion activists embrace and articulate an antiracist politics that rightly critiques black women's past and present experiences of discrimination in the healthcare industry and the reproductive-rights movement. Put more concisely, "Black babies matter" is a sign that abortion is an arena where right-of-center politicians and activists can potentially make inroads with black voters. It is also a reminder that social groups, including black people, convey politically fluid experiential claims.

We should regard these claims not merely as exercises in political incoherence or short-term political gain but, rather, as serious attempts to craft public policy that warrant our sustained analysis and attention. As we have seen, the campaign to establish ABMSs constitutes just such an attempt. This book explores how black male supporters of these schools disturb the demarcation between progressive and antiprogressive politics. It focuses primarily, but not exclusively, on these supporters' claim that black schoolboys underachieve because they are taught by racist white women who are neither able nor willing to accommodate their black male students' gender-specific learning needs.

The logic that black supporters of ABMSs deploy reveals the political perils as well as the political possibilities of making experience-based claims—in this case, claims regarding how, why, and with what effect black boys are oppressed in the nation's schools. On the one hand, claiming that black boys experience gender-specific racism or that they are intersectionally oppressed because they are relegated to racist, female dominated classrooms is a worthwhile exercise. It allows black male supporters of ABMSs to illuminate important dimensions of structural racism in the classroom, including the troubling reality that the vast majority of the nation's teachers are white, even though more than half of their students are nonwhites. The campaign to open ABMSs also offers a much-needed antiracist critique of the disproportionately high numbers of black children, particularly black boys, who are suspended and expelled from school and who are placed in so-called "special education" classes.

On the other hand, striving to open ABMSs on the grounds that "endangered" black boys are victims of masculinized racism is perilous. There is no scientific evidence that indicates that boys learn differently than girls or that definitively demonstrates that boys, including black boys, perform better in single-gender schools. Not only that, even if they do perform better in such schools, the fact remains that the campaign in favor of ABMSs obscures the extent of black girls' own experiences of oppression in school. This includes but is certainly not limited to the fact that black girls are more likely to be suspended than girls of any race as well as most boys.

The challenge is not just that the campaign to establish ABMSs is premised on empirically shaky ground, but also that it draws on the widespread conversations about black males (rather than black females) as endangered in urban classrooms. These conversations, combined with the discourse that purports a transracial "boy crisis" in education, perpetuate harmful stereotypes about women and girls, especially black women and black girls, as either dysfunctional single mothers or "distracting" seductresses who steer black males from the path of racial uplift and respectability. Also troubling are the many black male supporters of ABMSs who conclude not only that black boys bear the greatest burden of racism's harms but also that said boys are thus more deserving of supposedly emancipatory neoliberal educational interventions than their female counterparts.

Where does this leave those of us whose primary concern is racial and gendered justice in the nation's classrooms and elsewhere? One response, which this book undertakes, is to better understand why the black-male-led push for ABMSs is so appealing to political liberals, conservatives, and others who are, in many other circumstances, political adversaries. What my research reveals is that the across-the-aisle appeal of the discourse in favor of ABMSs is far from surprising in a contemporary social, political, and economic context characterized by public support, from various quarters, for vouchers, charter schools, single-gender schools, and other "choice" based interventions *as well as* rallies, protests, and other efforts to challenge young black men's oppression in the criminal-justice system and the classroom. This material and discursive context fosters the ability of those black males who support ABMSs to critique structural racism in the classroom. It also legitimizes their contention that black boys are more endangered than black girls and that applying free-market principles to the nation's educational system is key to remedying these boys' poor educational outcomes.

Equally important is that black male proponents of these schools embrace an always-political but nevertheless fluid intersectional framework that highlights how racial, gendered, and other spheres of difference are co-constitutive, but that does not dictate which spheres are mutually constructing, who experiences oppression in the process, or how to challenge their oppression. These supporters are thus free to construct black boys rather than black girls as intersectionally disadvantaged, to suggest that the former are oppressed because they are victims of racist, overly feminized classrooms, and to offer ABMSs as the best solution to what ails black boys.

My argument, however, is not simply that black male supporters of ABMSs make simultaneously liberatory and oppressive experiential claims because they are intersectionally privileged and marginalized. Nor is it that they do so solely because of the particular material and discursive moment in which the movement in favor of ABMSs emerges. While both of these explanations are true, my more fundamental claim is that the very logic of intersectionality enables black male proponents of ABMSs to advance political ends whose liberatory versus oppressive qualities are often hard to untangle.

A similar dynamic is present among members of other social groups, including conservative black Christians who oppose gay marriage. These Christians take it for granted that they are oppressed not because they are black but also because they are blacks whose experience of racism is informed by other arenas of oppression—namely, increasing heterophobia and anti-Christian bias in contemporary American society. While there is scant evidence that heterophobia or anti-Christian bias actually harm the well-being of racially marginalized blacks, these conservative black Christians' logic is nevertheless as intersectional one.

The antiracist and antifeminist politics that undergirds the push for ABMSs is a function, too, of the dialectical relationship between experience and politics. Or, put more plainly, experiencing racism's harmful effects motivates black male supporters of such schools to identify and criticize systemic racial oppression in the classroom. At the same time, wider, gender-biased conversations about black males' increasingly endangered status and about a boy crisis in education shape these supporters' assumption regarding *why* black boys are racially oppressed—because they are taught by white women who are, by definition, unwilling and unable to accommodate their learning needs.

A Better Future Together

This book concludes that it is possible to forge emancipatory political coalitions among diverse social groups, including but not limited to black male supporters and feminist critics of ABMSs. Such coalitions are feasible when black male supporters of such schools embrace a normative-critical understanding of power that makes them willing to and capable of critically interrogating the political assumptions and political demands associated with their own and with others' experiential claims, including those of their feminist detractors. Engaging in this kind of interrogation can lead black male advocates of ABMSs to recognize that they, like their feminist critics, lay claim to experience in ways that help *and* harm their efforts to resist oppression, and that what consequently unites them is not a shared experience of oppression but a shared problem—how to reap the benefits without succumbing to the limitations of their experience-based politics.

My aim in outlining this coalition-building process is not to change minds or to somehow persuade feminist critics that their rejection of ABMSs is fundamentally flawed. Having such a goal ignores the degree to which feminists' stance on ABMSs is not determined by black popular support, or the lack thereof, for such schools. It also denies an important reality—that feminist commentators are right that the push for ABMSs is often predicated on a distinctly patriarchal politics that is detrimental to black girls' social, psychological, and academic flourishing. Likewise, the ultimate aim of the kind of cooperative educational reform that I discuss is not necessarily to halt the push for ABMSs. Such a goal denies the powerful academic, corporate, and nonprofit allegiances that make such schools possible. It also ignores the possibility that the push for ABMSs reflects an important reality—that gender-specific, antiracist politics is valid, albeit in a radically revised form.

Furthermore, any attempt to persuade black male supporters of ABMSs to fully reject such schools overlooks the extent to which these supporters' embrace of normative-critical theory is often only partial. For example, when Webb, Green, and other black male advocates of ABMSs say that they subscribe to the notion that it is impossible to challenge one form of oppression without challenging others, what they generally mean is that it is important to challenge how gendered racism is manifest in *straight* black males' lives. Similarly, when these advocates claim to be suspicious of dominative harm, they usually mean that they are suspicious of and committed to challenging the kinds of harm that affect heterosexual black males. Put more concisely, most black male advocates of ABMSs are unwilling to critically interrogate the *full* range of issues—be it the privatization of public education or homophobia in all-male classrooms[1]—that might encourage them to seriously contemplate rejecting single-gender schools for black boys.

I recognize also that the kind of coalition building I have presented in this book is a "thin" one. Indeed, I spend more time discussing what makes coalition building possible between proponents of ABMSs and their feminist challengers and less time detailing exactly how such coalitions, once established, would accomplish their stated goals. My own concern, however, centers less on advocating an ideal model of coalition building and more on presenting a model that is realistic. Central to my project is the recognition that attempts to formulate and achieve "ideal" political coalitions, however defined, are meaningless if these attempts are not cognizant of the specific contexts in which people, including supporters and critics of ABMSs, live their lives. To this end, the actual process of coalition building that I outline suggests a concrete means by which black male advocates and feminist critics of these schools can navigate a nuanced material and discursive reality—one that makes it difficult, if not impossible, for them to conclude definitively that casting black boys as victims of racist, female-dominated classrooms facilitates or stymies a politics of resistance.

My broad assumption is that a multiplicity of insights is necessary for social groups to critically assess the political assumptions and political demands associated with their own and with others' experiential claims. It is also the case that while these insights alone cannot overcome oppression, they do provide potentially fruitful space in which the disadvantaged can collectively explore how to survive or to navigate a world where their own and others' appeals to experience unsettle the line between liberatory and oppressive politics. Put another way, collectively and successfully navigating the political "messiness" of making experiential claims is less about transcendence and more about acceptance. What I mean and what this book demonstrates is that emancipatory coalition building is possible among social groups who accept that their own and others' appeals to experience foster and impede a politics of resistance and among those who attempt to critically interrogate the political assumptions and political demands linked to these appeals. In the discursive arena of ABMSs, black male supporters and feminist detractors of such schools engage in this kind of interrogation when they explore the political risks and political rewards that come with constructing black boys as academic underachievers in racist, "overly" feminized classrooms.

The desire and ability of black males who support ABMSs to do exactly this raises the possibility that they might try to remedy at least some of the erroneous, ill-informed, or otherwise harmful claims they make about black girls and black boys. If and when these supporters try to enact such remedies, they are likely to do so not because they have had some kind of feminist epiphany but because they recognize that achieving their main goal—improving black boys' educational outcomes—requires doing the same or also improving the educational outcomes of black girls. In sketching this pragmatic yet potentially progressive understanding of coalition building, I have resisted the temptation to conclude either that disadvantaged social groups' political interests necessarily perpetuate the oppressive status quo or that oppressed groups are always politically interested, first and foremost, in helping others. Instead, I intend my reading of how to potentially forge coalitions among oppressed groups, including black male supporters and feminist critics of ABMSs, to function as a productive reference point for realizing a politics of resistance in a variety of socioeconomic and political circumstances—whether they are "ideal" or otherwise.

Spacing, Placing, and the Critical Eye

It is not sufficient, however, to simply conclude that black male advocates of ABMSs and other social groups can successfully accept and navigate the contradictory politics of their experience-based claims. I say this because while the AMIS roundtable I describe in chapter 4 serves as a concrete example of what such navigation looks like, roundtables are not necessarily the most feasible or the most desirable arenas for black males and other social groups to critically interrogate their own as well as others' appeals to experience. Not all black men and black boys, or their feminist critics, have the resources (transportation, paid vacation, affordable childcare, physical ability, and so on) to participate in roundtables, workshops, panel discussions, and other similar gatherings regarding the merits of ABMSs. In addition, the public-speaking skills, literacy, as well as the "middle class" demeanor and decorum often required to fully participate in these kinds of gatherings might mean that when people do attend, only a small number of supporters and critics of ABMSs are able to speak and have their voices heard. In short, exactly where black male proponents and feminist critics of such schools should cast a critical eye on the political assumptions and political demands associated with each other's experiential claims is far from clear.

What *is* clear is that both sets of commentators are well positioned to decipher what this space and place should look like. To this end, Menah Pratt-Clarke (2010), a black feminist critic of ABMSs, suggests that successfully interrogating one's own and others' appeals to experience requires a community-based, "decentralized," and "non-hierarchical" arena that makes use of but is not dependent, spatially or otherwise, on the resources of the National Organization of Women, the National Urban League, and other formal entities. This is the case, Pratt-Clarke emphasizes, because "transformative applied research" or "creating new knowledge" about schools, including ABMSs, requires being situated not at the center but, rather, "at the borders and boundaries" of power, including antiracist and feminist power (160). How else, Pratt-Clark rightly concludes, can we freely and effectively assess either our own and others' claims regarding the relationships among students, teachers, administrators, and parents in the nation's ABMSs?

Many black male advocates of ABMSs also know about the kind of spaces that are conducive to community-based, critical interrogation of their own and their feminist critics' appeals to experience. At first glance, this is a curious statement to make given what this book illuminates—that many of the principal players in the black-male-led push for ABMSs are antiracist but also embrace a neoliberal, antifeminist politics that is anything but "bottom up" in its orientation. A closer reading, however, reveals that "neoliberal," "antifeminist," "antiracist," and "community-based" are not mutually exclusive concepts or terms within the discourse in favor of ABMSs or beyond.[2] Indeed, many black male supporters of ABMSs who presume that women teachers harm black boys and/or that said boys are victims of structural racism come to embrace such views via a variety of community-based contexts—be it informal conversations in black barbershops, listening to and talking about black musical forms, posting on "black twitter," frequenting a neighborhood laundromat or library, and so on (Harris-Lacewell 2010; Collins 2008; Neal 2013).

These same community-grounded spaces are fruitful arenas for an array of black male supporters of ABMSs to critically assess both their own and their feminist critics' experiential claims. This is because beauty salons, laundromats, libraries, and other such informal, community-based domains attract and are accessible to a wide cross-section of black people. Not only that, while these arenas are often where black patriarchal and neoliberal ideals are normalized, history tells us that they have also served as incubators for antiracist, anticapitalist, and other kinds of politics that challenge existing hierarchies of power. It thus stands to reason that they are well-equipped to handle conversations about the political risks and political rewards of constructing black boys as victims of masculinized racism in the nation's classrooms.

Educational Advocacy and the Way Forward

Using community-based spaces to interrogate their own and their detractors' experiential claims enables black male advocates of ABMSs and other social groups to accept and navigate the contradictory politics associated with their appeals to experience. This reality, as the preceding pages make clear, portends a new kind of coalition building between these advocates and their feminist critics, particularly their black feminist critics. A tangible and important question nevertheless remains—How can those who engage in this kind of coalition building foster black children's academic and social well-being in the classroom? The answer is that achieving this goal requires black male supporters and feminist critics of ABMSs to collectively embark on a particular kind of educational advocacy—one that emphasizes the importance of public schools while challenging the quality of such schools available to black children.

My argument rejects the notion that public schools' aim is either to advance the well-being of already-privileged white, middle-class, and/or male students or to teach nonwhites, the working class, and other supposedly inferior groups the modes of communication, ideals, and other practices that middle-class whites deem normative. In short, I eschew past and present elements of conservative progressivism. Paramount among these elements is the notion that because "science and experience" dictate that white women, nonwhites, non-Christians, homosexuals, and/or working-class people cannot determine the parameters of the public good, these groups should not benefit from the political rights, economic opportunities, and other dimensions of this good, however defined (Gould 2014). A case in point are the many Progressive Era whites who disenfranchised blacks and severely limited their access to taxpayer-funded education on the grounds that doing so was key to rooting out social, moral, and intellectual "impurity" in the voting and educated public.

My call for emphasizing both the significance of public schools *as well as* the shortcomings of the public schooling afforded to black children is, instead, aligned with antiracist, feminist understandings of progressive politics. On the one hand, I assume, as do other antiracist and feminist progressives, that pursuing publicly funded education, housing, healthcare, libraries, and other public goods is key to ameliorating the oppression borne by the nation's disadvantaged citizens. Or, as philosopher Cornel West (2001) explains:

> About one out of every five children in this country lives in poverty, including one out of every two black children. . . . Faced with these facts, how do we expect ever to constitute a vibrant society? One essential step is some form of large-scale public intervention to ensure access to basic social goods—housing, food, health care, education, child care, and jobs. . . . We must focus our attention on the public square. (7, 6)

A similar sentiment informs feminist Nancy Holmstrom's (2011) conclusion: "In the United States, a struggle for public goods like universal medical care, childcare, and eldercare would enhance the interests of all women who are not rich" (Cudd and Holmstrom 2011, 258).

Within the specific context of the classroom, this kind of progressive politics rightfully guides many to conclude that public schools are key to challenging black children's oppression not because of what such schools have provided black children but because of what they have the capacity to provide. Black feminist Patricia Hill Collins (2009) suggests exactly this when she argues that "because public schools must take everyone," we should "think creatively about education as a protector of fairness and a facilitator of equity . . . [r]ather than examining [it] primarily as a gatekeeper for privilege" (88). Political philosopher Danielle Allen (2016a, 2016b) concurs that public schools can provide all children with "participatory readiness" or with the capacity to engage in a three-pronged process of "civic agency" that involves reasoned deliberation regarding the nation's challenges, redefining dominant norms and values in ways that resist rather than reproduce existing inequalities, and publicly pursuing one or more socioeconomic or political causes.

Other commentators contend that public schooling enables the nation's most disadvantaged children to actively resist their oppression. Pauline Lipman (2011) argues such schools can function as "a tool for liberation" when they "teach oppressed people's true histories," validate disadvantaged "communities' cultures, languages, experiences, and social contributions," and, in the process, provide a diversity of oppressed social groups with the "critical consciousness" necessary for challenging and "transforming injustice" (165). Historian Manning Marable (2011) is even more specific. He contends not only that public schools can help foster a white citizenry that is more amenable to racial equality and inclusiveness, but also that such schools can enhance black children's critical-reasoning skills in ways that heighten the possibility of "Black empowerment and Black freedom":

> A vigorous defense of public education is directly connected with the struggle for Black community empowerment. Despite the many arguments now circulating in favor of privatization and "school choice" in many African-American neighborhoods, only a strong public school system will produce real results for our children. . . . More than a century ago, African Americans understood this. The newly freed men, after Emancipation and the celebration of Jubilee, desired two things: land and education. The formerly enslaved African Americans were absolutely clear that knowledge was power and that the resources of the government were essential to provide the educational context and social space for their collective advancement. It is for this reason that so many of the decisive struggles against Jim Crow segregation in the 20th century focused around our access to quality public education.

On the other hand, my insistence on critiquing the kind of public schooling afforded to black children also recognizes, as do many antiracist and feminist progressives, that oppressed groups often bear the unfair burden of living with subpar public goods (Fabricant and Fine 2012, 2015). Flint, Michigan's overwhelmingly black and working-class residents have access to water provided by the state, but it, unlike the publicly funded water available in wealthier white municipalities, is tainted with lead (Welburn and Seamster 2016). While all Americans have legal access to taxpayer-funded streets and sidewalks, it is also true that a disproportionately high number of women, including black women, are physically and/or sexually harassed on these same streets and sidewalks (Kearl 2014). In short, contrary to what much of the literature on progressive politics suggests, public goods are not necessarily a panacea for those who are disadvantaged.

Public schools are no exception. A typical example is what I describe throughout this book—that black boys and black girls in public schools are far more likely than their white classmates to be suspended, placed in "special education" classes, and stereotyped as physical and/or moral threats to the social order. Public schools are also sites of a less explicit but equally harmful color-blind ethos, which mistakenly presumes that teachers can and should fail to see the race and ethnicity of their students. The problem with this approach is that "by claiming not to notice [race], the teacher is saying that she is dismissing one of the most salient features of the child's identity" and, ultimately, failing to "account for it in her curricular planning and instruction" (Ladson-Billings 2013, 36).

Most public schools also have a "hidden" gender-biased curriculum that holds children, including black children, to patriarchal standards of dress and decorum, that fuels competition between boys and girls, and that encourages students to believe that certain areas of study, extracurricular activities, and career paths are "natural" for men or for women (Harbach 2016; Sadker and Zittleman 2009; Crenshaw, Ocen, and Nanda 2015). Finally, public school districts' dependence on property taxes for funding combined with poor, racially segregated neighborhoods means that most black children attend schools that are grossly underfunded relative to those of their white peers. The practical reality is that schools in predominantly black neighborhoods are more likely to have outdated textbooks and technology, rundown physical facilities, as well as a high number of inexperienced and uncertified teachers (Kozol 1991; Hochschild 2003; White 2015).

Black Self-Determination against Intersectional Oppression

The process of educational advocacy I have outlined thus far—articulating how public schools help and hinder black students' well-being—is only successful when those who embrace it abide by two norms. The first norm is that good public schools foster black self-determination in the face of intersectional oppression. While the meaning of black self-definition is subject to interpretation, I use the term, as does philosopher Tommie Shelby, to describe what occurs when black people strive for "self-realization" or otherwise attempt to "flourish in the modern world" without "being unjustly constrained or interfered with by outside forces" (Shelby 2009, 249–50). To be effective, such striving must occur without the flawed, essentialist assumption that blacks are a homogenous group united by their shared "primordial" African ancestry and with a focus on real, as opposed to "utopian," social and political realities.

That schooling is successful when it enables blacks to pursue lives of their own choosing is a well-entrenched concept (Franklin and Berry 1992). Blacks who established "secret" or "self-help" schools during and after the Civil War did so not just to enable black children to read and write but also out of a "deep-seated desire to control and sustain schools for themselves and their children." Put another way, the "values of self-help and self-determination" were central to slaves and "ex-slaves' educational movements" (Anderson 2010, 5). A similar ethos motivated the small but powerful group of black philanthropists who exercised significant influence over black educational institutions during the late 1800s and throughout the first half of the 1900s. Unlike their white peers who focused almost exclusively on raising funds to support black vocational and technical education, these philanthropists emphasized the need for black liberal-arts colleges on the assumption that such institutions fostered blacks' own intellectual development and concomitant ability to combat high rates of poverty, early mortality, and other socioeconomic disparities between blacks and whites (Leak and Reid 2010).

The black power and civil-rights movements of the 1960s provided new opportunities for blacks to articulate this notion that schooling is effective when it fosters black self-determination. Consider the following declaration from Stolkey Carmichael, former chairperson of the Student Nonviolent Coordinating Committee (SNCC):

> Too often the goal of "integration" has been based on a complete acceptance of the fact that *in order to have* a decent house or education, Negroes must move into a *white* neighborhood or go to a *white* school. What does this mean? . . . [I]t allows the nation to focus, for example, on a handful of Negro children who finally get by Southern racism mobs and into white schools, and to ignore the 94% who are left behind in unimproved, all-black schools. Such situations will not change until Negroes have political power—to control their own school boards, for example. (qtd. in Ogbar 2005, 24)

On Carmichael's account, schools are successful not when they are racially integrated or when they encourage blacks' socioeconomic and political advancement but, rather, when they enable black people to decide for themselves what this advancement looks like.

Carmichael and other black leaders during the 1960s not only articulated but took concrete steps to realize this particular vision of black schooling. Examples of their efforts include but are not limited to SNCC's Freedom Schools for children in the Mississippi delta, the national network of Pan-African and Afrocentric primary and secondary schools established during the late 1960s and 1970s, as well as the black-parent-led movement for "community control" of schools. Such control was widely presumed to encompass the ability to install black teachers and administrators, to implement a culturally relevant curriculum, and to manage the school budget of predominantly black public schools (Johnson 2000; Lomotey 1992; Rickford 2016).

The contemporary push for and popularity of ABMSs is firm evidence that many black people remain wedded to the belief that successful schooling necessarily fosters black self-determination. Scholar Verna Williams (2004) captures this important reality when she notes that for many blacks the push to open separate schools for black boys is not only about "sex" or interrogating the gendered dimensions of racism in the classroom. It is also about "black people [and] their right to self-determination" (16). Sociologists Anthony

Mitchell (2013) and James B. Stewart exemplify this reality. They argue that ABMSs are worth establishing because they provide students with "a greater degree of educational self-determination" or more opportunity to define for themselves what "progressive" education looks like than do traditional schools. It is unsurprising then, Mitchell and Stewart go on to explain, that blacks from all walks of life, including "K-12 and higher-education experts and practitioners," have "overwhelmingly affirmed" the establishment of ABMSs (388).

Like Verna Williams and other feminist critics, I am of the view that ABMSs are premised on and perpetuate a masculinized vision of antiblack racism that obscures black women's and black girls' experience of oppression in the nation's schools. Unlike Williams and other, similarly minded commentators, I want to emphasize that the self-determinist aspect of this vision is worth preserving and expanding upon. My argument here is twofold. First, as the process of educational advocacy I outline above makes clear, traditional public schools have long failed to identify, much less address, black students' educational and social needs. Given this, Mitchell, Stewart, and other supporters of ABMSs are right to suggest that blacks can and should exercise more control over their education.

Second, there is evidence, albeit limited, that focusing on black self-determination has enabled some black male supporters of ABMSs to reconfigure their classrooms as antiracist spaces. For instance, teachers at the Eagle Academies' Bronx campus utilize a curriculum that fosters students' ability to not just recite important happenings in black history but to also think critically about what constitutes effective resistance against antiblack racism. Journalist Tiffany Lankes (2014) explains:

> The questions posted on the screen prompt the students to contemplate their heritage. Students in this eighth-grade humanities class spent the year studying topics such as the slave trade, the Harlem Renaissance and race and culture in this country. They read the works of black scholars and leaders including Marcus Garvey and Booker T. Washington. Now, they will decide whether they agree or disagree with them. What should be the place of the Negro ("Black and Brown people") in White America? What were the strengths and weaknesses of each scholar's plan for improving the Negro? What philosophy would be more acceptable to White America then? White America now? The questions that guide the discussion are edgy, but they force the students to think about their identity, culture and place in society—historically and now.

This emphasis on critical analysis, as Eagle Academies' head David Banks explains, is key to ensuring that unlike their enslaved ancestors, today's black boys "don't have shackles on" and are instead free to engage in self-determination or to declare: "I am the master of my fate" (qtd. in Lankes 2014).

To be clear, black self-determination, as I understand it, is worth pursuing if and when it is focused on all rather than some black people's experience of intersecting oppressions. Without this broad focus, such self-determination is attainable only for the most advantaged black people or for those—like middle-class heterosexual black men—with one primary source of oppression. I am making the case for the kind of self-determination that Maria Stewart, Nannie Burroughs, Ella Baker, and other black feminist educators have long pursued—one that recognizes and resists the reality that racism, patriarchy, and other intersecting oppressions impede black people's, including black women's, ability to decide how and why they are educated (Collins 2009; Johnson 2013; Ransby 2003).

Consider Lucy Slowe's insistence that patriarchy and racism intersect in ways that hinder young black women's capacity to determine the parameters of their social and intellectual advancement. Slowe, who served as Howard University's first woman dean during the 1930s, argues that "segregation on account of race" not only limited young black women's ability to attend colleges of their own choosing but also provided black male leaders of Howard and other historically black colleges with ample opportunities for exercising gender-based power and privilege over black women (Perkins 1996). Slowe, in response, gave public lectures and engaged in years-long activism that challenged male faculty members' belief that women students who went off-campus without male chaperones threatened the respectability of the race, that women students should not study "masculine" subjects, and that equally qualified women faculty were undeserving of the same pay as their male peers (Rasheed 2009; Perkins 1996).

Analyzing educators' widespread assumption that black schoolgirls are hypersexual, overly defiant, and thus in need of discipline and criminal punishment also leads contemporary social justice scholar Monique Morris (2016) to a similar conclusion—that "sexism . . . intersects with racism" in ways that limit young black women's autonomy. "What suffers," Morris emphasizes, is not just their "ability to shape their identities as young scholars but also their ability to develop agency in shaping professional and personal futures where they can live with dignity, respect, and opportunity" (13). It is thus imperative, Morris argues, that the road ahead includes cultivating black girls' "self-determination" in the classroom and beyond (187). She concludes that such self-determination is not an unrealizable goal but one that all black children can achieve when they have access to schools that, among other things, encourage conversations about positive student–teacher and other relationships; provide family counseling, healthcare, and other "wraparound" services; award academic credit for learning that takes place in juvenile detention centers; and implement "racial justice practice" that is "gender inclusive" (187).

Of course, being attentive to intersectionality will not automatically lead black male supporters of ABMSs to embrace a kind of black self-determination that focuses on a variety of black people's needs. Indeed, this book has demonstrated that intersectionality's political fluidity means that such an outcome is far from guaranteed. My analysis, however, also reveals something else—that some black male advocates of ABMSs are willing to challenge black women's and black girls' intersecting race- and gender-based oppression when they recognize that doing so is conducive to achieving their own goals. Given this reality, it is not unreasonable to assume that a similar realization—that self-determined black women and black girls foster black males' own capacity to achieve the same status—might motivate these advocates to embrace a more rather than less intersectionally informed vision of black self-determination.

Reconceptualizing Life in a Democratic Polity

Black men and black women can collectively communicate how public schools help as well as harm black students if and when they embrace a second norm—that such schools are successful when they prepare black children to continually evaluate what life looks like in a democratic polity. As I demonstrate in the paragraphs to come, adhering to this normative standard makes it possible to recognize that the kind of democratic choice public schools make available to black students is limited, at best, *and* that there is a relationship between public schooling and democracy.

The latter claim, or the notion that public schools are important incubators for things democratic, is as old as public schools themselves. In 1816 Thomas Jefferson proposed a publicly financed school system as part of a larger plan for decentralized government that would "fortify us against the degeneracy of our government, and the concentration of all its powers in the hands of the one, the few, the well-born or the many" (Jefferson [1816] 1984, 1381). Thirty-two years later, Horace Mann, secretary of Massachusetts's first board of education and a prominent advocate of taxpayer-funded and locally run "common" schools, argued that such institutions were "the great equalizer of the conditions of men—the balance-wheel of the social machinery" (Mann

[1848] 1957, 87). By 1920, the number of public-school graduates was three times that of the 1890s (Herrick and Stewart 2005). This was somewhat expected, given the many Progressive Era educators, including Thomas Dewey, who concluded that "Democracy has to be born anew every generation, and education is its midwife" precisely because "[o]nly free and continued education can counteract those forces which are always at work to restore, in however changed a form, feudal oligarchy" (Dewey [1916] 1980).

Notwithstanding, or more precisely because of, whites' well-established presumption that blacks have no place in public schools, the latter have also been instrumental in constructing such schools as central to democratic life. After the Civil War, ex-slaves joined forces with Southern white Republicans and the Freedman's Bureau to open common schools in the South (Faulkner 2004; Morris 1981). The result was not only, as Du Bois notes, that "the first great mass movement for public education at the expense of the state, in the South, came from Negroes" (Du Bois [1935] 2013, 570).[3] It was also the dawn of a major strain in black politics, which presumes that racially equitable public schools and democracy go hand in hand. Historian Carter G. Woodson, on this note, asserts that ex-slaves were pivotal in establishing "the first free public school system[s]" for blacks in the South and, by extension, "the first democratic education" the region "had ever had" (Woodson 1947, 382). Educator Nannie Burroughs's conclusion that "education and justice are democracy's only life insurance" (qtd. in Johnson 2013, 65) and Martin Luther King's 1964 assertion of a link between blacks' access to "education" and the "road to equality and citizenship" strike a similar chord (qtd. in Green 2015, 12).

Several contemporary social and political theorists similarly presume that public schools foster democracy. Wendy Brown's (2010) impassioned defense of public schooling as that which allows citizens to "check the powers that govern us" is typical of many of these theorists:

> Without quality public education, we the people cannot know, handle, let alone check the powers that govern us. Without quality public education, there can be no substance to the promise of equality and freedom, no possibility of developing and realizing individual capacities, no possibility of children overcoming disadvantage, or of teens reaching for the stars, no possibility of being a people guiding their own destiny or of individuals choosing their own course. Above all, there is no possibility of being a self-governing people, a democracy.

Danielle Allen (2016b) contends, more recently, not just that taxpayer-funded schools prepare students for "civic agency" but also that this agency involves resisting "oligarchical social and political arrangements." Put more plainly, Allen believes that "education is a causal force behind democracy" or the type of social and political arrangement that enables all to participate equally and competently "in the life of a polity." Michael Fabricant and Michelle Fine (2015) agree that "the larger collective project of public education" is "to develop critical thinkers and effective citizens in a democracy" (62). Amy Gutmann (1999) concludes, too, that publicly supported schools are successful when they provide students with the "skills and virtues" necessary for deliberate democracy or a world in which "citizens and their accountable representatives offer one another morally defensible reasons for mutually binding laws in an ongoing process of mutual justification" (xii, xiii).

Burroughs, Allen, and Gutmann shed important light on why public schools are widely regarded as key to providing students, especially disadvantaged students, with access to life in a more democratic polity. It is nevertheless important to be wary about the sort of democratic life public education makes available to disadvantaged students, particularly disadvantaged black students. Such wariness is warranted because, as is the case with the broader concept of the public good, taxpayer-funded schools have long defined democracy in ways that help but also harm black students. The past and present push for "differentiated curricula" is a typical example. Numerous black public-school teachers and administrators have used this notion—that all students should be offered the opportunity to learn in ways that are tailored to their specific intellectual, social, and cultural needs—to implement antiracist, Afrocentric curricula that privilege rather than ignore or demonize African histories and cultures (Binder 2009; Cohen 2016). It is also true, however, that when Progressive Era educators implemented curricula supposedly designed to meet the interests of all students instead of only those who were college bound, the result was a new, racist model of teaching and learning that persists today—one in which white teachers "stream" or differentiate black children into general education or vocational classes that impart few of the analytical skills required to succeed at the tertiary level or in the white-collar labor market (Ladson-Billings 2013; Ravitch 2000).

How public schools have implemented differentiated curricula strongly suggests that these institutions offer black students a vision of democracy that can but does not always further their social and academic well-being. This is not shocking given that the liberatory potential of democratic choice, within public schools and beyond, is very much subject to debate. The perils of "school choice" or of the contemporary effort to enroll children, especially black children, in publicly funded but privately managed charter schools, which I detail in chapter 1, is a case in point. The broader issue is that the continued reality of systemic racial, gendered, and other oppressions in public schools means that the potential of these schools to foster democratic life, within or beyond the classroom, remains challenging, at best.

It thus follows that public schools are at their best not when they prepare black students to realize an ideal, already established understanding of democracy—be it deliberative or otherwise—but, rather, when they imbue these students with the ability to (re)define the parameters of democracy in a given space and time. Put in more tangible terms, public schools succeed when their students, particularly their black students, are able to discern either the criteria by which already existing "democratic" educational initiatives advance their well-being or their ability to fashion their own, new understandings of what education for life in a democratic polity looks like.

As is the case with black self-determination, broadly defined, black students are best positioned to continually (re)assess democracy's meaning when they pay attention not only to some but, rather, to all of each other's intersectionally informed experiential claims. Doing otherwise risks enabling those among them who are *not* situated at the crossroads of race, gender, class, and other axes of oppression to determine what democracy looks like. This prospect must be avoided not just because it is undemocratic but also because it runs counter to what this book ultimately reveals—that black people can forge antiracist and feminist coalitions by interrogating the liberatory as well as the less-than-liberatory potential of their own and of others' intersectionally informed appeals to experience.

Appendix

AMBSs Proposed or Established to Date*

Proposed

Martin Luther King Jr. African American Immersion Academy (Milwaukee, Wisconsin, 1990)

Malcolm X African American Immersion School (Milwaukee, Wisconsin, 1990)

Ujaama Institute—Medgar Evans College (Brooklyn, New York, 1991)

Madison Preparatory Academy (Madison, Wisconsin, 2010)

Coastal STEAM (Charleston, South Carolina, 2015)

Established

Malcolm X African Centered Academy (Detroit, Michigan, 1991)

Marcus Garvey African Centered Academy (Detroit, Michigan, 1991)

Paul Robeson African Centered Academy (Detroit, Michigan, 1991)

Urban Prep Charter Academy for Young Men - Englewood Campus (Chicago, Illinois, 2002)

Eagle Academy for Young Men (Bronx, New York, 2004)

Excellence Charter School - Elementary Academy (Bedford Stuyvesant, New York, 2004)

Excellence Charter School - Middle Academy (Bedford Stuyvesant, New York, 2004)

Academy of Business and Development (Brooklyn, New York, 2005)

Alpha: School of Excellence (Youngstown, Ohio, 2005)

The Urban Assembly Academy for History and Citizenship for Young Men (Bronx, New York, 2005)

The Young Men's Leadership School at Thomas Fitzsimons (Philadelphia, Pennsylvania, 2005)

Dayton Boys Prep Academy (Dayton, Ohio, 2006)

Dr. Bernard C. Watson Academy for Boys (Gary, Indiana, 2006)

B.E.S.T. (Business, Engineering, Science, and Technology) Academy - High school (Atlanta, Georgia, 2007)

B.E.S.T. (Business, Engineering, Science, and Technology) Academy - Middle School (Atlanta, Georgia, 2007)

Bluford Drew Jemison STEM Academies - East (Baltimore, Maryland, 2007)

Boys' Latin of Philadelphia Charter Schools - High School (Philadelphia, Pennsylvania, 2007)

Boys' Latin of Philadelphia Charter Schools - Middle School (Philadelphia, Pennsylvania, 2007)

Ginn Academy (Cleveland, Ohio, 2007)

KIPP Polaris Academy for Boys (Houston, Texas, 2007)

Capitol Pre-College Academy for Boys (Baton Rouge, Louisiana, 2008)

Eagle Academy for Young Men (Ocean Hill/Brownsville, New York, 2008)

Green Tech High Charter School (Albany, New York, 2008)

Miller McCoy Academy for Mathematics and Business (New Orleans, Louisiana, 2008)

Bluford Drew Jemison STEM Academies - West (Baltimore, Maryland, 2009)

Urban Prep Charter Academy for Young Men - West Campus (Chicago, Illinois, 2009)

Eagle Academy for Young Men (South Queens, New York, 2010)

Fulton Leadership Academy (Atlanta, Georgia, 2010)

Urban Prep Charter Academy for Young Men - Bronzeville Campus (Chicago, Illinois, 2010)

Barack Obama Male Leadership Academy (Dallas, Texas, 2011)

Ivy Preparatory Young Men's Leadership Academy at Kirkwood (Atlanta, Georgia, 2011)

100 Black Men Community School (Oakland, California, 2012)

Eagle Academy for Young Men (Newark, New Jersey, 2012)

Eagle Academy for Young Men (Harlem, New York, 2013)

Eagle Academy for Young Men (Staten Island, New York, 2014)

Valor Academies of Leadership - Elementary School (Jacksonville, Florida, 2014)

Valor Academies of Leadership - High School (Jacksonville, Florida, 2014)

Valor Academies of Leadership - Middle School (Jacksonville, Florida, 2014)

Prestige Academy (Charleston, South Carolina, 2016)

Ron Brown Preparatory High School (Washington, D.C., 2016)

---

*There is no official list of all-boys schools, including ABMSs (Williams 2016). The above list of ABMSs was gleaned from an August 2016 internet search using Google Books, Google Scholar, International Index of Black Periodicals, Education Resources Information Center, Ethnic NewsWatch, Pro Quest Historical Black Newspaper Index, Lexis/Nexis Academic Search Engine, and the Reader's Guide to Periodical Literature. I used search terms Black Male School(s), African American Male School(s), Black Male Academy(ies), Single Sex School(s), Single Gender School(s), Same Sex School(s), Same Gender School(s), black boy(s), black male(s), African American boy(s), African American male(s).

Notes

Introduction

1. While a larger proportion of black women have college degrees than black men, it is also the case that black women continue to be less educated than many other groups. For instance, 24.3 percent of black women, age twenty-five and older, have a college degree compared with 36.1 percent of white women and 55.6 percent of Asian/Pacific Islander men (U.S. Department of Education 2015a).

2. Black male advocates of ABMSs often speak of "girls" in race-neutral terms. However, given that most black boys attend racially segregated schools, it is safe to presume that when these advocates bemoan the havoc that "girls" supposedly wreak in the classroom, they have black girls in mind (Pratt-Clarke 2010).

3. Men have long feared the feminizing and purportedly harmful effects of women teachers. In the early 1900s, when women rapidly began entering what had been the male-dominated teaching profession, many male commentators expressed concern that boys were being emasculated and otherwise rendered unfit to function as future patriarchs (Blount 2006, Carter 2005). The reasons for this gendered shift in the teaching force and the corresponding panic about schoolboys' well-being included but were not limited to the combination of low pay and increased educational requirements for teachers in the decades after the Civil War era, the wider availability of "masculine" work with advent of the industrial revolution, and new constructions of "true" men as those whose schooling, work, and other daily activities existed in a separate sphere from that which is feminine.

4. Put more succinctly, the experiential claims associated with women's "situated knowledges" reflect "multiple and often contradictory realities" that are "both critical of and vulnerable to the dominant culture" (Hartsock 1990, 29).

Chapter 1. Choice, Crisis, and Urban Endangerment

1. Other commentators argue that all American men as well as boys are in crisis. Leaders of the "mythopoetic" men's movement contend that today's men are psychologically scarred by a "defective mythology of manhood" that deprives them of traditionally close "ties with each other, their families, communities and the earth" (Kimbrell 1991; Bly 1990; Kindlon and Thompson 1999). Another school of thought presumes that American men will no longer be adrift if and when they re-embrace an explicitly Christian and patriarchal understanding of masculinity (Groothuis and Groothuis 1996). More recent, "fathers' rights" commentators argue that the courts are biased against male parents when it comes to custody agreements and child support payments and that this bias is particularly egregious given the growing number of men who want to sustain or rekindle their bond with their offspring (Williams and Williams 2013).

2. Jawanza Kunjufu is an important exception. He believes that while white boys also "suffer" in female-dominated classrooms, not all women and girls exercise power over men and boys. This is the case, Kunjufu asserts, because "white male supremacy" prevents black women and black girls from enjoying any authority over whites, including white males (qtd. in Brooks 1990; Kunjufu 2004, 25–26). In other words, Kunjufu disagrees with purveyors of the boy crisis discourse who assume that all women are complicit in all boys' academic failure.

3. More broadly, even if we accept that black women are more successful in the professional workplace than black men, it does not follow that they succeed because black men fail. "Government enforcement agencies" do not give "double credit" for hiring a black woman, and even if employers mistakenly believe that such a double credit exists, there is no evidence that they act on this belief in ways that harm black men (Sokoloff 1992, 94).

4. Black men have long constructed experiencing and resisting racism as a masculine phenomenon. Frederick Douglass declared that physically defeating his white overseer "revived" his "sense" of "manhood" (qtd. in Estes 2005, 4). W. E. B. Du Bois (1903) lamented the fact that racism not only bars the best black men or "Talented Tenth" from ordinary socioeconomic and political life, it also thwarts these men's ability to lead the race to a higher plane of social, economic, and "moral" living (311). Malcolm X concluded that civil rights era sit-ins were meaningless because: "Anybody can sit. An old woman can sit. A coward can sit. . . . It takes a man to stand" (qtd. in Estes 2005, 97).

5. See, for instance, Tractenberg (2013), Delpit (2012), and Kenny (2000). Important exceptions include scholars who emphasize that suburban schools are also frequently beset by the "abysmal curricula, laggard instruction and cultures of mediocrity" associated with urban schools (Biddle 2011) as well as those (Posey-Maddox 2012; Lewis-McKoy 2014) who argue that white gentrification of city centers and the growing number of black suburbanites undermine the notion that "black" schools are urban and "white" schools are suburban.

6. ABMSs' black male advocates are not alone in embracing neoliberal educational reform for politically diverse ends. Many liberals use school "choice" to appeal to white, middle-class voters, while many conservatives do so to appear antiracist without having to eradicate systemic inequality in the classroom (see, for instance, Angelo 2015).

7. Some scholars argue that the ideological ascendancy of markets and individuals over governments and communities was evident as early as the 1960s and 1970s; others contend that neoliberal tenets, like monetarism and the dismantling of the welfare state, first emerged during Jimmy Carter's administration. Another explanation is that the 1980 election of Ronald Reagan was neoliberalism's defining moment (Gamble 2001; Small 1994).

8. One example is black pastors' use of entrepreneurship and budgeting "workshops" to convince congregants that their poverty stems from their own "problematic mental states" (Spence 2012, 153). Another example is charter-school teachers' use of cellphones, cash, and other enticements to persuade inner-city black children that whether they succeed or fail in school and in life is ultimately a function of their own self-discipline and drive to achieve (Spence 2012).

9. Tim King similarly argues that the infusion of private funds from "national foundations as well as corporations" is what allows his Urban Prep Academies and other charter schools to "base our delivery of instruction on the . . . kinesthetic, competitive, and collaborative . . . learning styles of boys" (King 2008, 1, 3). King not only embraces the neoliberal mantra that the best public schools are those that are privatized; he also assumes such schools succeed because they recognize and cater to students' supposedly gender-specific learning needs.

Chapter 2. Antiracist, Antifeminist Intersectionality

1. Hancock argues, for instance, that when viewed through an intersectional lens, working-class lesbians are subordinated by individually heterosexist and misogynist men who sexually or verbally assault them and are structurally disadvantaged by welfare reform measures, including efforts to garnish the wages of "deadbeat dads," which mistakenly assume that all impoverished children stem from heterosexual unions.

2. Collins (2006) is not the only scholar to cast intersectionality as a heuristic or lens for understanding the social world; see also Crenshaw (2011) and Weldon (2008). Collins is, however, the first intersectional theorist to suggest that intersectionality's status as a heuristic means that it can be used for antiprogressive ends.

3. This is in contrast to "racialization" as a sociological concept, which entails not only difference but also marginalization or hierarchical distinctions of power and value.

4. Of course, any white supremacist can argue that this is the case without providing the kind of structural or historical evidence that academics generally require to validate such a claim. My argument is that the logic of intersectionality does not necessarily require white supremacists or others to provide such evidence.

5. Collins' (2008) specific argument is that the scholarship of black women theorists of intersectionality "is influenced by the merger of action and theory" precisely because they have long been "[d]enied positions as scholars and writers which allow [them] to emphasize purely theoretical concerns." In addition, these women's very existence at the junction of race, class, and gender subordination renders them particularly amenable to "both/and conceptual orientation[s]" including the notion that thought and action are necessarily interdependent (37, 221).

6. See Brown (2013) and Morris (2016) for discussions of how white women teachers discriminate against black girls.

7. Why many black males are now expressing a fear of white women teachers is debatable. One explanation is that this fear is a function of gender-related changes in the global economy, including the contraction of male-dominated manufacturing labor and the concomitant rise of a female-dominated service sector, that have eliminated many of the masculinized manufacturing jobs that not just males but black males have traditionally occupied.

8. This is hardly surprising given that only 23 percent of black males with education degrees go into teaching (the comparable figure for black women, white women, and white men is 41 percent, 42 percent, and 27 percent, respectively) (Hawkins 2015). Furthermore, black males account for only 1.8 percent of the nation's teachers (7.5 percent of teachers are black women, 62.4 percent are white women, and 16.5 percent are white men) (Toldson 2013).

9. While Urban Preparatory Academies' Englewood campus has an impressive 94 percent four-year graduation rate, fewer than 5 percent of all Urban Preparatory Academies' students meet or exceed state reading and math standards and fewer than 20 percent are prepared for college (Illinois State Board of Education 2016). The four-year graduation rate at the Eagle Academy–Ocean Hill/Brownsville campus is an impressive 89 percent. However, only 25 percent of the school's students successfully finished "approved college or career preparatory courses and exams" and only 16 percent of its students are college ready. At the Eagle Academy–Bronx campus the four-year graduation rate is 79 percent, but only 31 percent of the student body has completed approved college and/or career preparatory courses and tests and only 9 percent are officially college ready. Finally, at Eagle middle schools no more than 23 percent of students meet state achievement standards in English, and no more than 20 percent of students meet the standards in math (New York Department of Education 2016).

10. It is important to note that most black Christians rank the economy as their greatest political worry. Not only that, they are more likely than the general population to identify as "liberals" and to believe that the government is obligated to help the needy. Moreover, a near-majority of black Christians (46 percent) support gays and lesbians serving openly in the military (Pew Research Center for Religion and Public Life 2009; Pew Research Center 2010). At the same time, a near-majority of black Christians (44 percent) also oppose gay marriage (Pew Research Center 2017). There is evidence that this opposition exists among black Christians who attend services

weekly (69 percent), who attend less regularly (59 percent), who identify as evangelical Protestants (73 percent), and who define themselves as mainline Protestants (52 percent). Furthermore, black Christians are two and a half times more likely to oppose gay marriage than their religiously unaffiliated peers even when controlling for the age, education, political ideology, biblical views, and religious attendance of the former (Pew Research Center for Religion and Public Life 2009; Pew Research Center 2010).

11. Many white critics of affirmative action argue that it boosts racial minorities' and/or women's academic and job prospects at the expense of better qualified white *men* (Lynch 1989; Pulera 2006). By this reasoning, white men, unlike white women and/or racial minorities, receive no "special" treatment under the law. While this argument clearly ignores white men's systemic privileges in the labor market and beyond—as evidenced by their higher average hourly earnings ($21) relative to white women's ($17) and black men's ($15) (Patten 2016)—it nevertheless rests on the decidedly intersectional presumption that racism is gendered. Many of President Donald Trump's white working-class supporters similarly suggest that undocumented immigrants increase foreigners' socioeconomic status at the expense of American-born, white *working class men's*. The intersectional assumption here is not that immigrant laborers undercut the well-being of all white Americans, including, for example, middle-class white women. It is, rather, that such labor has a particularly harmful effect on whites who are *working class* and *male* (Luna 2016, Katz 2016).

12. In 2007 several black religious leaders submitted an amicus brief against efforts to legalize gay marriage in California (Wadsworth 2011). In addition, the National Black Church Initiative, a nationwide coalition of thirty thousand black churches, sponsors "Family Strengthening Circles," which aim to persuade participants that "the success of the black community depends on the Church's vigorous defense of the traditional family" (National Black Church Initiative 2012). Other black church leaders have established the Maryland Marriage Alliance, one of the main sponsors of a petition drive and letter-writing campaign aimed at overturning the Maryland General Assembly's recent approval of gay marriage (Maryland Marriage Alliance 2012).

Chapter 3. *The Double Dialectic between Experience and Politics*

1. Other dialectic tensions are present in the neoliberal politics of those black males who support ABMSs. For instance, many of these supporters are critical of "zero-tolerance," tracking, test-driven teaching, and other harmful effects of neoliberal governmentality in the classroom. At the same time, the sheer pervasiveness of neoliberal thought and practice means that when these supporters attempt to challenge the systemic dimensions of black males' experience of racism in the classroom, they often do so by reproducing the flawed neoliberal assumption that oppression is best ameliorated via individualized and psychologized remedies. Chief among these remedies is replacing one set of educators (racist, "overly" feminized white women), whose intentions are flawed, with another (antiracist black men), whose goals and

outlook are supposedly superior. Of course, hiring more black male teachers who espouse antiracist values is a laudable and worthy goal. The problem is that this kind of neoliberal-inspired remedy often ends up masking the structural factors—including racist disciplinary and curricular practices that proponents of ABMSs themselves recognize as responsible for black boys' oppression in school.

2. Hartsock (1983) is careful to emphasize that the political "standpoint" she has in mind is "not generated unproblematically by simple existence in a particular social location" (237). Instead, it is the "possibility of new thinking" inherent in mothering and women's other-specific subsistence and reproductive activities that produces an explicitly feminist political standpoint. Also see phenomenologist Linda Alcoff's (2005) conclusion that experiencing racial, gendered, and other kinds of objectifying gazes motivates oppressed groups to view their own and others' bodies in new, emancipatory ways (189), as well as political philosopher Sonia Kruks's (2001) claim that "common experiences of feminine embodiment" provide or "furnish" an "affective predisposition to act on behalf of women other than and different from oneself" in ways that ultimately foster "feminist solidarity" (151).

3. Numerous intellectuals and activists associated with gay rights, antiracist, and other social movements have long argued that social groups who recognize and articulate the fact that they are united by a shared set of characteristics are well positioned to: legitimize their racial, ethnic, religious, and other experiences in the face of systematic efforts to invalidate these experiences (Taylor 1989; Kymlicka 1989); help foster societies premised on the "inclusion of different social groups in democratic discussion and decision-making" (Young 2002, 83; see also Young 1990 and Alcoff 2005); and avoid the psychosocial problems that arise from trying to live without a core self (Layton 1998). In contrast, critics of so-called identity politics characterize it as a rigid, homogenizing, and ahistorical concept that: does little to illuminate the diverse experiences of or to foster an emancipatory politics among those who are oppressed (Phelan 1989); obscures the "real" material bases of exploitation (Harvey 1996); and fuels the racial and cultural cleavages that undermine the sort of independent, rational thought, which is purportedly the cornerstone of democratic life (Schlesinger 1991, Elshtain 1995).

4. Although White (1990) limits most of her analysis to Afrocentricism, she briefly acknowledges that it is not the only narrative with a double-edged nature that connects it to dominant discourse as well as "oppositional voices." She also makes passing reference to: the "Chicano nationalist movement" that, in her view, fights racism and perpetuates patriarchy (81); the white feminist movement that challenges patriarchy and perpetuates racism; and the black feminist movement that resists gendered racism but does so on the mistaken, essentialist presumption that black women share a trans-historical or fixed identity.

5. Angela Davis contends that when black women slaves communicated their pride in rearing children, cleaning, and engaging in other kinds of domestic labor for fellow slaves, they challenged racism by helping to ensure all black people's social and physical survival in the face of white supremacy *and* did so in ways that normalized

their patriarchal oppression, including the presumption that it was their duty to do "women's" or domestic work (A. Davis 1972). Bonnie Thornton Dill (1979) notes, too, that the "harsh deprivations of slavery, farm, factory, and domestic work" have long constituted both black women's "oppressive experiences of work" and the conditions that facilitate their "liberating attitudes" toward "personal autonomy and sexual equality" (554, 555).

6. Scholars debate whether Afrocentricism first emerged in the eighteenth century or if it is a manifestation of the cultural black nationalism of the 1960s and 1970s (Bay 2000; Joseph 1998). Others query whether Afrocentricism sheds important light on or homogenizes the diversity of languages, cultures, and histories across Africa and the African diaspora (Gates 1992; Asante 1990).

7. White also notes that even when black women try to articulate their experiences of oppression by way of a less antifeminist Afrocentrism, their appeals to experience nevertheless remain mired in a simultaneously antiracist and antifeminist politics. White (1990) cites, as examples, Filomina Steady (1987) and Rosalyn Terborg-Penn (1987), whose claims about black women's shared experience of oppression during and after "slavery and colonization" challenge overly simplistic, racist accounts of black women's lives across the African diaspora *and* reinscribe patriarchy by embracing "the ideology of complementarity" or the notion that black men and black women will be free from oppression when they engage in separate but equal gender-specific tasks (86–87, 91).

8. Wendy Brown (1995) argues for a politics of "I want this for us" instead of "I am." Her goal is to "destabilize" the kind of experiential claim that mistakenly regards "the formulation of identity as fixed position" *and* to validate and "affirm 'position' and 'history'" as ways of understanding and communicating about ourselves and others (75). Johanna Oksala (2014) asserts that women can "recognize" that they have "communal experiences" as "women" and understand that these experiences are culturally contingent and politically constituted" (388, 399).

9. Michael Kauth and Dan Landis (1996) also allude to this notion when they note that the "overt maneuvering and energy expended in keeping people separated by skin color may also have made it easier [during the Civil Rights Movement] to recognize racial discrimination as a problem and attempt to resolve it" (101).

10. My argument is not, as philosopher Allison Stone (2007, 22) suggests, that Young's (1994) theorizing is wedded to the flawed, *universal* notion that gender is binary and that heterosexuality is "normative." A closer examination reveals that when Young speaks of two gendered series, "men" and "women," and contends that "female bodies have something to do with the constitution of the series women," she assumes that this is so because of the machinations of socioeconomic structures, like compulsory heterosexuality and the gendered division of labor, in *this* particular space and time (729). Hence, Young's assertion that while she is "inclined to say that the series includes all female human beings in the world, and others of the past," she also recognizes the need to "draw" definitive "historical lines" when considering women as a series (737).

11. Put more specifically, if the very notion of a coherent social group is a fiction that requires persistent critique, how can members of heterogeneous groups strategically agree about what constitutes their shared experience of oppression or how best to resist this oppression? One potential response is that groups can and do have multiple strategic interests. Women can strategically embrace their experience as women in ways that privilege challenging racism and patriarchy. Blacks can strategically embrace their experience as blacks in ways that prioritize feminist and antiracist activism. Yet even if we recognize that women and those in other diverse groups can have multiple strategic interests, this does little to address the fact that not all group members are equally well positioned to define and articulate these interest(s). At issue here is "secondary marginalization," or the process by which some group members dismiss the experiential claims of other members who exist at the junction of multiple, intersecting types of oppression (Cohen 1999; Strolovitch 2007). Another response is that if subalterns are not equally well positioned to define or articulate their strategic interests, then perhaps someone else, like the Subaltern Studies Group itself, can and should do so on their behalf (Spivak 1988). But if it is the case that a cadre of experts are best suited to make the oppressed visible, then women and other disadvantaged groups are apparently excluded from the very mode of resistance—subalterns themselves articulating and continually critiquing their own experiential claims—that Spivak claims to espouse (Alcoff 2000).

12. There is a distinction between Aristotle's syllogistic method or use of multiple premises to arrive at or deduce a specific truth and Plato's inductive approach or use of dialogue to increasingly subdivide a single concept with the ultimate goal of identifying the universal truth that governs these subdivisions (Golden 1984; Keyt 2009). My claim is that both Plato and Aristotle take it for granted that to embrace the dialectical is to adhere to a particular means or set of guidelines, however defined, for understanding the social and political world. It is this fundamental notion of "dialectical" as a methodological as well as an ontological and epistemological approach to reality that animates my specific conception of coalition building in the ensuing discussion.

Chapter 4. Building Progressive Coalitions around Experience-Based Politics

1. Other such gatherings include Saving the Black Male, a 1990 Detroit-based community meeting; Black Male Schools and Other Opportunities, a 1991 forum sponsored by the National Council of African American Men; the University of Cincinnati College of Law's 2004 conference, "Title IX and Gender Equity in Education: The Unfinished Agenda"; Wheelock College's 2007 conference, "A Contemplation on the Education of Black Male Students"; the Black Star Project's 2011 National Conference on Educating Black Males; the Center for Law and Social Policy's 2012 "Partnership Circle Meeting," and "Is Separation the Solution?" a 2015 gathering sponsored by the African American Policy Forum, Department of Gender Studies, and Center

for Intersectionality and Social Policy Studies at the University of California—Los Angeles.

2. Also see Collins (2006), Hardman-Cromwell (1995), and Mutua (2006).

3. See, for instance, Green's call (mentioned herein) for "gender specific programming" that includes courses on "family life skills." This call hints at the possibility of classes on the virtues of patriarchal family life—a vision that definitely does not accord with feminist sensibilities.

4. Green's argument is also a departure point for obtaining a broader understanding of how feminists and black male supporters of ABMSs understand the relationship between these schools and separate educational institutions for girls. The answer is threefold. First, a significant minority of feminists, including Susan Estrich (1998) and fellow legal scholar Rosemary Salomone (2003), support ABMSs on the grounds that they, like all-girls schools, provide same-gender "role models" who increase students' "social competence," self-confidence, and academic performance. Far more feminists, however, cite ABMSs as further evidence of what they regard as the chief limitation of *all* single-gender schools—that their very existence rests on the flawed assumption that girls and boys have different learning styles and needs (Halpern et al. 2011; Feminist Majority Foundation 2014; Pahlke, Hyde, and Allison 2014). Finally, unlike Green, several other black male supporters of ABMSs embrace all-girls schools for the following two reasons that are not necessarily feminist-inspired: to emphasize that *all* single-gender schools, including those for black boys, are legally sound and to highlight the notion some girls have specific social needs, including the need to continue their educations during and after their pregnancies—that are best met in single-gender and presumably de-sexualized learning environments. See, for instance, Hopkins (1997), Watson and Smitherman (1996), and Detroit Board of Education (1991).

Conclusion

1. Two important but rare examples include Warren's (2012) and Oeur's (2013) recognition and embrace of gay black boys in ABMSs. Further research is clearly required to better identify what particular understandings of gay and other masculinities inform the push for ABMSs.

2. Teach for America's emphasis on "deregulation, market reforms, and collaboration between the public and private sectors" as it assigns recent college graduates to teach and instigate change in underperforming public schools, is a form of "grassroots neoliberalism" (Lahann and Reagan 2011, 17; Friedrich 2014). Others have characterized Phyllis Schlafly's successful effort to defeat the 1972 Equal Rights Amendment (ERA) as grassroots anti-feminism. The nationwide STOP ERA campaign, which Schlafly founded, was composed of local, women-led chapters whose members used the administrative and oratorical skills they frequently acquired in their churches to lobby politicians, solicit donations from community-based businesses, create and mail flyers, and write letters to newspaper editors (Critchlow 2005).

3. In December 1864, for instance, leaders of Savannah, Georgia's black community met with Secretary of War Edwin M. Stanton and General William Tecumseh Sherman to press for a system of public schools throughout the state (Riegel 2015). Two years later, former slaves petitioned Mississippi's constitutional convention for free, universal public education for all children regardless of their race and gender (Span 2012).

References

Alcoff, Linda Martín. 2000. "Who's Afraid of Identity Politics?" *Linda Martín Alcoff.* http://www.alcoff.com/content/afraidid.html.

———. 2005. *Visible Identities: Race, Gender, and the Self.* Studies in Feminist Philosophy. New York: Oxford University Press.

Alexander-Floyd, Nikol G. 2007. *Gender, Race, and Nationalism in Contemporary Black Politics.* New York: Palgrave Macmillan.

———. 2012. "Disappearing Acts: Reclaiming Intersectionality in the Social Sciences in a Post-Black Feminist Era." *Feminist Formations* 24 (1): 1–25.

Allan, Elizabeth J. 2012. *Policy Discourses, Gender, and Education: Constructing Women's Status.* New York: Routledge.

Allen, Amy. 1998. "Rethinking Power." *Hypatia* 13 (1): 21–40.

———. 1999. *The Power of Feminist Theory: Domination, Resistance, Solidarity.* Boulder, Colo.: Westview.

Allen, Danielle. 2016a. *Education and Equality.* Chicago: University of Chicago Press.

———. 2016b. "What Is Education For?" *Boston Review*, May 9.

American Association of University Women. 2015. *Where the Girls Are: The Facts about Gender Equity in Education.* Washington, D.C.: AAUW Educational Foundation.

———. 2016. *The Simple Truth about the Gender Pay Gap.* Washington, D.C.: AAUW.

American Civil Liberties Union. 2011. "Letter of Concern Regarding Madison Preparatory School." November 7. https://www.aclu.org/letter/letter-madison-metropolitan -school-district-regarding-madison-preparatory-school.

———. 2012. "ACLU Launches 'Teach Kids, Not Stereotypes' Campaign against Single-Sex Classes Rooted in Stereotypes." May 21. https://www.aclu.org/news/ aclu-launches-teach-kids-not-stereotypes-campaign-against-single-sex-classes -rooted-stereotypes.

Amos, Denise Smith. 2014. "Six Single-Gender Charter Schools Taking Shape in Jacksonville." *Florida Times Union*, April 17.

Anderson, James D. 2010. *The Education of Blacks in the South, 1861–1935*. Chapel Hill: University of North Carolina Press.

Anderson, Kristin J. 2014. *Modern Misogyny: Anti-Feminism in a Post-Feminist Era*. London: Oxford University Press.

Angelo, Nathan. 2015. "What Happened to Educational Equality? Tracing the Demise of Presidential Rhetoric on Racial Inequality in Higher Education." *New Political Science* 37 (2): 221–40.

Anthias, Floya. 1998. "Rethinking Social Divisions: Some Notes towards a Theoretical Framework." *Sociological Review* 46 (3): 505–35.

Asante, Molefi K. 1990. *Kemet, Afrocentricity, and Knowledge*. Trenton, N.J.: Africa World.

———. 2007. *An Afrocentric Manifesto: Toward an African Renaissance*. Cambridge U.K.: Polity.

Bacchi, Carol Lee. 1999. *Women, Policy and Politics: The Construction of Policy Problems*. New York: Sage.

Banks, David. 2014. "There's Hope: How to Transform the Lives of Black Boys." Interview by Denene Millner. *My Brown Baby*, November 18. http://mybrownbaby.com/2014/11/educating-black-boys.

———. 2015. *Soar: How Boys Learn, Succeed, and Develop Character*. New York: Atria / 37 Ink.

Barnard, Ian. 2004. *Queer Race: Cultural Interventions in the Racial Politics of Queer Theory*. New York: Peter Lang.

Baronov, David. 2006. "Globalization and Urban Education." *Encounter: Education for Meaning and Social Justice* 19 (4): 12–18.

Becerril, Crystal Stella, and Arielle Zionts. 2015. "Teachers Say 17 Firings at Urban Prep Charter Schools Were Retaliation for Unionization." *In These Times*, July 1.

Becker, Abigail. 2015. "Wisconsin's Black-White Achievement Gap Worst in Nation Despite Decades of Efforts." *WisconsinWatch.org*, December 16. http://wisconsinwatch.org/2015/12/wisconsins-black-white-achievement-gap-worst-in-nation.

Bell, Ella L. J. Edmondson, and Stella M. Nkomo. 2003. *Our Separate Ways: Black and White Women and the Struggle for Professional Identity*. Boston: Harvard Business School Press.

Berger, Michelle, and Kathleen Guidroz. 2009. "A Conversation with Founding Scholars of Intersectionality." In *The Intersectional Approach: Transforming the Academy through Race, Class, and Gender*, edited by Michele Tracy Berger and Kathleen Guidroz, 61–80. Chapel Hill: University of North Carolina Press.

Berman, Edward. 1977. "American Philanthropy and African Education: Towards an Analysis." *African Studies Review* 20 (1): 71–85.

Bernard, Jessie. 1966. *Marriage and Family among Negroes*. Englewood Cliffs, N.J.: Prentice-Hall.

Bhavnani, Ravi, and David Backer. 2000. "Localized Ethnic Conflict and Genocide: Accounting for Differences in Rwanda and Burundi." *Journal of Conflict Resolution* 44 (3): 283–306.

Biddle, Rishawn. 2011. *The Myth of Differences between Urban and Rural Schools. This Is Dropout Nation, August 2.* http://dropoutnation.net/2011/08/02/the-myth-of-differences-between-urban-and-rural-schools.

Biewener, Carole, and Marie-Hélène Bacqué. 2015. "Feminism and the Politics of Empowerment in International Development." *ASPJ Africa and Francophonie* 6 (2): 51–75.

Bilge, Selma. 2013. "Intersectionality Undone." *Du Bois Review: Social Science Research on Race* 10 (2): 405–24.

Binder, Amy J. 2009. *Contentious Curricula: Afrocentrism and Creationism in American Public Schools.* Princeton, N.J.: Princeton University Press.

Blacknews.com. 2008. "Gurian Institute Programs Help Schools, Parents, and Communities Solve Issues Faced by African-American Boys." http://www.blacknews.com/news/gurian_institute_programs_help_black_boys101.shtml#.V-Ld5zvsflI.

Blacks for Marriage. 2011. "About Us." *BlacksforMarriage.org.* Accessed December 1, 2011. http://www.blacksformarriage.org/about-us.html (now defunct).

Blaska, David. 2011. "Blaska's Blog Says Madison Schools Need a Caire Package." *Isthmus,* Blaska's Blog, November 11. http://isthmus.com/archive/blaskas-blog/blaskas-blog-says-madison-schools-need-a-caire-package.

Blount, Jackie. 2006. *Fit to Teach: Same-Sex Desire, Gender, and School Work in the Twentieth Century.* Albany: State University of New York Press.

Bly, Robert. 1990. *Iron John.* New York: Addison-Wesley.

Bonilla-Silva, Eduardo. 2013. *Racism without Racists: Color-Blind Racism and the Persistence of Racial Inequality in America.* Lanham, Md.: Rowman and Littlefield.

Boser, Ulrich. 2014. *Teacher Diversity Revisited: A New State-by-State Analysis.* Issue brief. https://cdn.americanprogress.org/wp-content/uploads/2014/05/TeacherDiversity.pdf.

Brah, Avtar, and Ann Phoenix. 2004. "Ain't I a Woman? Revisiting Intersectionality." *Journal of International Women's Studies* 5 (3): 71–86.

Brathwaite, Jessica. 2016. "Neoliberal Education Reform and the Perpetuation of Inequality." *Critical Sociology* 43 (3): 429–48.

Brewer, Rose, Cecilia A. Conrad, and Mary C. King. 2002. "The Complexities and Potential of Theorizing Gender, Caste, Race, and Class." *Feminist Economics* 8 (2): 1–18.

Bridges, Lois. 2013. *Make Every Student Count: How Collaboration among Families, Schools, and Communities Ensures Student Success.* New York: Scholastic. http://teacher.scholastic.com/products/face/pdf/research-compendium/Compendium.pdf.

Bronner, Stephen Eric. 2011. *Critical Theory: A Very Short Introduction.* New York: Oxford University Press.

Bronner, Stephen, and Douglas Kellner. 1989. *Introduction to Critical Theory and Society: A Reader*, edited by Stephen Eric Bronner and Douglas Kellner, 1–24. New York: Routledge.

Brooks, Darius. 1990. "Educator Examines Status of Blacks in the U.S." *Stanford Daily*, February 5.

Brooks, Pamela E. 2008. *Buses, Boycotts, and Passes: Black Women's Resistance in the U.S. South and South Africa*. Amherst: University of Massachusetts Press.

Brothawolf. 2012. "Urban Prep." *Agabond (blog)*, April 9. https://abagond.wordpress.com/2012/04/09/urban-prep.

Brown, Kevin. 1993. "Do African-Americans Need Immersion Schools? The Paradoxes Created by Legal Conceptualization of Race and Public Education." *Iowa Law Review* 78:811–81.

Brown, Ruth Nicole. 2013. *Hear Our Truths: The Creative Potential of Black Girlhood*. Urbana: University of Illinois Press.

Brown, Wendy. 1995. *States of Injury: Power and Freedom in Late Modernity*. Princeton, N.J.: Princeton University Press.

———. 2010. "Commentary: Without Quality Public Education, There Is No Future for Democracy." *California Journal of Politics and Policy* 2 (1): 1–3.

Brubaker, Rogers. 2004. *Ethnicity without Groups*. Cambridge, Mass.: Harvard University Press.

Butler, Judith. 1988. "Performative Acts and Gender Constitution: An Essay in Phenomenology and Feminist Theory." *Theatre Journal* 40 (4): 511–31.

———. 1990. *Gender Trouble: Feminism and the Subversion of Identity*. New York: Routledge.

Butler, Judith, and Joan W. Scott. 1992. *Feminists Theorize the Political*. New York: Routledge.

Butler, Paul. 2013. "Black Male Exceptionalism? The Problems and Potential of Black Male-Focused Interventions." *Du Bois Review* 10:481–511.

Campaign for Black Male Achievement. 2016. *Strategy and Core Beliefs*. http://blackmaleachievement.org/about/cbma.

Carbado, Devon. 1999. "Introduction: When and Where Black Men Enter." In *Black Men on Race, Gender and Sexuality: A Critical Reader*, edited by Devon Carbado, 1–17. New York: New York University Press.

Carter, Patricia. 2005. "Becoming the New Women: The Equal Rights Campaigns of New York City Schoolteachers, 1901–1920." In *The Teacher's Voice: A Social History of Teaching in 20th Century America*, edited by Richard Altenbaugh, 31–57. London: Falmer.

Causey, James. 2010. "It's Time for the City to Mobilize." *Milwaukee Journal Sentinel*, April 3.

———. 2015. "Taki S. Raton, a Molder of Young Minds." *Milwaukee Journal Sentinel*, July 10.

Childress, Clenard. 2009. "Gay Rights Struggle Not the Same as African-Americans." *NJ.Com: True Jersey (blog)*, December 11. http://blog.nj.com/njv_guest_blog/2009/12/gay_rights_struggle_not_the_sa.html.

Chiles, Nick. 2013a. "The Miseducation of Black Boys." *Ebony* (July), 121–27.

———. 2013b. "The State of Black Boys." *Ebony*, May, 121–42.

———. 2014. "6 Ways America's White Female Teaching Force Harms Black Boys." *Democracy and Class Struggle (blog)*, December 12. http://democracyandclasstruggle .blogspot.com/2014/12/usa-6-ways-americas-white-female.html.

Choo, Hae Yeon, and Myra Marx Ferree. 2010. "Practicing Intersectionality in Sociological Research: A Critical Analysis of Inclusions, Interactions, and Institutions in the Study of Inequalities." *Sociological Theory* 28 (2): 121–49.

Clough, Patricia, and Michelle Fine. 2007. "Activism and Pedagogies: Feminist Reflections." *Women's Studies Quarterly* 35 (3/4): 255–75.

Coalition of Schools Educating Boys of Color. 2015. *Standards and Promising Practices for Schools Educating Boys of Color: Executive Summary*. http://www.coseboc.org/ sites/coseboc.org/files/assets/Executive_Summary_Standards.pdf.

Coffee, Angela C., Erin Stutelberg, Colleen Clements, and Timothy J. Lensmire. 2017. "Precarious and Undeniable Bodies: Control Waste, and Danger in the Lives of a White Teacher and Her Students of Color." In *White Women's Work: Examining the Intersectionality of Teaching, Identity, and Race*, edited by Stephen Hancock and Chezare A. Warren, 41–70. Charlotte, N.C.: Information Age.

Cohen, Cathy J. 1999. *The Boundaries of Blackness: AIDS and the Breakdown of Black Politics*. Chicago: University of Chicago Press.

Cohen, Rachel M. 2016. "The Afrocentric Education Crisis." *American Prospect*, September 2. http://prospect.org/article/afrocentric-education-crisis.

Collins, Patricia Hill. 1998. *Fighting Words: Black Women and the Search for Justice*. Minneapolis: University of Minnesota Press.

———. 2006. "Some Group Matters: Intersectionality, Situated Standpoints, and Black Feminist Thought." In *A Companion to African-American Philosophy*, edited by Tommie L. Lott and John P. Pittman, 201–29. Malden, Mass.: Blackwell.

———. 2008. *Black Feminist Thought: Knowledge, Consciousness, and the Politics of Empowerment*. New York: Routledge.

———. 2009. *Another Kind of Public Education: Race, Schools, the Media, and Democratic Possibilities*. Boston: Beacon.

Collins, Patricia Hill, and Sirma Bilge. 2016. *Intersectionality*. Cambridge: Polity.

Combahee River Collective. 1983. "A Black Feminist Statement." In *Home Girls: A Black Feminist Anthology,* edited by Barbara Smith, 191–208. New York: Kitchen Table Women of Color.

Comp, Nathan. 2011. "Madison school board faces a divided public over Madison Prep." *Isthmus*, October 4. http://isthmus.com/news/news/madison-school-board -faces-a-divided-public-over-madison-prep.

Cooper, Anna Julia. 1892. *A Voice from the South*. Xenia, Ohio: Aldine.

Cooper, Brittney. 2016. *Beyond Respectability: The Intellectual Thought of Race Women*. Urbana: University of Illinois Press.

Cose, Ellis. 1997. *Color-Blind: Seeing beyond Race in a Race-Obsessed World*. New York: HarperCollins.

———. 2015. "Baltimore Cries Out for End to Denial." *USA Today*, April 29.

Crellin, Olivia. 2004. "Captain David Banks: Starting at the Finishing Line." *Olivia Crellin* (blog). http://oliviacrellin.com/captain-david-banks-starting-at-the-finishing -line.

Crenshaw, Kimberlé. 1991. "Mapping the Margins: Intersectionality, Identity Politics, and Violence against Women of Color." *Stanford Law Review* 43 (6): 1241–99.

———. 2000. "Demarginalizing the Intersection of Race and Sex: A Black Feminist Critique of Antidiscrimination Doctrine, Feminist Theory and Antiracist Politics." In *Black Feminist Reader*, edited by Joy James and T. Denean Sharpley-Whiting, 208–38. Malden, Mass.: Blackwell.

———. 2016. Postscript to *Framing Intersectionality: Debates on a Multi-Faceted Concept in Gender Studies*, edited by Helma Lutz, Maria Teresa Herrera Vivar, and Linda Supik, 221–34. Abingdon, U.K.: Ashgate.

Crenshaw, Kimberlé Williams, Priscilla Ocen, and Jyoti Nanda. 2015. *Black Girls Matter: Pushed Out, Overpoliced, and Unprotected*. African American Policy Forum, Center for Intersectionality and Social Policy Studies. https://static1.squarespace.com/ static/53f20d90e4b0b80451158d8c/t/54dcc1ece4b001c03e323448/1423753708557/ AAPF_BlackGirlsMatterReport.pdf.

Critchlow, Donald T. 2005. *Phyllis Schlafly and Grassroots Conservatism: A Woman's Crusade*. Princeton, N.J.: Princeton University Press.

Cudd, Ann L., and Nancy Holmstrom. 2011. *Capitalism, For and Against: A Feminist Debate*. Cambridge: Cambridge University Press.

Cunningham, Paige Winfield. 2015. "'Black Babies Matter': The Black Anti-Abortion Movement's Political Problems." *Washington Examiner*, September 28.

Dahl, Robert A. 1961. *Who Governs? Democracy and Power in an American City*. New Haven, Conn.: Yale University Press.

Dalton, Deron. 2015. "How 4 Black Lives Matter Activists Handle Queerness and Trans Issues." *Daily Dot*, October 11. http://www.dailydot.com/politics/black-lives -matter-queer-trans-issues.

Davies, Raymond Calvin, Jr. 2005. *The Extinction Coefficient: The Systematic Feminization of African American Males*. Lincoln, Neb.: IUniverse.

Davis, Angela. 1972. "Reflections on the Black Woman's Role in the Community of Slaves." *Massachusetts Review* 13 (1/2): 81–100.

———. 2000. "Women and Capitalism: Dialectics of Oppression and Liberation." In *The Black Feminist Reader*, edited by Joy James and T. Denean Sharpley-Whiting, 141–82. Malden, Mass.: Blackwell.

Davis, Martin A., Jr. 2006. "A Right to Single-Sex Education?" Thomas B. Fordham Institute, November 1. http://edexcellence.net/commentary/education-gadfly -weekly/2006/november-2/a-right-to-single-sex-education.html.

Dawson, Michael C. 2001. *Black Visions: The Roots of Contemporary African-American Political Ideologies*. Chicago: University of Chicago Press.

"The Debate Surrounding Single-Sex Schools Isn't Over." 1992. *Philadelphia Tribune*, April 7.

Delpit, Lisa. 2012. *"Multiplication Is for White People": Raising Expectations for Other People's Children*. New York: New Press.

Deskins, Donald. 1996. "Economic Restructuring, Job Opportunities, and Black Social Dislocation in Detroit." In *Social Polarization in Post-Industrial Metropolises*, edited by John O'Loughlin, and Jürgen Friedrichs, 1251–82. Berlin: Walter de Gruyter.

Detroit Board of Education. 1991. "Male Academy Resolution." February 26. Unpublished resolution presented at a general board meeting.

Dewey, John. (1916) 1980. "The Need of an Industrial Education in an Industrial Democracy." In *John Dewey: The Middle Works, 1891–1924 (vol. 10, 1911–1917)*, edited by Jo Ann Boydston, 137–43. Carbondale: Southern Illinois University Press.

Dhamoon, Rita. 2011. "Considerations on Mainstreaming Intersectionality." *Political Research Quarterly* 64 (1): 230–43.

Dill, Bonnie Thornton. 1979. "The Dialectics of Black Womanhood." *Signs* 4 (3): 543–55.

Diop, Mateen Ajala. 2009. "A Case Study of the Impact of Single-Gender Schooling on Student Achievement, Self-Esteem, and School Climate." Ed.D. diss., Texas A&M University.

DiPrete, Thomas A., and Claudia Buchmann. 2013. *The Rise of Women: The Growing Gender Gap in Education and What It Means for American Schools*. New York: Russell Sage Foundation.

"District Leaders Learn More about Boys-Only Charter School." 2010, December 7. Video retrieved from https://www.youtube.com/watch?v=uptKCk2Wp74.

Du Bois, W. E. B. 1903. *The Souls of Black Folk*. Chicago: McClurg.

Duckworth, Angela. 2016. *Grit: The Power of Passion and Perseverance*. New York: Simon and Schuster.

Dumas, Michael J. 2016. "My Brother as 'Problem': Neoliberal Governmentality and Interventions for Black Young Men and Boys." *Educational Policy* 30 (1): 91–113.

Durham, Joseph T. 2003. "The Other Side of the Story: The World of African-American Academies in the South after the Civil War." *Negro Educational Review* 54 (1–2): 1–16.

Dwarte, Marquis. 2014. "The Impact of Single-Sex Education on African American Reading Achievement: An Analysis of an Urban Middle School's Reform Effort." *Journal of Negro Education* 83 (2): 161–72.

Eichenbaum, Luise, and Susie Orbach. 1982. *Outside In, Inside Out: Women's Psychology; A Feminist Psychoanalytic Approach*. Harmondsworth, Middlesex: Penguin.

Elshtain, Jean Bethke. 1995. *Democracy on Trial*. New York: Basic.

Emdin, Christopher. 2016. *For White Folks Who Teach in the Hood . . . and the Rest of Y'all Too: Reality Pedagogy and Urban Education*. New York: Beacon.

English, Holly. 2003. *Gender on Trial: Sexual Stereotypes and Work/Life Balance in the Legal Workplace*. New York: ALM.

Equiano, Olaudah. 1789. *The Interesting Narrative of the Life of Olaudah Equiano; or, Gustavus Vassa, the African*. Vol. 1. London. http://docsouth.unc.edu/neh/equiano1/equiano1.html.

Estes, Steve. 2005. *I Am a Man: Race, Manhood, and the Civil Rights Movement*. Chapel Hill: University of North Carolina Press.

Estrich, Susan. 1998. "Ideologues Decry Single-Sex Education, But Girls Benefit." *Denver Post*, May 22.

Fabricant, Michael, and Michelle Fine. 2012. *Charter Schools and the Corporate Makeover of Public Education: What's at Stake?* New York: Teachers College Press.

———. 2015. *Changing Politics of Education: Privatization and the Dispossessed Lives Left Behind*. New York: Routledge.

Fanon, Frantz. 1967. *Black Skin, White Masks*. Translated by Charles Lam Markmann. New York: Grove.

Farley, Reynolds, Sheldon Danzinger, and Harry J. Holzer. 2000. *Detroit Divided*. New York: Russell Sage Foundation.

Faulkner, Carol. 2004. *Women's Radical Reconstruction: The Freedmen's Aid Movement*. Philadelphia: University of Pennsylvania Press.

Fearon, James D., and David D. Laitin. 1996. "Explaining Interethnic Cooperation." *American Political Science Review* 90 (4): 715–35.

Feminist Majority Foundation. 2014. "Identifying US K-12 Public Schools with Deliberate Sex Segregation." December 11. http://feminist.org/education/pdfs/IdentifyingSexSegregation12-12-14.pdf.

Fergus, Edward, Pedro Noguera, and Margary Martin. 2014. *Schooling for Resilience: Improving the Life Trajectory of Black and Latino Boys*. Cambridge, Mass.: Harvard Education Press.

Fergus, Edward, Katie Sciurba, Margary Martin, and Pedro Noguera. 2009. "Single-Sex Schools for Black and Latino Boys: An Intervention in Search of Theory." *In Motion*, October 31. http://inmotionmagazine.com/er/fsmn_09.html.

Ferguson, Ann. 2001. *Bad Boys: Public Schools in the Making of Black Masculinity*. Ann Arbor: University of Michigan Press.

———. 2009. "How Is Global Gender Solidarity Possible?" In *Sexuality, Gender and Power: Intersectional and Transnational Perspectives*, edited by Anna G. Jónasdóttir, Valerie Bryson, and Kathleen B. Jones, 243–58. New York: Routledge.

Firestone, Shulamith. 1970. *The Dialectic of Sex: The Case for Feminist Revolution*. New York: Bantam.

Fish, Jennifer, and Jennifer Rothchild. 2010. "Intersections of Scholar-Activism in Feminist Fieldwork: Reflections on Nepal and South Africa." In *The Intersectional Approach: Transforming the Academy through Race, Class, and Gender*, edited by Michele Tracy Berger and Kathleen Guidroz, 267–77. Chapel Hill: University of North Carolina Press.

Fletcher, Glynetta. 2013. "Voices of African American Male High School Graduate Participants in Single-Sex Programs." Ed.D. diss., California State University.

Floyd, Carlos. 2015. *Missouri's Young Adult Black Males: An Endangered People*. New York: Page.

Ford, Donna Y. 1996. *Reversing Underachievement among Gifted Black Students: Promising Practices and Programs*. New York: Teachers College Press.

Fordham, Signithia. 1993. "'Those Loud Black Girls': (Black) Women, Silence, and Gender 'Passing' in the Academy." *Anthropology and Education Quarterly* 24 (1): 1–32.

Franklin, V. P., and Mary Berry. 1992. *Black Self-Determination: A Cultural History of African-American Resistance.* Chicago: Lawrence Hill.

Fraser, Nancy. 2013. *Fortunes of Feminism: From State-Managed Capitalism to Neoliberal Crisis.* London: Verso.

Frazier, E. F. 1939. *The Negro Family in America.* Chicago: University of Chicago Press.

Freire, Paulo. 1970. *Pedagogy of the Oppressed.* Translated by Myra Bergman Ramos. New York: Herder and Herder.

Fremon, Celeste, and Stephanie Renfrow Hamilton. 1997. "Are Schools Failing Black Boys?" *Parenting,* April.

Friedman, Thomas L. 2007. *The World Is Flat 3.0: A Brief History of the Twenty-First Century.* New York: Macmillan.

Friedrich, Daniel S. 2014. "Global Microlending in Education Reform: Enseñá por Argentina and the Neoliberalization of the Grassroots." *Comparative Education Review* 58 (2): 291–321.

Fuss, Diana. 1989. *Essentially Speaking: Feminism, Nature and Difference.* New York: Routledge.

Gaitskell, Deborah. 1983. "Housewives, Maids or Mothers: Some Contradictions of Domesticity for Christian Women in Johannesburg, 1903–39." *Journal of African History* 24 (2): 241–25.

Gale, Daryl. 2006. "All-Boy School Deserves a Chance." *Philadelphia Tribune,* December 22.

Gamble, Andrew. 2001. "Neo-Liberalism." *Capital and Class* 25 (3): 127–34.

Gammill, Shellie, and Courtney Vaughn. 2011. "Lessons for a Rural Female Superintendent: Gender, Leadership, and Politics." *Advancing Women in Leadership* 31: 111–23.

Gatling, R. Perez, Veleka Gatling, and Leroy Hamilton Jr. 2014. *An Inexcusable Absence: The Shortage of Black Male Teachers.* Bloomington, Ind.: Author House.

Gause, C. P. 2008. *Integration Matters: Navigating Identity, Culture, and Resistance.* New York: Peter Lang.

Gershenson, Seth, Stephen B. Holt, and Nicholas W. Papageorge. 2016. "Who Believes in Me? The Effect of Student–Teacher Demographic Match on Teacher Expectations." *Economics of Education Review* 52: 201–24.

Giddens, Anthony. 1984. *The Constitution of Society: Outline of the Theory of Structuration.* Berkeley: University of California Press.

———. 1998. *The Third Way: The Renewal of Social Democracy.* Malden, Mass.: Polity Press.

Gilchrist, Brenda. 1991. "All-Male Schools Anguish Civil Rights Veterans." *Detroit Free Press,* September 3.

Ginsberg-Schutz, Maggie. 2010. "Kaleem Caire: Change Agent." *Isthmus* (Madison, Wisc.), December 23.

Giroux, Henry A. 2015. *Against the Terror of Neoliberalism: Politics beyond the Age of Greed.* New York: Routledge.

Gladden, Miriam Paula. 1992. "The Constitutionality of African-American Male Schools and Programs." *Columbia Human Rights Review* 24 (1): 239–71.

Goff, Wilhelmina D., and Norman J. Johnson. 2008. "Beyond Insanity: Creating All Male Classrooms and Schools as a Policy Option in the Portfolio of Local School Districts." *Forum on Public Policy* 2 (Summer).

Goodmark, Leigh. 2012. *A Troubled Marriage: Domestic Violence and the Legal System.* New York: New York University Press.

Gordon, Linda. 1988. *Heroes of Their Own Lives: The Politics and History of Family Violence; Boston, 1881–1960.* Urbana: University of Illinois Press.

Gottweis, Herbert. 2003. "Theoretical Strategies of Poststructural Policy Analysis." In *Deliberative Policy Analysis: Understanding Governance in the Network Society,* edited by Hajer A. Maarten and Hendrik Wagenaar, 241–65. Cambridge: Cambridge University Press.

Gould, Lewis L. 2014. *America in the Progressive Era, 1891–1914.* New York: Routledge.

Green, Les. 2015. "Germaine Greer Is Right about Trans-Women." *Semper Viridis (blog),* November 1. https://ljmgreen.com/2015/11/01/germaine-greer-is-right-about-trans-women.

Green, Robert L. 2015. *At the Crossroads of Fear and Freedom: The Fight for Social and Educational Justice.* East Lansing: Michigan State University Press.

Greene, Stuart. 2013. *Race, Community, and Urban Schools: Partnering with African American Families.* New York: Teachers College Press.

Greenwood, Janette Thomas. 2001. *Bittersweet Legacy: The Black and White "Better Classes" in Charlotte, 1850–1910.* Chapel Hill: University of North Carolina Press.

Greer, Germaine. 1999. *The Whole Woman.* New York: Doubleday.

Groothuis, Rebecca Merrill, and Douglas Groothuis. 1998. "Women Keep Promises, Too!" *Christian Ethics Today* (February), 17–25.

Gurian Institute. 2017. "How Can Single-Gender Schooling Help Boys?" Single Gender Successful Education Programs. Accessed May 1. http://www.gurianinstitute.com/single-gender.html.

Gurian, Michael. 2007. *The Minds of Boys: Saving Our Sons from Falling Behind in School and Life.* San Francisco: Jossey-Bass.

———. 2014. "Single-Sex Education Challenge: A Response by Michael Gurian to the Article 'Single-Sex Education's Benefits Challenged in Study.'" Gurian Institute, February 18.

Gutmann, Amy. 1999. *Democratic Education.* Princeton, N.J.: Princeton University Press.

Habermas, Jürgen. 1996. *Between Facts and Norms.* Cambridge: MIT Press.

Hajdukowski-Ahmed, Maroussia. 2013. "A Dialogical Approach to Identity: Implications for Refugee Women." In *Not Born a Refugee Woman: Contesting Identities, Rethinking Practices,* edited by Maroussia Hajdukowski-Ahmed, Nazilla Khanlou, and Helene Moussa, 21–54. New York: Berghahn.

Halpern, Diane F., Lise Eliot, Rebecca S. Bigler, Richard A. Fabes, Laura D. Hanish, Janet Hyde, Lynn S. Liben, and Carol Lynn Martin. 2011. "The Pseudoscience of Single-Sex Schooling." *Science* 333 (6050): 1701–7.

Hampton, Ilandus. 2015. "Creating a Framework for Success for High School African American Males: A Policy Advocacy Document." Ed.D. diss., National Louis University.

Hancock, Ange-Marie. 2007a. "Intersectionality as a Normative and Empirical Paradigm." *Politics and Gender* 3 (2): 248–54.

———. 2007b. "When Multiplication Doesn't Equal Quick Addition: Examining Intersectionality as a Research Paradigm." *Perspectives on Politics* 5 (1): 63–79.

———. 2016. *Intersectionality: An Intellectual History*. New York: Oxford University Press.

Haraway, Donna. 1990. "A Manifesto for Cyborgs: Science, Technology and Socialist Feminism in the 1980s." In *Feminism / Postmodernism*, edited by Linda J. Nicholson, 190–233. New York: Routledge.

Harbach, Meredith. 2016. "Sexualization, Sex Discrimination, and Public School Dress Codes." *University of Richmond Law Review* 50 (1039–1062).

Harding, Sandra G. 1991. *Whose Science? Whose Knowledge? Thinking from Women's Lives*. Ithaca, N.Y.: Cornell University Press.

Hardman-Cromwell, Youtha C. 1995. "Living in the Intersection of Womanism and Afrocentrism: Black Women Writers." In *Living in the Intersection: Womanism and Afrocentrism in Theology*, edited by Cheryl J. Sanders, 105–20. Minneapolis: Fortress.

Hardy, Nakia. 2010. "Portraits of Success: Effective White Female Teachers of Black Male Middle School Students." Ed.D. diss., University of North Carolina at Chapel Hill. https://cdr.lib.unc.edu/indexablecontent/uuid:2c398662-9ce5-40a9-9b29-b785fbf71a50.

Hare, Julia. 1995. *How to Find and Keep a BMW: Black Man Working*. San Francisco: Black Think Tank.

Hare, Nathan, and Julia Hare. 1984. *The Endangered Black Family: Coping with the Unisexualization and Coming Extinction of the Black Race*. San Francisco: Black Think Tank.

———. 1991. *The Hare Plan to Overhaul the Public Schools and Educate Every Black Man, Woman and Child*. San Francisco: Black Think Tank.

Harper, S. R., and Associates. 2014. "Succeeding in the City: A Report from the New York City Black and Latino Male High School Achievement Study." Philadelphia: University of Pennsylvania, Center for the Study of Race and Equity in Education. https://www.opensocietyfoundations.org/sites/default/files/succeeding-city-20130930.pdf.

Harris-Lacewell, Melissa Victoria. 2010. *Barbershops, Bibles, and BET: Everyday Talk and Black Political Thought*. Princeton, N.J.: Princeton University Press.

Hartigan, John, Jr. 1997. "Name Calling: Objectifying 'Poor Whites' and 'White Trash' in Detroit." In *White Trash: Race and Class in America*, edited by Annalee Newitz and Matt Wray, 41–56. New York: Routledge.

Hartsock, Nancy C. M. 1983a. "The Feminist Standpoint: Developing the Ground for a Specifically Feminist Historical Materialism." In *Discovering Reality: Feminist*

Perspectives on Epistemology, Metaphysics, Methodology, and Philosophy of Science, edited by Sandra G. Harding and Merrill B. Hintikka, 281–310. Dordrecht, Holland: Reidel.

———. 1983b. *Money, Sex, and Power: Toward a Feminist Historical Materialism*. Boston: Northeastern University Press.

———. 1990. "Postmodernism and Political Change: Issues for Feminist Theory." *Cultural Critique* 14 (Winter): 11–33.

Harvey, David. 1996. *Justice, Nature and the Geography of Difference*. Oxford: Blackwell.

———. 2007. *A Brief History of Neoliberalism*. Oxford: Oxford University Press.

Hawkins, Denise. 2015. "Where Are All the Black Male Teachers?" National Educational Association, September 22. http://neatoday.org/2015/09/22/where-are-all-the-black-male-teachers.

Hegel, G. W. F. 1979. *Phenomenology of Spirit*. Translated by A. V. Miller. Oxford: Clarendon.

Hegewisch, Ariane, Claudia Williams, and Vanessa Harbin. 2012. "The Gender Wage Gap by Occupation." Institute for Women's Policy Research, April 16. https://iwpr.org/publications/the-gender-wage-gap-by-occupation-2.

Hekman, Susan. 2013. *Feminism, Identity, Difference*. New York: Routledge.

Henderson, Nia-Malika. 2014. "Study: Black Girls Suspended at Higher Rates than Most Boys." *Washington Post*, March 21.

Henry, Paget. 2005. "Africana Phenomenology: Its Philosophical Implications." *CLR James Journal* 11 (1): 79–112.

Herrick, John M., and Paul H. Stuart. 2005. *Encyclopedia of Social Welfare History in North America*. New York: Sage.

Hicks, Reginald E. 2010. *Hidden in the Shadow of Truth: Why Our Black Boys Choose Criminality, Prison, and Enslavement*. Bloomington, Ind.: IUniverse.

Hochschild, Jennifer. 2003. "Social Class in Public Schools." *Journal of Social Issues* 59 (4): 821–40.

Honneth, Axel. 1999. *Pathologies of Reason: On the Legacy of Critical Theory*. New York: Columbia University Press,

hooks, bell. 1984. *Feminist Theory: From Margin to Center*. Cambridge, Mass.: South End.

———. 1996. *Killing Rage*. New York: Macmillan.

———. 2000. *Feminism Is for Everybody: Passionate Politics*. London: Pluto.

———. 2004. *We Real Cool: Black Men and Masculinity*. New York: Routledge/Psychology.

Hope, John. 1899. "Speech Notes from Speech to Wheat St. Baptist Church Women's Mission." Reel 21. John and Lugenia Burns Hope Papers. Atlanta University Center Archives Collection, Atlanta, Ga.

Hopkins, Ronnie. 1997. *Educating Black Males: Critical Lessons in Schooling, Community, and Power*. Albany: State University of New York Press.

Horkheimer, Max. 1982. *Critical Theory*. New York: Seabury.

Horkheimer, Max, and Theodor Adorno. 2002. *Dialectic of Enlightenment*. Trans. Edmund Jephcott. Stanford, Calif.: Stanford University Press.

Howard, Tyrone. 2013. *Black Male(d): Peril and Promise in the Education of African American Males*. New York: Teachers College Press.

Howard, Tyrone, and Clarence L. Terry Sr. 2011. "Culturally Responsive Pedagogy for African American Students: Promising Programs and Practices for Enhanced Academic Performance." *Teaching Education* 22 (4): 341–62.

Howell, William G., Martin R. West, and Paul E. Peterson. 2008. "The 2008 Education Next-PEPG Survey of Public Opinion." *Education Next* 8 (4): 11–26.

Hudson-Weems, Clenora. 2004. *Africana Womanism: Reclaiming Ourselves*. Troy, Mich.: Bedford.

Hunt, N. R. 1990. "Domesticity and Colonialism in Belgian Africa: Usumbura's Foyer Social, 1941–1960." *Signs* 15 (3): 441–47.

Hursh, D. 2007. "Assessing No Child Left Behind and the Rise of Neoliberal Education Policies." *American Educational Research Journal* 44 (3): 493–518.

Illinois State Board of Education. 2016. "Illinois State Report Card." https://www.illinoisreportcard.com.

Irby, Decoteau. 2014. "Revealing Racial Purity Ideology Fear of Black–White Intimacy as a Framework for Understanding School Discipline in Post-Brown Schools." *Educational Administration Quarterly* 50 (5): 783–95.

Jackson, Jacqueline. 2014. "The Black Male: An Endangered Species?" *Neon Tommy: Annenberg Digital News*, January 20. http://www.neontommy.com/news/2014/01/black-male-endangered-species.

James, Jennifer C. 2012. *A Freedom Bought with Blood. African American War Literature from the Civil War to World War II*. Raleigh: University of North Carolina Press.

James, Joy. 2014. *Transcending the Talented Tenth: Black Leaders and American Intellectuals*. New York: Routledge.

James, Marlon. 2010. "Never Quit: The Complexities of Promoting Social and Academic Excellence at a Single-Gender School for Urban African American Males." *Journal of African American Males in Education* 1 (3): 161–95.

Jefferson, Thomas. (1816) 1984. *Thomas Jefferson: Writings*. Edited by Merrill D. Peterson. New York: Library of America.

Johnson, Karen. 2013. *Uplifting the Women and the Race: The Lives, Educational Philosophies and Social Activism of Anna Julia Cooper and Nannie Helen Burroughs*. New York: Routledge.

Johnson, Norman. 2010. "Literacy and the Male Brain: The Path to Success." *Education 2.0*. https://mobilismobili.com/2010/02/03/gurian-institute-literacy-and-the-male-brain.

———. 2015. "Gurian Institute Programs Help Schools, Parents, and Communities Solve Issues Faced by African-American Boys." *BlackNews.com*, accessed October 29. http://www.blacknews.com/news/gurian_institute_programs_help_black_boys101.shtml#.VLbTeycXqQE.

Johnson, Stanley L., Jr. 2011. "An Interview with Dr. Jawanza Kunjufu." *Journal of African American Males in Education*, Leading Educators Series 2 (1/2): 141–45. http://saabnational.org/sites/all/themes/corporateclean/pdf/Jawanza-Kunjufu2.pdf.

Johnson, Umar. 2012. "Black Man's Burden: Myth of the Deadbeat." *A Voice for Men: Changing the Cultural Narrative*, October 17. http://www.avoiceformen.com/men/fathers/black-mans-burden-myth-of-the-deadbeat.

———. 2014. "Why I Want to Purchase an HBCU and Use It as a Boarding School to Serve Black Boys." *BlackNews.com*, June 2. http://www.blacknews.com/news/umar-johnson-why-i-want-to-purchase-hbcu-boarding-school-black-boys/#.VjGVG6K-uQE.

Johnston, Hank. 2002. "Verification and Proof in Frame and Discourse Analysis." In *Methods of Social Movement Research*, edited by Bert Klandermans and Suzanne Staggenborg, 62–91. Minneapolis: University of Minnesota Press.

Jones, Edward A. 1967. *A Candle in the Dark: A History of Morehouse College*. Valley Forge, Penn.: Judson.

Jones, James. 2014. "Raising Our Daughters and Loving Our Sons: How Female Headed Households Contribute to the Manufacturing of Sorry Black Men." *Manhood, Race, and Culture*, December 29. http://www.manhoodraceculture.com/2014/12/29/raising-our-daughters-and-loving-our-sons-how-female-headed-households-contribute-to-the-manufacturing-of-sorry-black-men.

Jones, Joy. 2015. "A Conversation with Tim King—Founder of Urban Prep Academies." *Black Wall Street Magazine*. http://blackwallstreetmagazine.com/2015/06/10/a-conversation-with-tim-king-founder-of-urban-prep-academies.

Jordan, Kathy-Anne. 2005. "Discourses of Difference and Overrepresentation of Black Students in Special Education." *Journal of African American History* 90 (1/2): 128–49.

Jordan-Zachery, Julia S. 2007. "Am I a Black Woman or a Woman Who Is Black? A Few Thoughts on the Meaning of Intersectionality." *Politics and Gender* 3 (2): 254–63.

———. 2014. "'I Ain't Your Darn Help': Black Women as the Help in Intersectionality Research in Political Science." *National Political Science Review* 16:19–30.

Karenga, Maulana. 1995. "Afrocentricity and Multicultural Education: Concept, Challenge, and Contribution. In *Toward the Multicultural University*, edited by Benjamin P. Bowser, Terry Jones, and Gale Auletta Young, 41–61. Westport, Conn.: Greenwood.

———. 2007. "Not Just in Jena: Resurgent Racism Everywhere." *Los Angeles Sentinel*, October 18.

Katz, Jackson. 2016. *Man Enough? Donald Trump, Hillary Clinton, and the Politics of Presidential Masculinity*. Northampton, Mass.: Interlink.

Kauth, Michael R., and Dan Landis. 1996. "Applying Lessons Learned from Minority Integration in the Military." In *Out in Force: Sexual Orientation and the Military*, edited by Gregory M. Herek, Jared B. Jobe, and Ralph M. Carney, 81–105. Chicago: University of Chicago Press.

Kearl, Holly. 2014. *Unsafe and Harassed in Public Spaces: A National Street Harassment Report*. Reston, Va.: Stop Street Harassment. http://www.stopstreetharassment.org/wp-content/uploads/2012/08/2014-National-SSH-Street-Harassment-Report.pdf.

Kenny, Lorraine Delia. 2000. *Daughters of Suburbia: Growing Up White, Middle Class, and Female*. New Brunswick, N.J.: Rutgers University Press.

Keyes, Alan. 1996. *Our Character, Our Future: Reclaiming America's Moral Destiny*. Washington, D.C.: Zondervan.

Kimbrell, Andrew. 1991. "A Male Manifesto: Men Should Not Accept Roles Society Demands of Them." *St. Louis Post-Dispatch*, June 10.

Kimmel, Michael S., and Michael Kaufman. 1994. "Weekend Warriors: The New Men's Movement." In *Theorizing Masculinities*, edited by Harry Brod and Michael Kaufman, 259–88. London: Sage.

Kindlon, Dan, and Michael Thompson. 1999. *Raising Cain: Protecting the Emotional Life of Boys*. New York: Ballantine.

King, Deborah K. 1988. "Multiple Jeopardy, Multiple Consciousness: The Context of a Black Feminist Ideology." *Signs* 14 (1): 41–72.

King, Ryan, and Marc Mauer. 2004. *The Vanishing Black Electorate: Felony Disenfranchisement in Atlanta, Georgia*. Atlanta: Sentencing Project.

King, Tim. 2008. "A New Hope for Change: Black Boys and Boys Schools." *Strategies: A Newsletter from the Chicago Urban League's Department of Policy and Research* 1 (3): cover story.

———. 2011. "Swords, Shields, and the Fight for Our Children: Lessons from Urban Prep." *Journal of Negro Education* 80 (3): 191–92.

———. 2015. "Letter to Parents and Guardians." Urban Prep Academy for Young Men–West Campus, February 20. https://drive.google.com/file/d/0B8RpkGJdu8iy NWFkRE8wV0YzR1JKLUs2RndYUkQoUzQoWW1N/view.

Klein, Sue, Jennifer Lee, Paige McKinsey, and Charmaine Archer. 2014. *Identifying US K-12 Public Schools with Deliberate Sex Segregation*. Feminist Majority Foundation. http://feminist.org/education/pdfs/IdentifyingSexSegregation12-12-14.pdf.

Kozol, Jonathan. 1991. *Savage Inequalities: Children in America's Schools*. New York: Crown.

Kruks, Sonia. 2001. *Retrieving Experience: Subjectivity and Recognition in Feminist Politics*. Ithaca, N.Y.: Cornell University Press.

Kunjufu, Jawanza. 2002. *Black Students, Middle Class Teachers*. Chicago: African American Images.

———. 2004. *Countering the Conspiracy to Destroy Black Boys*. 4 vols. in 1 [originally published 1985–95]. Chicago: African American Images.

———. 2005. *Keeping Black Boys out of Special Education*. Chicago: African American Images.

———. 2008. *State of Emergency: We Must Save African American Males*. Chicago: African American Images.

———. 2011. *Understanding Black Male Learning Styles*. Chicago: African American Images.

————. 2013. *Changing School Culture for Black Males*. Chicago: African American Images.

————. 2014. *Educating Black Girls*. Chicago: African American Images.

————. 2015. "Reading Scores and Prison Growth." Chicago: African American Images.

Kymlicka, Will. 1989. *Liberalism, Community and Culture*. New York: Oxford University Press.

La Caze, Marguerite. 2014. "Iris Marion Young's Legacy for Feminist Theory." *Philosophy Compass* 9 (7): 431–40.

Ladson-Billings, Gloria. 1995. "But That's Just Good Teaching! The Case for Culturally Relevant Pedagogy." *Theory into Practice* 34 (3): 159–65.

————. 2000. "Racialized Discourses and Ethnic Epistemologies." In *Handbook of Qualitative Research*, edited by Norman K. Denzin and Yvonna S. Lincoln, 257–78. 2nd ed. Thousand Oaks, Calif.: Sage.

————. 2013. *The Dreamkeepers: Successful Teachers of African American Children*. New York: Wiley.

Lahann, Randall, and Emilie Mitescu Reagan. 2011. "Teach for America and the Politics of Progressive Neoliberalism." *Teacher Education Quarterly* 38 (1): 7–27.

Laing, Tony. 2010. "Virtual Learning: A Solution to the All-Black Male School Debate and the Challenge of Black Male K-12 Outcomes." *Journal of African American Males in Education* 1 (3): 211–30.

Lankes, Tiffany. 2014. "How Bronx's Eagle Academy Helps Inner-City Kids Soar." *Buffalo News*, June 22.

Layton, Lynne. 1998. *Who's That Boy? Who's that Girl? Clinical Practice Meets Postmodern Gender Theory*. Northvale, N.J.: Aronson.

Leak, Halima N., and Chera D. Reid. 2010. "'Making Something of Themselves': Black Self-Determination, the Church and Higher Education Philanthropy." *International Journal of Educational Advancement* 10 (3): 231–44.

Legette, Willie M. 1999. "The Crisis of the Black Male: A New Ideology in Black Politics." In *Without Justice for All: The New Liberalism and Our Retreat from Racial Equality*, edited by Adolph Reed Jr., 291–324. Boulder, Colo.: Westview.

Leonhardt, David. 2014. "A Link between Fidgety Boys and a Sputtering Economy." *New York Times*, April 28.

Levine, Marc, and Sandra Callaghan. 1998. *The Economic State of Milwaukee: The City and the Region*. Milwaukee: Center for Economic Development.

Lewis, Evans. 2016. "Statement Regarding National Labor Relations Board, Chicago ACTS and Urban Prep Settlement." January 12. http://3ix98v4jkk22r5onw14w6xx1 .wpengine.netdna-cdn.com/wp-content/uploads/2016/01/MediaStatementNLRB FINAL.pdf.

Lewis, Hylan. 1967. *Culture, Class and Poverty*. Washington, D.C.: Cross-Tell.

Lewis-McKoy, R. L'Heureux. 2014. *Inequality in the Promised Land: Race, Resources, and Suburban Schooling*. Stanford, Calif.: Stanford University Press.

Lindsay, Constance, and Cassandra Hart. 2017. "Teacher Race and School Discipline." *Education Next* 17 (1): 72–78.

Lindsay, Keisha. 2013. "God, Gays, and Progressive Politics: Reconceptualizing Intersectionality as a Normatively Malleable Analytical Framework." *Perspectives on Politics* 11: 441–60.

Lipman, Pauline. 2013. *The New Political Economy of Urban Education: Neoliberalism, Race, and the Right to the City*. New York: Taylor and Francis.

Lohmann, Bill. 2013. "Preserving the History of a Life-Changing Place before It Crumbles." *Richmond Times-Dispatch*, March 24.

Lomotey, Kofi. 1992. "Independent Black Institutions: African-Centered Education Models." *Journal of Negro Education* 61 (4): 455–62.

Lorde, Audre. 1984. *Sister Outsider: Essays and Speeches*. Berkeley: Crossing.

Lukes, Steven. 1974. *Power: A Radical View*. London: Macmillan.

Luna, Jenny. 2016. "These Lifelong Republicans Explain Why They're Not Voting for Donald Trump: Why Some Voters Are Abandoning the GOP, and Others Are Jumping Onboard." *Mother Jones*, November 6. http://www.motherjones.com/politics/2016/11/arlie-hochschild-trump-voters-inquiring-minds.

Lynch, Frederick. 1989. *Invisible Victims: White Males and the Crisis of Affirmative Action*. Westport, Conn.: Greenwood.

Mack, Ryan. 2009. "Endangered: Young Black Males." *Black Star News*, May 8. http://www.blackstarnews.com/others/extras/endangered-young-black-males.html.

MacKinnon, Catharine A. 1989. *Toward a Feminist Theory of the State*. Cambridge, Mass.: Harvard University Press.

Madison [Wisc.] Metropolitan School District. 2016. "Annual Report on the MMSD Strategic Framework." https://www.madison.k12.wi.us/files/2015-16-MMSD-Annual-Report.pdf.

Majors, Richard, and Janet Mancini Billson. 1993. *Cool Pose: The Dilemmas of Black Manhood in America*. New York: Simon and Schuster.

Mann, Horace. 1957. *The Republic and the School: The Education of Free Men*. Edited by Lawrence A. Cremin. New York: Teachers College Press.

Manuel, Tiffany. 2006. "Envisioning the Possibilities for a Good Life: Exploring the Public Policy Implications of Intersectionality Theory." *Journal of Women, Politics and Policy* 28 (3/4): 171–203.

Marable, Manning. 2001. "Public Education and Black Empowerment." *People's Weekly World*, April 13.

Marcuse, Herbert. (1937) 1989. "Philosophy and Critical Theory." In *Critical Theory and Society: A Reader*, edited by Stephen Eric Bronner and Douglas McKay Kellner, 51–76. New York: Routledge.

Martin, Renee. 2011. "Are Black Students Better Off with Black Teachers?" *Clutch*. http://www.clutchmagonline.com/2012/03/are-black-students-better-off-with-black-teachers.

Marx, Karl. (1867) 1983. *Capital: A Critique of Political Economy*. Edited by Frederick Engels. Vol. 1. London: Lawrence and Wishart.

Maryland Marriage Alliance. 2012. Petition, accessed June 3. https://petition.marylandmarriagealliance.com/mma/petition/hb438;http://act.marylandmarriagealliance.com/5407/tell-maryland-lawmakers-protect-marriage.

Massey, Douglas and Nancy Denton. 1993. *American Apartheid: Segregation and the Making of the Underclass*. Cambridge, Mass: Harvard University Press.

Mathis, Greg. 2007. "Black Men Must Fight Back against Obstacles." *Ebony*, February, 38.

Matthews, Karen. 2013. "In New York City, All-Male Public Schools Aim to Help At-Risk Boys." *Washington Post*, November 17.

Mattox, W. 1995. "Stacking the Deck against Black Men." *Atlanta Constitution*, August 18.

Maxwell, Bill. 2006. "Midtown's Collective Attitude Is Changing." *Tampa Bay Times*, August 27.

———. 2013. "All-Black School, All Going to College." *Tampa Bay Times*, April 5.

May, Vivian M. 2012. *Anna Julia Cooper, Visionary Black Feminist: A Critical Introduction*. New York: Routledge.

———. 2015. *Pursuing Intersectionality, Unsettling Dominant Imaginaries*. New York: Routledge.

McAuliffe, Dante. 2015. "The Emasculation and Feminization of the Black Man." https://spacejamkev23.tumblr.com/post/130400371212/the-emasculation-and-feminization-of-the-black-man.

McCall, Leslie. 2005. "The Complexity of Intersectionality." *Signs* 30 (3): 1771–800.

McCluskey, Audrey T. 1993. "The Historical Context of the Single-Sex Schooling Debate Among African Americans." *Western Journal of Black Studies* 17 (4): 193–201.

McWhorter, John. 2014. "Equality Matters More Than Integration in Schools." *Daily Beast*, May 15. http://www.thedailybeast.com/articles/2014/05/15/equality-matters-more-than-integration-in-schools.html.

Mertz, Thomas J. 2011. "Some Truth about Urban Prep and Why It Matters." AMPS, October 11. https://madisonamps.org/2011/10/11/some-truth-about-urban-prep-and-why-it-matters.

Messner, Michael A. 1997. *Politics of Masculinities: Men in Movements*. Thousand Oaks, Calif.: Sage.

Meyers, Michael. 1992. "Separate Is Not Equal." *Washington Post*, September 23.

Mezirow, Jack. 1981. "A Critical Theory of Adult Learning and Education." *Adult Education Quarterly* 32 (1): 3–24.

Midgette, Thomas E., and Eddie Glenn. 1993. "African-American Male Academies: A Positive View." *Journal of Multicultural Counseling and Development* 21 (2): 69–78.

Milloy, Courtland. 1993. "A Frustrating Quest for Manhood Has Resulted in an Epidemic Loss of Life among Young Black Men." *Sun Sentinel*, April 4.

Mink, Gwendolyn. 2010. "Women's Work, Mother's Poverty: Are Men's Wages the Best Cure for Women's Economic Insecurity?" *New Politics* 12 (4). http://newpol.org/content/women%E2%80%99s-work-mother%E2%80%99s-poverty-are-men%E2%80%99s-wages-best-cure-women%E2%80%99s-economic-insecurity.

Mirza, Heidi Safia. 1997. "Introduction: Mapping a Genealogy of Black British Feminism." In *Black British Feminism: A Reader*, edited by Heidi Mirza, 1–30. London: Routledge.

Mitchell, Anthony, and James Stewart. 2010. "The Westinghouse Experiment: African-American Educators Think All-Male Schools Might Improve Prospects for Black Males." *Pittsburgh Post-Gazette*, September 30.

———. 2012. "The Effects of Culturally Responsive Mentoring on the High School to College Matriculation of Urban African American Males." *Spectrum: A Journal on Black Men* 1 (1): 71–93.

———. 2013. "The Efficacy of All-Male Academies: Insights from Critical Race Theory (CRT)." *Sex Roles* 69 (7/8): 382–92.

Mohanty, Chandra Talpade. 1984. "Under Western Eyes: Feminist Scholarship and Colonial Discourses." *boundary 2* 12 (3): 333–58.

———. 2003. *Feminism without Borders: Decolonizing Theory, Practicing Solidarity.* Durham, N.C.: Duke University Press.

Morris, Monique W. 2016. *Pushout: The Criminalization of Black Girls in Schools.* New York: New Press.

Morris, Robert C. 1981. *Reading, 'Riting, and Reconstruction: The Education of Freedmen in the South, 1861–1870.* Chicago: University of Chicago.

Morton, Carol. 1975. "The Prep School: Alternative in Education." *Ebony* (October), 102–13.

Moynihan, Daniel P. 1965. *The Negro Family. The Case for National Action.* Washington, D.C.: U.S. Government Printing Office.

Muhammad, Nisa Islam. 2016. "Developing a Quality Education for Black Children." *Final Call*, September 8.

Murrell, Peter. 1993. "Afrocentric Immersion: Academic and Personal Development of African American Males in Public Schools." In *Freedom's Plow: Teaching in the Multicultural Classroom*, edited by Theresa Perry and James W. Fraser, 231–59. New York: Routledge.

Mutua, Athena D. 2006. "Theorizing Progressive Black Masculinities." In *Progressive Black Masculinities,* edited by Athena D. Mutua, 1–42. New York: Routledge.

National Association for Single-Sex Public Education. 2017. "Single-Sex Education." Accessed April 1. http://www.singlesexschools.org.

National Black Church Initiative. 2012. "Current NBCI Programs." Accessed June 1. www.naltblackchurch.com/healingfamily.html.

National Commission of Excellence in Education. 1983. *A Nation at Risk: The Imperative for Education Reform.* Washington, D.C.: Government Printing Office.

National Organization for Women. 2006. "NOW Opposes Single-Sex Public Education as 'Separate and Unequal.'" *San Francisco Bay Area Independent Media Center.* October 24. http://www.indybay.org/newsitems/2006/10/24/18323109.php.

National Organization for Women Legal Defense and Education Fund. 1991. *Public Education Programs for African American Males: A Women's Educational Equity Perspective.* July. Copy on File at the Harvard Law School Library, Cambridge, Mass.

National Urban League. 1992. *African American Male Immersion Schools: Segregation?* Transcript. New York: National Urban League. http://files.eric.ed.gov/fulltext/ED377287.pdf.

Neal, Mark Anthony. 2013. *What the Music Said: Black Popular Music and Black Public Culture*. New York: Routledge.

Neuborne, Helen R. 1991. "Girls Are Drowning, Too." *Baltimore Sun*, August 27.

New York Department of Education. 2016. "New York City Quality Snapshots." http://schools.nyc.gov/FindASchool/reportsearch.htm?name=&repname=SchoolQuality SnapShot.

"No Boys Allowed: Garrison Elementary Pilots Same-Sex Classrooms." 2002. *Savannah Morning News*, October 29.

Noguera, Pedro. 2008. *The Trouble with Black Boys . . . and Other Reflections on Race, Equity, and the Future of Public Education*. San Francisco: Wiley.

———. 2012. "Saving Black and Latino Boys." *Phi Delta Kappan*, February 3.

Nott, Jemma. 2015. "Germain Greer: Transphobia Is All in Your Mind." *Green Left Weekly*, February 6. https://www.greenleft.org.au/content/germain-greer-transphobia -all-your-mind.

Oeur, Freeden. 2012. "The Men You Will Become: Single-Sex Public Education and the Crisis of Black Boys." Ph.D. diss., University of California, Berkeley.

———. 2013. "It's Not How Regular Boys are Supposed to Act: The Nonnormative Sexual Practices of Black Boys in All-Male Public High Schools." In *Gender and Sexualities in Education: A Reader*, edited by Elizabeth J. Meyer and Dennis Carlson, 357–69. New York: Peter Lang.

Ogbar, Jeffery. 2005. *Black Power: Radical Politics and African American Identity*. Baltimore, Md.: Johns Hopkins University Press.

Oksala, Johanna. 2014. "In Defense of Experience." *Hypatia* 29 (2): 388–403.

Oliver, Roland. *1952. Missionary Factor in Africa*. London: Longmans.

Omi, Michael, and Howard Winant. 2014. *Racial Formation in the United States: From the 1960s to the 1980s*. New York: Routledge.

Ong, Aihwa. 2006. *Neoliberalism as Exception: Mutations in Citizenship and Sovereignty*. Durham, N.C.: Duke University Press.

O'Sullivan, Rory, Konrad Mugglestone, and Tom Allison. 2014. "Closing the Race Gap: Alleviating Young African American Unemployment through Education." June. Washington, D.C.: Young Invincibles.

Overbeek, Henk. 1993. *Restructuring Hegemony in the Global Political Economy: The Rise of Transnational Neo-Liberalism in the 1980s*. New York: Routledge.

Pahlke, Erin, Janet Sibley Hyde, and Carlie M. Allison. 2014. "The Effects of Single-Sex Compared with Coeducational Schooling on Students' Performance and Attitudes: A Meta-analysis." *Psychological Bulletin* 140 (4): 1042–72.

Patten, Eileen. 2016. "Racial, Gender Wage Gaps Persist in U.S. Despite Some Progress." Pew Research Center, July 1. http://www.pewresearch.org/fact-tank/2016/07/01/ racial-gender-wage-gaps-persist-in-u-s-despite-some-progress.

Payne, Ruby K. 2001. *A Framework for Understanding Poverty*. 3rd ed. Highlands, Tex.: aha! Process.

Penny, Laurie. 2009. "Moving towards Solidarity: Transphobic Feminism Makes No Sense, Argues Laurie Penny." *The F Word*, December 6. https://www.thefword.org.uk/ 2009/12/cis_feminists_s.

Perkins, Linda M. 1996. "Lucy Diggs Slowe: Champion of the Self-Determination of African-American Women in Higher Education." *Journal of Negro History* 81 (1/4): 81–104.

Perpich, Diane. 2010. "Black Feminism, Poststructuralism, and the Contested Character of Experience." In *Convergences: Black Feminism and Continental Philosophy*, edited by Maria del Guadalupe Davidson, Kathryn T. Gines, and Donna-Dale L. Marcano, 13–34. Albany: State University of New York Press.

Pettigrew, Thomas F. 1964. *A Profile of the Negro American*. Princeton, N.J.: Van Nostrand.

Pettit, Phillip. 1999. *Republicanism: A Theory of Freedom and Government*. New York: Oxford University Press.

Petzen, Jennifer. 2012. "Queer Trouble: Centring Race in Queer and Feminist Politics." *Journal of Intercultural Studies* 33 (3): 289–302.

Pew Research Center. 2010. *Gay Marriage Gains More Acceptance: Majority Continues to Favor Gays Serving Openly in Military*. October 6. http://pewresearch.org/pubs/1755/poll-gay-marriage-gains-acceptance-gays-in-the-military.

Pew Research Center for Religion and Public Life. 2009. *A Religious Portrait of African Americans*. January 30. http://www.pewforum.org/A-Religious-Portrait-of-African-Americans.aspx.

Pew Research Center for U.S. Politics and Policy. 2017. *Support for Same-Sex Marriage Grows, Even among Groups That Had Been Skeptical*. June 26. http://www.people-press.org/2017/06/26/support-for-same-sex-marriage-grows-even-among-groups-that-had-been-skeptical/.

Phelan, Shane. 1989. *Identity Politics: Lesbian Feminism and the Limits of Community*. Philadelphia: Temple University Press.

———. 1994. *Getting Specific: Postmodern Lesbian Politics*. Minneapolis: University of Minnesota Press.

Pollack, William. 1999. *Real Boys: Rescuing Our Sons from the Myths of Boyhood*. New York: Owl Books.

Pope, Jacqueline, and Janice Joseph. 1997. "Student Harassment of Female Faculty of African Descent in the Academy." In *Black Women in the Academy: Promises and Perils*, edited by Lois Benjamin, 251–60. Gainesville: University Press of Florida.

Posey-Maddox, Linn. 2012. *Middle- and Upper-Middle-Class Parent Action for Urban Public Schools: Promise or Paradox?* Chicago: University of Chicago Press.

Potter, Jackson. 2008. "Perspectives and Urban Prep Charter Schools Dump 'Failing' Students Back into Public High Schools?" *Substance News*, September. http://www.substancenews.net/articles.php?page=560.

Poussaint, Alvin. 1996. "Reaching All Children." Interview by Jim Carnes. *Teaching Tolerance*, Spring. https://www.tolerance.org/magazine/spring-1996/reaching-all-children.

Pratt-Clarke, Menah A. E. 2010. *Critical Race, Feminism, and Education: A Social Justice Model*. New York: Palgrave Macmillan.

Pulera, Dominic J. 2006. *Sharing the Dream: White Males in Multicultural America*. New York: Continuum International.

Ransaw, Theodore S., Richard Majors, and Mikel D. C. Moss. 2016. "Turning Negatives into Positives: Cool Ways to Implement Successful Expectation Violations in Black Male Classrooms," In *Closing the Education Achievement Gaps for African American Males*, edited by Theodore S. Ransaw and Richard Majors, 123–42. East Lansing: Michigan State University Press.

Ransby, Barbara. 2003. *Ella Baker and the Black Freedom Movement: A Radical Democratic Vision*. Durham, N.C.: University of North Carolina Press.

Rasheed, Lisa. 2009. "Lucy Diggs Slowe, Howard University Dean of Women, 1922–1937: Educator, Administrator, Activist." Ph.D. diss., Georgia State University. http://scholarworks.gsu.edu/eps_diss/55.

Raspberry, William. 1987. "Male Teachers Could Fill Void in the Lives of Inner-City Boys." *Sun Sentinel*, March 6.

———. 2005. "Why Our Black Families Are Failing." *Washington Post*, July 25.

Raton, Taki S. 2012. "School Psychologist Speaks to Realities of Growing Up Black and Male in America." *Milwaukee Community Journal*, March 29. http://community journal.net/school-psychologist-speaks-to-realities-of-growing-up-black-and -male-in-america.

Ravitch, Diane. 2000. *Left Back: A Century of Failed School Reforms*. New York: Simon and Schuster.

———. 2016. *The Death and Life of the Great American School System: How Testing and Choice Are Undermining Education*. 3rd ed. New York: Basic.

Reese, Renford. 2004. *American Paradox: Young Black Men*. Durham, N.C.: Carolina Academic.

Reuters. 2010. "South Carolina Survey Positive on Single-Gender Classes." November 30. http://www.reuters.com/article/us-education-southcarolina-gender-idUSTRE 6AT61N20101130.

Rickford, Russell. 2016. *We Are an African People: Independent Education, Black Power, and the Radical Imagination*. New York: Oxford University Press.

Riegel, Joshua. 2015. "Constitutional Literacy." http://webcache.googleusercontent .com/search?q=cache:2wn0bmZm9GgJ:www.law.nyu.edu/sites/default/files/ upload_documents/Riegel%2520Constitutional%2520LiteracyCLEAN.docx+&cd =1&hl=en&ct=clnk&gl=us.

Robert, Sarah A. 2015. *Neoliberal Education Reform: Gendered Notions in Global and Local Contexts*. New York: Routledge.

Rollins, James C., and Brandy M. Hicks. 2011. *From Moses to the Joshua Generation*. Lulu.com.

Roper, Shani. 2013. "Educating Wards of the State: Gender-Based Vocational Curriculum in Jamaican Industrial Schools 1890–1940." Summer Workshop on the Comparative History of School Accountability, University of South Florida. http://scholarcommons.usf.edu/compaccountability2013/Papers/PreConference Submissions/6.

Ruff, Allen. 2012. "The Company One Keeps: Kaleem Caire's Rightward Connections, Part #2." *Ruff Talk: Commentary on the State of the World, Political and Historical Ob-*

servations and an Occasional Tale (blog). February 6. http://allenruff.blogspot.com/
2012/02/company-one-keeps-kaleem-caires.html.

Sadker, David, and Karen R. Zittleman. 2009. *Still Failing at Fairness: How Gender
Bias Cheats Girls and Boys in School.* New York: Simon and Schuster.

Salomone, Rosemary. 2003. *Same, Different, Equal: Rethinking Single-Sex Schooling.*
New Haven, Conn.: Yale University Press.

Samad, Anthony Asadullah. 2009. "Weighing In on 'Black Strategic Alternatives'
for Education (and Anything Else)." *LA Progressive,* October 14. https://www
.laprogressive.com/weighing-in-on-black-strategic-alternatives-for-education
-and-anything-else.

Sanchez, Melissa. 2015. "Union Accuses Urban Prep of Retaliatory Firings." *Chicago
Reporter,* June 26.

Sangster, Joan. 2011. *Through Feminist Eyes: Essays on Canadian Women's History.*
Edmonton: Athabasca University Press.

Sax, Leonard. 2016. *Boys Adrift: The Five Factors Driving the Growing Epidemic of
Unmotivated Boys and Underachieving Young Men.* New York: Basic.

Schlesinger, Arthur M., Jr. 1991. *The Disuniting of America: Reflections on a Multicultural Society.* Knoxville, Tenn.: Whittle.

Schneider, Elizabeth M. 2000. *Battered Women and Feminist Lawmaking.* New Haven,
Conn.: Yale University Press.

Schubert, Sunny. 2011. "Saving Young Black Men." *Wisconsin Policy Research Institute:
WI Magazine* 20 (1). http://www.wpri.org/WPRI/WI-Magazine/Volume20No1/
Saving-Young-Black-Men.htm.

Scott, Joan W. 1991. "The Evidence of Experience." *Critical Inquiry* 17 (4): 771–97.

———. 1999. *Gender and the Politics of History.* Rev. ed. New York: Columbia University Press.

Sergent-Shadbolt, Jean. 2015. "Germaine Greer's Dirty Feminism: Necessary Evils
and the Advancement of a Social Epistemology." *New Zealand Sociology* 30 (1):
141–54.

Severson, Don. 2011. "Approve Madison Prep Non-Instrumentality." December 15.
http://www.schoolinfosystem.org/2011/12/15/approve_madison.

Sewell, William H., Jr. 1980. *Work and Revolution in France: The Language of Labor
from the Old Regime to 1848.* Cambridge: Cambridge University Press.

Shabazz, Nimrod Malik. 1994. "The Need and Justification for All-Black Academies
in Urban Areas." Master's thesis, Langston University. http://dclu.langston.edu/
mccabe_theses/32.

Shah, Seema and Grace Sato. 2015. *Quantifying Hope: Philanthropic Support for Black
Men and Boys.* New York: Foundation Center. http://bmafunders.org/wpcontent/
uploads/2015/04/quantifying-hope-web-final.pdf.

Shange, Ntozake. 1977. *For Colored Girls Who Have Considered Suicide / When the
Rainbow Is Enuf.* New York: Macmillan.

Shapiro, Ian. 2012. "On Non-Domination." *University of Toronto Law Journal* 62 (3):
293–335.

Shelby, Tommie. 2009. *We Who Are Dark: The Philosophical Foundations of Black Solidarity*. Cambridge, Mass.: Harvard University Press.

Simmons, Dan. 2011. "Kaleem Caire Draws on Personal Experience to Support School Alternatives for Blacks." *Wisconsin State Journal*, September 20.

Small, Stephen. 1994. *Racialized Barriers: The Black Experience in the United States and England in the 1980s*. London: Routledge.

Smith, Barbara. 1985. "Some Home Truths on the Contemporary Black Feminist Movement." *Black Scholar* 16 (2): 1–13.

Smith, Pamela J. 1992. "Comment: All-Black Male Schools and the Equal Protection Clause: A Step Forward toward Education." *Tulane Law Review* 66 (6): 2004–55.

Smith, Valerie. 1998. *Not Just Race, Not Just Gender: Black Feminist Readings*. New York: Routledge.

Smith-Evans, Leticia, Janel George, Fatima Goss Graves, Lara S. Kaufmann, and Lauren Frohlich. 2014. *Unlocking Opportunity for African American Girls: A Call to Action for Educational Equity*. New York: NAACP Legal Defense and Educational Fund; Washington, D.C.: National Women's Law Center.

Soares, Rachel, Baye Cobb, Ellen Lebow, Allyson Regis, Hannah Winsten, and Veronica Wojnas. 2011. *2011 Catalyst Census: Fortune 500 Women Executive Officers and Top Earners*. New York: Catalyst.

Sokoloff, Natalie J. 1992. *Black Women and White Women in the Professions: Occupational Segregation by Race and Gender, 1960–1980*. New York: Routledge.

Sommerfeldt, Chris, and Ginger Adams Otis. 2016. "Hillary Clinton Embraced as Keynote Speaker at Fundraiser for All-Boys Eagle Academy She Helped Establish." *New York Daily News*, April 29. http://www.nydailynews.com/new-york/hillary -clinton-embraced-all-boys-eagle-academy-fund-raiser-article-1.2619008.

Sommers, Christina Hoff. 2013a. "The Bizarre, Misguided Campaign to Get Rid of Single-Sex Classrooms." *Atlantic*, October 4. https://www.theatlantic.com/ education/archive/2013/10/the-bizarre-misguided-campaign-to-get-rid-of-single -sex-classrooms/280262.

———. 2013b. *The War against Boys: How Misguided Feminism Is Harming Our Young Men*. New York: Simon and Schuster.

———. 2016. "A Necessary Option." *New York Times*, September 6.

Span, Christopher M. 2012. *From Cotton Field to Schoolhouse: African American Education in Mississippi, 1862–1875*. Durham, N.C.: University of North Carolina Press.

Spence, Lester K. 2012. "The Neoliberal Turn in Black Politics." *Souls: A Critical Journal of Black Politics, Culture, and Society* 14 (3–4): 139–59.

Spivak, Gayatri Chakravorty. 1988a. "Can the Subaltern Speak?" In *Marxism and the Interpretation of Culture*, edited by Cary Nelson and Lawrence Grossberg, 271–313. Urbana: University of Illinois Press.

———. 1988b. *In Other Worlds: Essays in Cultural Politics*. New York: Routledge.

———. 1993a. "An Interview with Gayatri Chakravorty Spivak." By Sara Danius and Stefan Jonsson. *Boundary 2* 20 (2): 21–50.

———. 1993b. *Outside in the Teaching Machine*. New York: Routledge/Psychology.

Spivak, Gayatri Chakravorty, and Sara Harasym. 1990. *The Post-Colonial Critic: Interviews, Strategies, Dialogues*. New York: Routledge.

Squires, David. 2012. "A Man-Up Talk to Single Moms." *Daily Press*, March 7. http://articles.dailypress.com/2012-03-07/news/dp-nws-squires-column-0308-20120307_1_single-moms-boys-and-girls-young-boys.

St. Jean, Yanick, and Joe R. Feagin. 2015. *Double Burden: Black Women and Everyday Racism*. New York: Routledge.

Staples, Robert. 1987. "Black Male Genocide: A Final Solution to the Race Problem in America." *Black Scholar* 18 (3): 1–11.

Steady, Filomina Chioma. 1987. "African Feminism: A Worldwide Perspective." In *Women in Africa and the African Diaspora: A Reader*, edited by Rosalyn Terborg-Penn, Andrea Benton Rushing, and Sharon Harley, 3–24. Washington, D.C.: Howard University Press.

Stiffman, Eden. 2015. "Foundation Support for Black Men and Boys Grows Sharply, Study Says." *Chronicle of Philanthropy*, April 14. https://www.philanthropy.com/article/Foundation-Support-for-Black/229337.

Stone, Alison. 2007. *An Introduction to Feminist Philosophy*. Cambridge: Polity.

Stone, David. 2015. "Union Busting, Chicago-Style." *Substance News*, June 25. http://www.substancenews.net/articles.php?page=5717.

Stiglitz, Joseph E. 2003. *Globalization and Its Discontents*. London: Penguin.

Strolovitch, Dara Z. 2007. *Affirmative Advocacy: Race, Class, and Gender in Interest Group Politics*. Chicago: University of Chicago Press.

Sugrue, Thomas. 2014. *The Origins of the Urban Crisis: Race and Inequality in Postwar Detroit*. Princeton, N.J.: Princeton University Press.

Sullivan, Nikki. 2003. *A Critical Introduction to Queer Theory*. New York: New York University Press.

Tatum, Beverly Daniel. 2003. *"Why Are All the Black Kids Sitting Together in the Cafeteria?" and Other Conversations about Race*. New York: Basic.

Taylor, Charles. 1989. *Sources of the Self: The Making of the Modern Identity*. Cambridge, Mass.: Harvard University Press.

Terborg-Penn, Rosalyn. 1987. "African Feminism: A Theoretical Approach to the History of Women in the African Diaspora." In *Women in Africa and the African Diaspora*, edited by Rosalyn Terborg-Penn, Andrea Benton Rushing, and Sharon Harley, 43–63. Washington, D.C.: Howard University Press.

Terry, Clarence L., Sr., Terry K. Flennaugh, Samarah M. Blackmon, and Tyrone C. Howard. 2014. "Does the 'Negro' Still Need Separate Schools? Single-Sex Educational Settings as Critical Race Counterspaces." *Urban Education* 49 (6): 661–97.

Theron, Stephen. 2013. *Hegel's Philosophy of Universal Reconciliation: Logic as Form of the World*. Cambridge: Cambridge Scholars.

"They Did It Again! Entire Senior Class at Urban Prep Chicago Is Headed to College." 2016. *Essence*, April 29.

Thomas-Whitfield, Chandra. 2011. "B.E.S.T. Men: Atlanta's All-Male Academy Seeks to Close Achievement Gap." *Juvenile Justice Information Exchange*, January 3. http://jjie .org/2011/01/03/best-men-atlantas-allmale-academy-seeks-close-achievement-gap.

Toldson, Ivory A. 2013. "Race Matters in the Classroom." In *Black Male Teachers: Diversifying the United States' Teacher Workforce*, edited by Chance W. Lewis and Ivory A. Toldson, 11–24. Bingley, U.K.: Emerald Group.

Toomer, Regan. 2007. "All-Boys Charter School Opens Its Doors." *Philadelphia Tribune*. September 7.

Tractenberg, Paul. 2013. "A Tale of Two Deeply Divided NJ Public School Systems." *NJSpotlight*, December 31. http://www.njspotlight.com/stories/13/12/30/a-tale-of -two-deeply-divided-new-jersey-public-school-systems/?p=all.

Tsoi-a-Fatt, Rhonda. 2001. *We Dream a World: The 2025 Vision for Black Men and Boys*. New York: Twenty-First Century Foundation. https://www.opensociety foundations.org/sites/default/files/we-dream-a-world-20110104.pdf.

Tyehimba, Agyei. 2015. "I Support Dr. Umar Johnson's Mission to Educate Black Boys." *My True Sense* (blog), June 15. https://mytruesense.wordpress.com/2015/06/15/i-support -dr-umar-johnsons-mission-to-educate-black-boys.

Tyre, Peg. 2006. "Education: Boys Falling Behind Girls in Many Areas." *Newsweek*, June 29.

United Presbyterian Church in the U.S.A. General Assembly. 1920. *Minutes of the General Assembly of the Presbyterian Church in the United States of America*. Philadelphia: Office of the General Assembly, Witherspoon Building.

U.S. Bureau of the Census. 1991. *Poverty in the United States: Current Population Reports; Consumer Income. Issue 171*. Washington, D.C.: U.S. Government Printing Office. https://www.census.gov/content/dam/Census/library/publications/1992/ demo/p60–181.pdf.

U.S. Department of Education. National Center for Education Statistics. 2007. *Digest of Education Statistics: Table 105*. August. http://nces.ed.gov/programs/digest/d07/ tables/dt07_105.asp.

———. Office for Civil Rights. 2006. *Nondiscrimination on the Basis of Sex in Education Programs or Activities Receiving Federal Financial Assistance; Final Rule*. Washington, D.C.: U.S. Government Printing Office. http://www2.ed.gov/legislation/ FedRegister/finrule/2006-4/102506a.html.

———. 2011. *Youth Indicators 2011: Table 14*. Washington, D.C.: U.S. Government Printing Office. https://nces.ed.gov/pubs2012/2012026/tables/table_14.asp.

———. 2012. *The Condition of Education 2012*. NCES 2012-045, Table A-33-1. Accessed October 25. https://nces.ed.gov/pubs2012/2012045.pdf.

———. Office for Civil Rights. 2014. "Civil Rights Data Collection: Data Snapshot; School Discipline." Issue brief no. 1, March 21. http://ocrdata.ed.gov/Downloads/ CRDC-School-Discipline-Snapshot.pdf.

———. 2015a. *Digest of Education Statistics: Table 104.10*. December. https://nces .ed.gov/pubs2016/2016014.pdf.

———. Office for State Support. 2015b. *Fundamental Change: Innovation in America's Schools Under Race to the Top*. Washington, D.C.: U.S. Government Printing Office. https://www2.ed.gov/programs/racetothetop/rttfinalrpt1115.pdf.

———. 2016. *Status Dropout Rates, 2015*. Accessed October 21. https://nces.ed.gov/programs/digest/d16/tables/dt16_219.70.asp.

U.S. Department of Labor. 2011. Bureau of Labor Statistics. "Unemployment Rates, by Race, and Hispanic or Latino Ethnicity, 1975–2010." *TED: The Economics Daily*, October 5. https://www.bls.gov/opub/ted/2011/ted_20111005_data.htm.

Wacquant, Loïc. 2009. *Prisons of Poverty*. Expanded ed. Minneapolis: University of Minnesota Press.

Wadsworth, Nancy D. 2011. "Intersectionality in California's Same-Sex Marriage Battles: A Complex Proposition." *Political Research Quarterly* 64 (1): 200–216.

Walker, Alice. 1982. *The Color Purple*. New York: Washington Square.

Walker, Vanessa Siddle. 2013. "Black Educators as Educational Advocates in the Decades before *Brown v. Board of Education*." *Educational Researcher* 42 (4): 207–22.

Wallace, Michele. 1979. *Black Macho and the Myth of the Black Superwoman*. New York: Dial.

Warren, Chezare A. 2012. "Empathic Interaction: White Female Teachers and Their Black Male Students." Ph.D. diss., University of Illinois at Chicago. http://indigo.uic.edu/bitstream/handle/10027/9470/Warren_Chezare.pdf?sequence=1.

———. 2015. "Conflicts and Contradictions: Conceptions of Empathy and the Work of Good-Intentioned Early Career White Female Teachers." *Urban Education* 50 (5): 572–600.

Watkins, Boyce. 2014a. "Black Children Are Not 'Future Criminals.'" *NewsOne*, http://newsone.com/1502905/black-children-future-criminals.

———. 2014b. "Dr. Boyce Watkins—The People's Scholar." November 10. https://www.facebook.com/thedrboycewatkins/posts/10152841373043609.

Watson, Clifford. 1991. "Wrong Fight Waged on School System." *Detroit Free Press*, August 31.

Watson, Clifford, and Geneva Smitherman. 1996. *Educating African American Males: Detroit's Malcolm X Academy Solution*. Chicago: Third World Press.

Weil, Elizabeth. 2008. "Teaching to the Testosterone." *New York Times Magazine*, March 2.

Welburn, Jessica, and Louise Seamster. 2016. "How a Racist System Has Poisoned the Water in Flint, Mich." *The Root*, January 9. http://www.theroot.com/articles/politics/2016/01/how_a_racist_system_has_poisoned_the_water_in_flint_mich.

Weldon, Laurel. "Intersectionality." 2008. In *Politics, Gender, and Concepts: Theory and Methodology*, edited by Gary Goertz and Amy G. Mazur, 191–218. New York: Cambridge University Press.

Weldon, Shawn. 2010. "The Other Drexel: Louise Drexel Morrell." *PAHRC: Philadelphia Archdiocesan Historical Research Center*, April 9. http://www.pahrc.net/tag/st-francis-industrial-school-for-boys.

Wells, Ida B. 1892. *Southern Horrors: Lynch Law in All Its Phases.* New York: New York Age Print.

West, Cornel. 2001. *Race Matters.* New York: Beacon.

Whitaker, Charles. 1991. "Do Black Males Need Special Schools?" *Ebony*, March, 11–22.

White, E. Frances. 1990. "*Africa on My Mind*: Gender, Counter Discourse and African-American Nationalism." *Journal of Women's History* 2 (1): 71–97.

White, Gillian B. 2015. "The Data Are Damning: How Race Influences School Funding." *Atlantic*, September 30. http://www.theatlantic.com/business/archive/2015/09/public-school-funding-and-the-role-of-race/408085.

Whitmire, Richard. 2011. "What's behind Education's 'Boy Problems'?" *Dallas Morning News*, September 6.

Wiley, Ed. 1993. "Too Few Higher Education Initiatives Aim to Reverse Plight of Young Black Males, Say Education Experts." *Black Issues in Higher Education,* no. 10: 18.

Williams, Brandi N. 2013. "Disrupting Discourses of Failure: Narratives of Black Male Students and Academic Success." Master's thesis, Syracuse University.

Williams, Claudette. 1993. "We Are a Natural Part of Many Different Struggles: Black Women Organizing." In *Inside Babylon: The Caribbean Diaspora in Britain*, edited by Winston James and Clive Harris, 153–64. London: Verso.

Williams, Gwyneth, and Rhys Williams. 2013. "Framing the Fathers' Rights Movement." In *Social Problems: Constructionist Readings*, edited by Donileen R. Loseke and Joel Best, 91–100. Piscataway, N.J.: Transaction.

Williams, Juliet A. 2013. "Girls Can be Anything . . . But Boys Will Be Boys: Discourses of Sex Difference in Education Reform Debates." *Nevada Law Journal* 13 (2): 513–46.

———. 2016. *The Separation Solution? Single-Sex Education and the New Politics of Gender Equality.* Oakland: University of California Press.

Williams, Verna L. 2004. "Reform or Retrenchment? Single Sex Education and the Construction of Race and Gender." *Wisconsin Law Review* 2004 (1): 15–79.

———. 2006. "Private Choices, Public Consequences: Public Education Reform and Feminist Legal Theory." *William and Mary Journal of Women and Law* 12 (3): 563–601.

Willis, Ellen. 1984. "Radical Feminism and Feminist Radicalism." *Social Text*, no. 9/10: 91–118.

Willis, Sharon. 1996. "In the Name of Theory." In *The Ends of Theory*, edited by Jerry Herron, Dorothy Huson, Ross Pudaloff, and Robert Strozier, 71–85. Detroit: Wayne State University Press.

Wisconsin Council on Children and Families. 2013. *Race to Equity: Baseline Report on the State of Racial Disparities in Dane County.* http://racetoequity.net/baseline-report-state-racial-disparities-dane-county.

Woo, David. 2015. "Why My Charter School Needs a Union." *Huffington Post*, May 8.

Woodson, Carter G. 1947. *The Negro in Our History.* Huntingdon, Tenn.: Associated.

Wright, Tim. 2013. "Why You Should Care about the 'Boy Crisis.'" *Tim Wright Blog*, December 4. http://sixseeds.patheos.com/timwright/2013/12/why-you-should -care-about-the-boy-crisis.

Wubbena, Zane. 2016. "Introduction—A Fight *for* Education and against Capital: Neoliberalism, New Media, and Educational Policy." In *News Media and the Neo-liberal Privatization of Education*, edited by Zane C. Wubbena, Derek R. Ford, Brad J. Porfilio, xi–xxxii. Charlotte, N.C.: Information Age.

Yamaguchi, Makiko. 2014. "Why Girls? A Report on the Status of Women and Girls in the U.S." July. Alameda, Calif.: Girls Incorporated.

Yeatman, Anna. 1997. "Feminism and Power." In *Reconstructing Political Theory: Feminist Perspectives,* edited by Mary Lyndon Shanley and Uma Narayan, 144–57. University Park: Pennsylvania State University Press.

Yoon, Irene H. 2016. "Trading Stories: Middle-Class White Women Teachers and the Creation of Collective Narratives about Students and Families in a Diverse Elementary School." *Teachers College Record* 118 (2): 1–54.

Young, Iris Marion. 1990. *Justice and the Politics of Difference*. Princeton, N.J.: Princeton University Press.

———. 1994. "Gender as Seriality: Thinking about Women as a Social Collective." *Signs* 19 (3): 713–38.

———. 2002. *Inclusion and Democracy*. New York: Oxford University Press.

Yuval-Davis, Nira. 2006. "Intersectionality and Feminist Politics." *European Journal of Women's Studies* 13 (3): 193–209.

Zerai, Assata. 2000. "Agents of Knowledge and Action: Selected Africana Scholars and Their Contributions to the Understanding of Race, Class, and Gender Inter-sectionality." *Cultural Dynamics* 12 (2): 182–222.

Index

KEISHA LINDSAY is an assistant professor of gender and women's studies and political science at the University of Wisconsin-Madison.

Dissident Feminisms

The University of Illinois Press
is a founding member of the
Association of American University Presses.

———————————————————————————

Composed in 10.5/13 Minion Pro
by Lisa Connery
at the University of Illinois Press
Cover designed by Jason Gabbert
Cover art by artist Gregory St. Amand (GOGO)
Manufactured by Sheridan Books, Inc.

University of Illinois Press
1325 South Oak Street
Champaign, IL 61820-6903
www.press.uillinois.edu